AIR
FORCE
ONE

ALSO BY KENNETH T. WALSH

Feeding the Beast: The White House Versus the Press
Ronald Reagan: Biography

AIR FORCE ONE

A History of the Presidents and Their Planes

KENNETH T. WALSH

Chief White House Correspondent
U.S. News & World Report

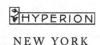

NEW YORK

Library of Congress Cataloging-in-Publication Data

Walsh, Kenneth T.
    Air Force One : a history of the presidents and their planes / Kenneth T. Walsh—1st ed.
        p. cm.
    Includes bibliographical references and index.
    ISBN 1-4013-0004-9
    1. Air Force One (Presidential aircraft)—History. 2. Presidents—Transportation—United States—History. 3. United States. President—History. I. Title.

TL723 .W35 2003
387.7'42'088351—dc21

2002038751

Hyperion books are available for special promotions and premiums. For details contact Hyperion Special Markets, 77 West 66th Street, 11th floor, New York, New York 10023-6298, or call 212-456-0133.

FIRST EDITION

10 9 8 7 6 5 4 3 2 1

*For Barclay
and Gloria*

ACKNOWLEDGMENTS

This book was conceived over brunch two years ago at Richard's Corner Grill in Shady Side, Maryland, an hour and a lifestyle away from Washington, D.C.

A happy trio sat at the table that sunny morning: me, my wife, Barclay Walsh, and our friend Marlin Fitzwater, the former press secretary for Ronald Reagan and George Herbert Walker Bush. We chatted about the weather, the growing season, and the joys of our Western Shore retreats, located a few miles from each other near the Chesapeake Bay. Eventually the conversation turned to the White House, as it usually does, since it has been such a big part of our lives for so long. We agreed that *Air Force One* was a relatively unplumbed topic in the media and in the history books. And we found ourselves agreeing that, as White House correspondent for *U.S. News & World Report* for nearly two decades, I was perfectly positioned to write a book about the presidents and their planes.

I must admit I had thought about this before, but by the time the second cups of coffee arrived I was well on my way to finally getting the project started. Maybe it was the inspiration provided by the uplifting beauty of the Western Shore. More likely it was the encouragement of Barclay and Marlin. But the more I looked into it, the more enthusiastic I became. After a few weeks of thinking and reporting, it was clear that writing a history of *Air Force One* would not only add to the historical record of the past six decades, but also might be fun. I was not disappointed on either score.

I would like to thank Brian Duffy, editor of *U.S. News & World Report*, and Terry Atlas, the magazine's nation and world editor, for giving me the opportunity to complete this project.

I also want to thank the many sources who were so generous with their time and insight. I interviewed more than 120 people for this book, and virtually all of them were immensely helpful. At the top of the list are President George W. Bush and former presidents Gerald Ford, Jimmy Carter, George Herbert Walker Bush, and Bill Clinton. All of them have traveled extensively on *Air Force One*, and their love for the airplane came across in my interviews with each man. Ronald Reagan could not participate because of his Alzheimer's disease, but his former aides and the staff at his library, where a permanent exhibition on *Air Force One* and presidential travel is being organized, provided invaluable assistance.

I tried to emphasize firsthand reporting whenever possible. I wish to thank Ralph Albertazzie, Ralph Alswang, Dan Bartlett, Sandy Berger, Mike Berman, Bob Boorstin, Doug Brinkley, Jim Bull, Mark Burson, Nick Calio, Andy Card, Joe Chappell, James Cross, Bob Dallek, Reed Dickens, Eric Draper, Ken Duberstein, Kris Engskov, Ari Fleischer, Howie Franklin, Al From, Bill Galston, Geoff Garin, David Gergen, Mike Gerson, Stan Greenberg, Tom Griscom, Bill Gulley, John Haigh, Karen Hughes, Harold Ickes, Ron Kaufman, Jim Kennedy, Tim Kerwin, Ken Khachigian, Josh King, Jim Kuhn, Joe Lockhart, Frank Luntz, Scott McClellan, Mike McCurry, Bill McInturff, Mack McLarty, Walter Mondale, Ron Nessen, Charlie Palmer, Leon Panetta, Julia Payne, Mark Penn, Anna Perez, John Podesta, Roman Popadiuk, Jody Powell, Noelia Rodriguez, Mark Rosenker, Karl Rove, Bob Ruddick, Fred Ryan, Brent Scowcroft, George Shultz, Elliott Sluhan, Doug Sosnik, Gene Sperling, Sheila Tate, Mark Tillman, Jeffery Underwood, David Valdez, Jack Valenti, Mike Waldman, Phil Wise, and Bruce Zanca.

Many other past and present advisers to the presidents were helpful but asked to remain anonymous.

I would like to express my gratitude to Will Schwalbe and Mark Chait, my editors at Hyperion, and to my agent, Jillian Manus, all of whom saw the value of this book and believed in it from the beginning.

Finally, my deepest thanks to Marlin and Barclay. Marlin is a professional in every sense, a talented author in his own right, and has become a good friend over the years.

Barclay is my partner in work and in life, and she provided invaluable research, insight, and support every step of the way. She is simply the best.

Kenneth T. Walsh
Bethesda, Maryland
November 2002

CONTENTS

FOREWORD

Starting with Theodore Roosevelt's presidency in 1901, the private lives of presidents became public property. TR cleverly used his large family to create unprecedented connections between the public and the First Family. In recent years, however, the rise of an irreverent press corps revealing presidential secrets has made private White House matters less an opportunity for political gains—as they generally remained from TR to Kennedy—than a struggle between presidential image makers and "gotcha" journalism.

As Kenneth T. Walsh makes clear in this impressive history of *Air Force One*, the last bastion of presidential privacy for chief executives from Franklin D. Roosevelt to George W. Bush has been the planes carrying them around the country and the world in search of political gains, relaxation, national security, and peace. Although each of the twelve presidents since FDR, who have logged millions of miles in the air, gave varying degrees of access to the press traveling with them, each accurately assumed that journalists invited into the inner sanctum of *Air Force One* would be respectful of presidential privacy. The plane was a kind of sanctuary from journalistic probing into the intimate detail of a president's life, sordid or otherwise.

The cloistered environment of *Air Force One* has given presidents the freedom to be more spontaneous than in any other public setting. During long wartime flights to meet Churchill and Stalin, Walsh observes, FDR "provided a glimpse into . . . [his] gregarious personality and his everyday challenges as a polio victim." Harry Truman aboard the "Sacred Cow," the plane he inherited from Roosevelt, faithfully "reflected his feisty personality and his down-to-earth approach to life," Walsh writes. Reflecting the style of the fifties, Eisenhower almost always traveled in a jacket and tie, which he rarely loosened. The unadorned state of the plane, "a simple, gray, utilitarian military-style aircraft . . . embodied the no-nonsense spirit of the cold war."

Kennedy's plane, like the man, "seemed to embody modernity itself." On board, he "spent hours swapping political stories, sharing gossip, talking about women, smoking cigars, and enjoying a few drinks." Lyndon Johnson was, by turns, more overtly "earthy, profane, selfish, devious, or rude, and then polite, considerate, affectionate, and downright charming" than he was at the White House or before guests at his Texas ranch. On *Air Force One,* Richard Nixon gave full voice to his affinity for both decisiveness and vacillation, finalizing major policy choices while in flight and descending into moods of self-doubt and personal pique. Ford, less guarded and political during flying trips, gave expression to his natural gregariousness and decency, habitually "wandering through the plane, chatting with staff members and guests." Jimmy Carter, an introverted, obsessive worker and micromanager, showed himself during plane trips to be a loner who often shut himself off from staff and reporters.

Reagan impressed everyone aboard *Air Force One* as more introspective and self-contained than he was on the campaign trail, at the White House, or at overseas conferences. In the confines of the plane, George H. W. Bush felt free to dress down in "a bizarre white jacket . . . white socks and slippers with the presidential seal on each toe." He also could cast aside "his own non-confrontational nature and discipline errant aides there." Bill Clinton "reflected all his positives and negatives," alternating "frenetic activity with periods of wasted time," working feverishly hard and holding all-night bull sessions. His traits of "brilliance, curiosity, and a will-ingness to make excuses for himself were on constant display during his airborne adventures." As for George W. Bush, he shows himself "to be more of an average Joe than most presidents like to admit." He reads little, displays small interest in the day's news, and manages feelings of restlessness at being confined on long plane trips he doesn't especially like by jogging on a treadmill.

Ken Walsh's book is not only a fascinating look into presidential behavior aboard *Air Force One* but also a thoughtful discussion of what the plane stands for in American and international politics. The Oval Office has become familiar to millions of Americans through photographs, television, and replicas in presidential libraries, but presidential planes remain largely unknown. Except for the famous still photograph of Lyndon Johnson taking the oath of office aboard *Air Force One* after Kennedy's assassination, the aircraft's décor and facilities remain little glimpsed by most Americans. Consequently, the plane has taken on mythic proportions that presidents have used to their advantage. According to a poll Walsh cites, two-thirds of Americans see the plane as "a symbol of the country and a reminder of history." Harry Truman "invented the use of the president's plane as a modern spectacle," Walsh writes, with thousands of Americans coming to airports to watch the president's arrival. Kennedy ordered that "United States of America" be painted "in huge, bold letters" on the plane's fuselage, making the aircraft a symbol of the presidency and the nation. Reagan used *Air Force One* as "a fabulous prop," instituting "The Walk, a carefully choreographed, dignified march [by himself] from his limousine or helicopter up the stairs and into the magnificent blue and white 707."

Carter, Reagan, and Bush 41 were all mindful of *Air Force One*'s power as an American symbol. Carter saw "within the eyes and the demeanor of those who welcomed us that they sensed that *Air Force One* at that moment *was* the United States of America." When he arrived back at the airport in a foreign city, Reagan recalled, "it's a little bit like hearing the national anthem and you swell a little with pride." The senior Bush remembered that "when you taxi up in our country or in some other country, there is great emotion. . . . It is the mobile symbol of the presidency and the country."

Walsh's book demonstrates that in the sixty years presidents have traveled by air, *Air Force One* has become an integral but all too neglected part of America's presidential history. His welcome history of the presidents and their planes will fill this gap and expand our understanding of the men and their administrations.

Robert Dallek

Washington, D.C.

October 2002

NOTE TO READERS

Since I started covering the White House in May 1986, I have traveled on *Air Force One* more than 200 times and visited all 50 states and 60 countries.

In the process, I became familiar not only with the planes available to the White House, but also with the presidents I observed on board—Ronald Reagan, George Herbert Walker Bush, Bill Clinton, and George W. Bush. These personal insights have been invaluable as a supplement to my research on the larger theme of the 12 presidents who have taken to the air since Franklin Roosevelt became the first of our leaders to fly, in 1943. As a result, I occasionally will enter the narrative of this book as an eyewitness to the events I describe.

All in all, I hope *Air Force One: A History of the Presidents and Their Planes* will provide a fresh perspective not only on these leaders, but also on the history of the past 60 years.

K. T. W.

I wish they had formed us like birds of the air, able to fly where we please. I would have exchanged for this many of the boasted preeminencies of man.

—THOMAS JEFFERSON,
third president of the United States
Letter to Maria Cosway, Paris, December 24, 1786

AIR
FORCE
ONE

CHAPTER ONE

THE ROLE OF *AIR FORCE ONE*

*A*IR FORCE ONE IS MORE than an airplane. It has become one of the most distinctive icons in the world.

As the personal jet of the president of the United States, it is a symbol of power, freedom, and prestige, immediately recognizable by virtually all Americans and by millions of people around the globe.

It has become part of our national mythology. It has emerged as a force in popular culture, appearing in top-rated television shows such as *The West Wing*, movies like Harrison Ford's 1997 hit, *Air Force One*, and even the comic strip "Doonesbury." It is seen regularly on the news as the president gives his famous wave from the top of the stairs. It is so glamorous that everyone from prime ministers to potentates, Hollywood actors to congressmen, urbane entertainers to hard-bitten journalists, wants to hitch a ride. And every president delights in showing off his very special airplane whenever he can.

With good reason. The bubble-topped 747—its blue-and-white skin waxed to a high gloss and its 231-foot, 10-inch fuselage bearing the oversized blue letters UNITED STATES OF AMERICA—is quite possibly the most unique plane ever built. The jumbo jet is not only reconfigured to accommodate the most powerful man in the world and his advisers, but it is also crammed with the latest technological advances, from communications to security. It is in the same league as the Statue of Liberty, the Lincoln Memorial, and the White House in its ability to inspire feelings of national pride. "It's a majestic symbol of our country," President George W. Bush told me in an interview for this book. "It reminds me of a bird, the bald eagle, in a way. It's just a powerful look. . . . Every time I see it, I'm proud of our country."

"It has," says pollster Bill McInturff, "become associated with incredibly powerful images," especially the instantly recognizable photograph of the swearing-in of President Lyndon Johnson a few hours after John F. Kennedy's assassination in 1963.

The American presidency would be a far different institution if not for the global reach that *Air Force One* has provided. The plane transported Richard Nixon on his path-breaking trip to China in February 1972 and to the Soviet Union in May 1972. In the 1980s, it took Ronald Reagan to his superpower summit meetings with Mikhail Gorbachev in Geneva, Reykjavik, and Moscow. It carried Bill Clinton on more foreign trips than any other president—133 over eight years. And it hopscotched George W. Bush from one secure location to another in the harrowing hours after the terrorist attacks of September 11, 2001.

LIKE ALL SUCCESSFUL institutions, the presidency adapts to the times. And since the Great Depression in the 1930s, the nation's chief executive has accommodated himself to more profound changes than ever before—in world affairs, politics, culture, the economy, and nearly every other aspect of national life. This period encompassed World War II and the cold war, cycles of prosperity and downturn, insularity and globalism, liberalism and conservatism.

One of the least noted but nevertheless important changes in the presidency has been generated by something that nearly every American today takes for granted: the ability to fly to any point on the globe, without undue strain or hardship, in a reasonable amount of time. This simple fact has made America's leader an international figure able to bring his ideas to places that presidents never dreamed of reaching a half century ago.

To that end, the president's plane has become an indispensable tool of his office, and the 12 chief executives who have taken to the air have logged 7 million miles since Franklin D. Roosevelt's first presidential flight, in 1943. "I can get more done on this plane!" Ronald Reagan said during a 1983 interview in his airborne office. "For example, I do a lot of letter writing, a lot of mail that I choose to answer myself, and I usually do it with a yellow tablet here. . . . I can come back with a tablet full and all the letters attached to it and hand it in to the office to be typed and for my signature. . . . There is instant communications and not only with the White House, but many times there've been international conversations on this plane. . . . But I have found that like in so many things domestically and so many things in every other part of our lives, face to face, getting to know the other heads of state, on a personal basis, I can actually say that we have established personal friendships with these people and . . . [*Air Force One*] has made it much more possible."

Bill Clinton told me: "I think in general a lot of presidents need more time alone than they get. You don't want it to be an excuse for avoiding hard decisions or the day-to-day work of the office. But my main times alone were on *Air Force One* and then when I was upstairs in the second-floor office in the White House. . . . I worked a lot late at night so I could be alone, read the things I wanted to read, and think about the things I thought I needed to think about. . . . Throughout the whole time I was president, I spent a lot of time alone on *Air Force One*. Especially when other people would sleep, I could just be there. Sometimes it was the first time in days I had been in a place where I could be away from the phones and away from mandatory meetings."

DWIGHT EISENHOWER, the third chief executive to fly, understood from the start that he was dealing with an important new dynamic. As he wrote more than four decades ago: "Behind all these other changes in the middle years of the 1950s loomed the changes of science, remaking the world and bringing new problems. More and more, the jet aircraft, the nuclear power plant, the hydrogen bomb, the ballistic missile were coming into the consciousness of all of us. When I entered the White House I traveled in a piston-driven plane, the *Columbine*. But before I left, my Air Force aide, Colonel Draper, had had to go to school to learn how to fly a new presidential airplane, a 707 jet."

It is significant that Ike mentioned jet travel in the same breath as nuclear power plants and the hydrogen bomb. He clearly saw it as one of the most important developments of his time, and he was right. It quickly became not only a symbol of the power of the presidency, but also what former Vice President Walter Mondale called, in an interview for this book, "an enormous symbol of American technological excellence."

IN ADDITION TO expanding the president's reach and serving as an international symbol, *Air Force One* has, over the past quarter century, become an invaluable window on the presidents themselves. It has evolved into a very special habitat, created by each president, that magnifies his virtues and flaws—and reveals that there is a real human being underneath the public façade.

Aboard *Air Force One*, a president has control over his surroundings without the intrusions, routines, and protocols of the West Wing. Presidents spend too much time within the confines of the plane, often under intense pressure and with little sleep, surrounded by confidants and friends, to keep their guard up for very long. As they cruise the endless skies during the course of endless hours, the essence of each individual will emerge.

As a result, *Air Force One* provides a unique view of a president's personality and character, a distillery of every quirk and foible, and a refuge where a chief executive can be observed in his natural state. If a president is a bully or a lout, as was Lyndon Johnson; if he is generous and kind, as was Gerald Ford; if he treats his subordinates with respect or disdain—all this will come across on the plane.

Historian Doug Brinkley says, "The White House is now a glass house. Everything is being watched and monitored, and it's very hard to create your own habitat there. But aboard *Air Force One*, a president is away from the media frenzy below. It's like commuting in a car. You get a contemplative space that you don't find anywhere else. You're getting a kind of tranquil oasis in a turbulent world, and a lot of decisions have been made in the sky."

In different ways, all 12 of the "flying presidents" used the plane to impress staff and guests with their power and personality and as a political instrument to lobby members of Congress and others to support their agendas. Several, especially Johnson, Richard Nixon, and Bill Clinton, seemingly used it to divert attention from their troubles in Washington by making high-profile trips abroad.

"In a sense, a president on *Air Force One* is a president more alone than he can be in the West Wing, whether he's winging his way to China or departing from the nation's capital for the final time," says Karl Rove, White House counselor to President George W. Bush. "On *Air Force One*, you see the president more as a single individual, not the great institution of the office. You see the presidents as they truly are."

Adds David Gergen, a journalist and political strategist who has advised presidents Nixon, Ford, Reagan, and Clinton: "This is a place where you can let your guard down very easily. . . . Part of it is you're physically much closer to people than you are sitting in the formal Oval Office setting. They're three feet away from you and there's almost a psychological tendency in a group like that to get into the spirit of intimacy. It's a setting which encourages more candid conversation."

"The most obvious thing is the degree to which some of these presidents become isolated up there in front of the plane," Gergen says. "In Nixon's case it was chosen. He wanted a private space. It was a carryover from the way he conducted his presidency. Nixon wanted to keep a wall. . . . Reagan tended to be more of a loner than people think. He was extremely affable but liked privacy. The mental picture one carries in his head is of Reagan and Nancy sitting forward in the plane. The mental picture you have of Nixon is Nixon alone in the plane.

"The mental picture you have of Clinton," Gergen continues, "is him staying up front part of the time but wanting to come back and watch movies with the staff, and sitting around playing cards. . . . What was certainly reinforced for me with Clinton was his need to be surrounded by people, how energized he was by talking."

Often a president's public persona is at odds with his private self. Once the president steps aboard and the big blue door slams shut, the veneer drops. Johnson, for example, may have been a great humanitarian in his public policies, but he was abusive to his subordinates and vulgar in the extreme when aboard the plane. Jimmy Carter also loved people in the abstract, but was aloof and sometimes inconsiderate to those around him.

Clinton had so many personas, both public and private, that it was impossible to tell which one would show up, the intellectual or the sports nut, the serious policy maker or everyone's pal. And as the most-traveled president in history, he conducted much of his business from his airborne White House. On the other end of the spectrum, Nixon was much the same person on and off the plane, a humorless workaholic and a solitary brooder who saw conspiracies everywhere.

Confirming his reputation, Reagan was just as disengaged from the details of governing in private as he was in public, although he never lost sight of his conservative ideals. And today, George W. Bush shows a similar conservative streak combined with a willingness to delegate large amounts of responsibility. Finally, Bush benefits from a Reagan-like affability that never disappears and a pervasive optimism.

A CLOSE LOOK at the flying presidents shows the remarkable diversity of America's leadership pool. They were all white men, of course, but if these chief executives are a guide, surely our democracy has no ruling class.

What other conclusion can one draw in a nation that turns for leadership to an eloquent Brahmin bred for power like FDR, then elects a failed haberdasher with a penchant for plain speaking and bold decision making like Harry Truman?

Next in line was a former general out of Kansas, Dwight Eisenhower, who had little in common with either of his immediate predecessors but provided an anchor of steadiness to national life. He was followed by a rich, telegenic career politician—and, for the first time, a Catholic—named John F. Kennedy who brought charisma, energy, and charm to the White House.

Then came a swaggering son of Texas, Lyndon Johnson, who was insecure about his ability to live up to the martyred Kennedy's legend but had big ideas about creating a Great Society.

Forced not to run again by an unpopular war, Johnson gave way to the brilliant but similarly insecure Nixon, another career politician with roots in California's middle class whose dark side led to the Watergate scandal and his resignation.

Gerald Ford, a former Michigan congressman who as vice president took office after Nixon resigned, was one of the most decent souls ever to serve. But he was defeated by a peanut farmer and ex-governor of Georgia, Jimmy Carter, who, like his two predecessors, lost the country's faith.

Ronald Reagan, an actor out of Hollywood, proved to be one of the twentieth century's most popular and influential presidents, a man who never forgot his Middle American background. Yet he passed his mantle to George H. W. Bush, another Brahmin with a penchant for public service, who was rejected after one term.

Bill Clinton, Southern-born son of the lower middle class, was the most gifted politician of his generation but one of the most self-indulgent of men. He took power from Bush by steering close to public opinion. But a dynasty was born when George W. Bush, of Yale, Harvard Business School, and Midland, Texas—the son of the former president—won the White House in 2000 after an extremely close election that was decided by a 5 to 4 vote in the Supreme Court.

Whatever their roots, all these men found that the presidential aircraft was one of the few places where they could feel a sense of privacy and create a unique atmosphere that reflected each one's personality, all reinforced by a staff that was always eager to please. "To the extent the plane is a traveling court, it is all oriented toward making sure the president has what he needs, and we were all there in that sense to serve the court," says Mark Penn, who was Clinton's pollster and a senior White House adviser.

Most newly elected presidents step aboard *Air Force One* and can't believe their good fortune. After spending a year or two bouncing around the country on small, leased aircraft as they seek the office, they tend to be overjoyed at the royal treatment they receive on their very own jet. Yet within a short time, they start thinking that they *deserve* such treatment. This can be a danger because it can inflate their already mammoth egos and insulate them from real life.

· · ·

THE PLANE HAS BEEN the venue for a wide range of behaviors, from the silly to the profound, fleshing out the human side of the presidency. There were Reagan's little-known practical jokes, and George W. Bush's bold decisions following the terrorist attacks on September 11. There were moments of high emotion, such as Clinton's moving tribute to Yitzhak Rabin that he delivered en route to the fallen Israeli leader's funeral, and whimsy, as in George Herbert Walker Bush's banning broccoli from the plane in 1989. The plane has been the perfect place for heavy-handed lobbying to pass the president's programs, a favorite technique of Johnson's. And it has served as a political reward, a specialty of Clinton, who gave scores of big donors rides on *Air Force One* during his eight years in power.

"I think you get a relatively complete picture of the president on *Air Force One*, especially on a long trip," says Andrew Card, White House chief of staff for George W. Bush, "because he does find time to eat, sleep, and be merry on the plane in addition to doing the job as president. . . . We don't get to see him sleep or eat very often or be merry very often in the Oval Office." Leon Panetta, White House chief of staff to President Bill Clinton, agrees. "Every *Air Force One* reflects the personality of the president. There's no question that it's as close as it gets to a family situation."

Air Force One has become, more than anywhere else, the place where a president can unwind immediately after a crisis, a high-pressure meeting, or a political showdown. He can kick back, have a drink or two, and relax with close advisers. "I rarely had that much unimpeded free time when I [was] not on the plane," Clinton said.

Often it is en route back home or to a vacation when a president's real personality and character clearly come into play, and where he can vent his innermost feelings. "There's something about the power and the majesty of that airplane that really reinforces to the presidents themselves that they are in charge," says Doug Sosnik, a former senior adviser to President Clinton who traveled frequently with him.

This dynamic was clear, for example, when President Kennedy traveled from Vienna to London after his confrontation with Soviet leader Nikita Khrushchev at their first summit meeting. "He had been through a trial by fire," says presidential historian Robert Dallek, who has written extensively about the Kennedy era. "Now he's in a little confined area on the airplane, he's with his friends, and he unburdens himself." As this book describes in Chapter Four, Kennedy's soul-searching monologue with aide Kenneth O'Donnell on that flight was one of the most revealing conversations of his presidency.

Air Force One had the same effect on Lyndon Johnson. Once, his aides said, he got "euphoric" during a May 22, 1964, flight to Washington after speaking at the University of Michigan in Ann Arbor. He was so delighted at the crowd's reaction to his use of the term the "Great Society" to define his social agenda that he even had a Scotch highball and pointed reporters to passages that he particularly liked so they could include them in their dispatches.

Clinton was known to be startlingly frank on late-night flights. Returning to Washington on Friday night, September 22, 1995, from California after a five-day fund-raising trip, he sauntered into the press compartment at the back of the plane wearing blue jeans, a casual shirt, and cowboy boots. Leaning against a bulkhead and then dropping into a crouch with his forearms resting on his knees, he talked gravely for 45 minutes about how America was in a "funk" because the world was changing so fast. "What makes people insecure is when they feel like they're lost in the funhouse," he told the puzzled journalists. "They're in a room where something can hit them from any direction any time. They always feel living life is like walking across a running river on slippery rocks and you can lose your footing at any time." He seemed to be blaming his fellow citizens for his own lack of leadership at a time when he was under attack from all sides. And even though he was mocked for it later, these were his true feelings, unmasked.

One thing all the recent presidents have had in common: a deep suspicion of the media. Few of the presidents have visited the press compartment very often, fearing that they might talk too much about sensitive policies or reveal too much of themselves. There is a standard warning that White House press secretaries have given to presidents in recent years: Beware of dropping by the media cabin, because you will be tempted by the casual, easy atmosphere to say too much, and nothing will be kept off the record (no matter what the reporters promise). Presidents who have disregarded this advice have done so at their peril.

AIR FORCE ONE IS ALSO a place where history is written. Clinton, for example, told me in January 2002: "We had actually quite a lot of eventful decisions that had to be made on *Air Force One*." As is discussed later in this book, he was talking about issues ranging from launching air strikes in the Middle East to ending a dangerous standoff in Miami over a Cuban boy named Elian Gonzalez.

Perhaps the best examples were the decisions made by George W. Bush aboard *Air Force One* on the day of the terrorist attacks in New York and Washington. Those choices set the course of the nation during a very trying time and set the tone for his presidency. It was probably the most dramatic day in *Air Force One*'s history.

FINALLY, *AIR FORCE ONE* is a place where extended periods of forced proximity can forge unique bonds among the world's most powerful and famous people. One such episode happened en route to the funeral of King Hussein of Jordan in February 1999, when the incumbent president, Bill Clinton, hosted three of his predecessors on the plane—George Herbert Walker Bush, Jimmy Carter, and Gerald Ford.

While Clinton occupied the presidential suite, Bush, Carter, and Ford, all in casual clothes, joined White House national security adviser Sandy Berger in the senior-staff compartment, which consists of four leather-upholstered seats, for the eight-hour flight from Washington to Amman. Eventually, Clinton appeared in the compartment and remained there for two hours, holding forth on the possibilities for peace in the Middle East, evaluating the region's leaders, and discussing the situations in Russia and Kosovo. At one point, Berger offered Clinton his chair, but the president declined and sat on a small ledge bordering the room.

In this rarified atmosphere—it's not often that current and former presidents get together—each of the four presidents was true to form.

Clinton immediately became the center of attention, analyzing the politics of the Middle East, explaining his policies, and displaying, as usual, a remarkable breadth of knowledge.

Ford, as Everyman, interrupted frequently to pose "straightforward questions that anyone might ask," according to an observer. "He just wanted to know more about what was going on. That was Ford's modus operandi."

Carter also would interrupt occasionally, but always to turn the conversation to himself. If Clinton mentioned Hussein, Carter would tell a story about his own relationship with the king. If Clinton talked about Egyptian leader Hosni Mubarak, Carter would tell a Carter–Mubarak story. It was as if he still had something to prove to this very select audience.

Bush didn't say a word for the entire two hours, but he listened carefully. Some Clinton aides felt he was gathering intelligence about the man who'd defeated him. Bush confidants later said he didn't want to meddle, and, just as important, didn't wish to appear deferential to his old antagonist. In any case, after Clinton left, the former president told Berger grudgingly, "He *is* a smart guy."

ANOTHER HISTORIC MOMENT was the remarkable partnership forged between former presidents Carter and Ford while aboard the plane.

It happened in October 1981, when newly inaugurated President Reagan asked his predecessors Carter, Ford, and Nixon to represent him at the funeral of assassinated Egyptian president Anwar el-Sadat. He sent them to Cairo aboard the same presidential jet that they had all used during their years in office. (The Secret Service advised Reagan and his vice president, George Herbert Walker Bush, not to attend because of security risks.)

The trip over was awkward, largely because of Nixon's brooding presence. Ford had endured ridicule for pardoning him for his role in the Watergate scandal and Carter had campaigned against his policies and character, so their relationships were difficult. Typically, Nixon kept mostly to himself. When he decided to stay behind to conduct some private business in the Middle East, Ford and Carter, the two adversaries from the 1976 campaign, were left to travel home together.

They sat for 18 hours inside a small conference room in comfortable leather-upholstered chairs, Ford, the big, balding former college football player, and Carter, the graying, diminutive lay preacher. They were interrupted a few times by courtesy calls from Alexander Haig, representing the Reagan administration as head of the U.S. delegation, and by a handful of other Reagan advisers and the flight stewards who served meals, snacks, coffee, and soft drinks. But as the hours melted away, so did the strictures of party, ideology, age, region, and background, and any lingering bitterness from their confrontation in 1976.

To their considerable surprise, by the end of that long flight, they had become close friends. They saw themselves, finally, as what they were: two battle-scarred public servants who had served with honor and good intentions but who lost the White House amid widespread criticism that their presidencies had failed. Aboard the plane, they became Jerry and Jimmy, old warriors who now yearned to make peace.

In an interview for this book, Carter told me: "Of course he had what I think was a friendly resentment—or maybe his family did—when I defeated him. That's an ordeal and a traumatic experience for anyone. And so we had very little relationship with each other until Sadat died.

"On the way back," Carter recalled, "President Ford and I just really got acquainted—about our children and our families and the difficulty of raising money to build presidential libraries. And we even talked about some of the events of those days, and the Camp David accords, and how he had been to Vladivostok and how my negotiations on the SALT II Treaty followed up on Vladivostok and how we dealt with cruise missiles."

Things got personal. "It was mostly consoling each other," Carter told me. "Both of us had been defeated after a rather short period of time, and [we talked about] how we reacted to post-presidential life." At one point, Ford confided that he needed to work hard on the lecture circuit and on corporate boards to earn money for his family. He had never accumulated a fortune, he explained, during his many years as a Republican congressman from Michigan and during his brief time as vice president and president.

"So by the time we got back home we realized that we hated to see the trip end. And after that we just became closer and closer," Carter said.

Ford has a similar recollection. "It was a very meaningful day-and-a-half, two-day trip under very trying circumstances," Ford told me in an interview. "On the way back, it was just President Carter and myself, and we had a lot of time to talk about things, what our plans were, what our differences might be, and how we could coordinate meetings at his library and do the same in mine. . . . We found that we had a lot of things in common where we would work together, and we have."

By the time the plane touched down at Andrews Air Force Base outside Washington, they had forged what Ford now calls "a very warm and constructive friendship" and Carter describes as an "intimate" friendship.

SIMILARLY, BOTH PRESIDENTS described *Air Force One* in almost reverential terms. Ford told me the plane had been invaluable to him. "It's the symbolism of the White House and of the presidency," he said, "and at the same time it's a very effective tool in how you deal with members of Congress, in how you deal with foreign dignitaries. It has a far broader impact than as just a mechanical piece of equipment."

Added Carter: "My most exhilarating moment as a governor [of Georgia] was when Richard Russell, our senator, died about two weeks after I became governor and Richard Nixon flew into Atlanta Airport in *Air Force One*. And I was overwhelmed with excitement and pride in my country. So I don't think there is any doubt that the aura of *Air Force One,* when I was in it going to the Mideast or when anyone uses it, is certainly an overwhelming factor of power and prestige."

Joe Lockhart, a regular traveling companion with President Clinton in the late 1990s as White House press secretary, says one reason for the unique atmosphere is that once a person gets inside *Air Force One*, pretense tends to fall away and everyone tends to act more naturally.

In recent years, jeans and sweat suits have been the favored form of dress on flights of more than an hour or two. Even Reagan, brought up with a sense of formality and dignity, would remove his carefully pressed jacket and trousers in his private cabin and slip into velour workout pants so he wouldn't wrinkle his outfit.

Once aboard, even the Secret Service agents can relax. The plane requires far less security than virtually anywhere else in the world because no one gets on without careful screening that includes sophisticated metal detectors and bomb-sniffer dogs; as a result, the dozen G-men and -women who accompany the president are essentially off duty, and feel no need to post themselves every few feet in the corridors and rooms, as they do in the West Wing. Instead, they plan the ground activities for the next stop, read, nap, listen to music, or watch movies. This contributes to the relaxed environment.

President George Herbert Walker Bush said *Air Force One* was an important tool during his four years in office. "I saw it as the symbol of the American presidency," Bush said in an interview for this book. ". . . People never forget that they rode on *Air Force One*. . . . And it was a very comfortable way in which to work and in which to relax.

"There's almost a kind of a wall in that plane," Bush told me. "You know, 'The president's up there. He's sleeping,' or 'He's working in his office right now. Do you think we ought to bother him?' I mean, you've got this kind of mystery about it like there is to the Oval Office, but it's a very different feeling. Their knees don't knock when you say, 'Get Joe up here. I want to talk to him.' "

"With President Clinton, you got to see the president in a different way," Lockhart added. "You could drop in to see him or sit at a table and play cards with him and ask him questions. You got a sense of what he was thinking, and you can't replicate that anywhere else. I learned a lot about his personal history and his political history, what he cared about, who he cared about."

Such insight is part of the unique atmosphere aboard *Air Force One*.

CHAPTER TWO

THE *AIR FORCE ONE* EXPERIENCE

S O, WHAT'S IT LIKE?

Riding *Air Force One* can be the thrill of a lifetime. Nearly every first-time guest, no matter how sophisticated, experiences a certain kid-in-a-candy-store awe.

Recalls journalist Hedrick Smith, a former *New York Times* correspondent: "Coming back from an economic summit meeting in Canada aboard *Air Force One* for an interview with Reagan, I remember being impressed by the high-backed luxury-style seats and a signal corps operator asking, 'Where would you like to call, sir?' Mentally, I imagined the click of military heels coming to attention at the other end of the line. Like an overawed tourist, I scooped up souvenirs: matchboxes, napkins, swizzle sticks, any item embossed with the presidential seal."

There are many theories about why it's so special. "It's almost a mythical place," says historian Doug Brinkley, who found flying aboard *Air Force One* more "awe inspiring" than visiting the White House. "The White House is no longer a residency. Hordes of people are turnstiling through, and there are endless photo ops. You feel much more privileged to be on *Air Force One*." And in that rarified atmosphere, visitors tend to bond with the president more intensely than anywhere else.

"The entire government of the United States is there in microcosm," says Stan Greenberg, who was President Clinton's pollster (and phoned his mother from the plane on his first trip). "The president is there with all his command authority and the infrastructure to wage war. You do things that are frivolous, like watch a movie, but you do it in the confines of this great concentration of power. And when you meet a president on *Air Force One* it's much more personal."

Greenberg explains that having an audience with the president in the Oval Office is less impressive because there is a pervasive sense that bodyguards, secretaries, senior-staff members, and others are ready to walk in at any moment. And the president is almost always rushed, with another appointment waiting in the wings. "On *Air Force One* you feel you're really there with him alone," Greenberg says in an observation shared by scores of people interviewed for this book. "There's something more intimate about it."

"For friends and supporters of the president, it's a very potent symbol of friendship, persuasion, and conciliation," adds Bill Galston, a political scientist and former White House adviser to Clinton. "For most people, it's a thrill. And when you come back you can share souvenirs of your trip on *Air Force One*— that's the coin of the realm." (Galston came away with an *Air Force One* notepad, which he still has at home.)

"Its role as a functioning, mobile White House should not be underestimated," the political scientist says. "It's a lot more conducive to work there than in the West Wing. You don't have phones ringing. You don't have people running in and out of your office.

"By White House standards it was luxurious. You felt pampered," Galston says. He tells a common tale: "You walk on *Air Force One* for the first time and you have to pinch yourself. You're feeling, 'Who am I to merit this?' I asked myself, 'How the hell did I get here?' Twenty years earlier I was an assistant professor teaching Plato and Aristotle. It was an existential experience."

.   .   .

THE AIRCRAFT HAS become so famous that virtually every American is familiar with it. Asked to name the plane that the president flies on, 78 percent of adults correctly identified *Air Force One*, according to a survey conducted in mid-2002 for this book by pollster Frank Luntz. Only 17 percent didn't know or refused to respond, and 4.5 percent gave other answers.

More than 82 percent of men correctly identified *Air Force One*, as did 74 percent of women. Frequent commercial travelers had an even higher recognition rate. Eighty-three percent of those who considered themselves "very likely" to take a trip in the next year correctly identified the president's plane.

For the first time, Luntz turned up evidence from survey research to demonstrate the aircraft's mystique and glamour. Asked how they would prefer to travel from the United States to Europe, Americans put *Air Force One* on a par with the *Queen Elizabeth 2* luxury cruise ship. About 38 percent of Americans said they would like to sail on the *QE2*, and 31 percent preferred *Air Force One*.

The mystique grows with a person's age. People between 50 and 64 were equally split, with 34 percent preferring to travel on *Air Force One* and 34 percent preferring the cruise ship—although women over age 50 chose *Air Force One* over the *QE2* by 37 percent to 33 percent. Men over age 50 were evenly split at 32.7 percent. Those over age 65, both men and women, favored the president's plane, 36.5 percent to 31.4 percent.

In a separate survey for this book conducted by pollster Bill McInturff of Public Opinion Strategies, 66 percent of Americans had a favorable impression of *Air Force One*, and only 4 percent had an unfavorable impression; the rest had no opinion or weren't sure. Asked to describe their feelings about the plane, the most common impression was that it was a symbol of the country and a reminder of history. Many volunteered that Lyndon Johnson was sworn in aboard the plane after President John F. Kennedy's assassination. Others remembered that George W. Bush began to direct the war on terrorism from *Air Force One* in response to the terrorist attacks of September 11, 2001.

IN THE MODERN presidency, two types of plane have stood out. The first was the sleek 707 used for three decades, with various modifications, by Eisenhower,

Kennedy, Johnson, Nixon, Ford, Carter, Reagan, and George H. W. Bush. It was the most modern jet in commercial use when it was introduced as the primary presidential aircraft in 1959, and carried 16 crew members and up to 50 passengers, including staff members, guests, Secret Service agents, and a handful of reporters and photographers called the press pool. It was capable of flying at 650 miles per hour but generally cruised at 580 mph with a range of 4,500 miles. The range gradually was increased to more than 7,000 miles. The journalists, then as now, were tucked into their own compartment so the president and his aides could avoid media snooping.

The second plane is the one in use today, a 747 jumbo jet that debuted with George Herbert Walker Bush in 1990. The 747 is a big improvement over the old 707 in various ways. For one thing, the jumbo jet can fly much farther without refueling; it has a range of 9,600 miles, a maximum cruising altitude of 45,100 feet, a cruising speech of 600 mph, and a maximum speed of 701 mph. That means it can travel nonstop all the way from Washington to Tokyo, for example. This saves the president lots of time, and has all but eliminated the need for trans-Pacific refueling stops.

The communications also are much improved, with added access to the Internet and to telephone service. There are 87 phones that can connect the president and all the passengers to nearly anyone in the world. The plane holds two pilots, a navigator, and flight engineer, a total of 26 crew members, and 76 passengers.

Journalist Hedrick Smith describes the huge entourage that has traveled with the president for many years, on the primary aircraft and several backup planes: "300 to 400 government officials: the President's senior staff plus echelons of policy advisers, negotiators, communiqué drafters, military aides, doctors, stewards, personal valets, even the first lady's hairdresser; plus several cabinet members with their lieutenants, specialists, secretaries, spokesmen, and miscellaneous handlers; and a phalanx of as many as 100 Secret Service agents ready to form a human wall, if need be, to insure the President's physical safety."

On major trips, a thousand pieces of luggage must be loaded and unloaded at each stop, transported to hotels, distributed to rooms, then brought back to the planes for departure. Finally, there is a separately chartered plane for the press (paid for on a prorated basis by the traveling journalists), which generally holds from 20 to several hundred reporters, editors, photographers, and technicians, and another dozen White House staff members and stenographers, depending on media interest in a particular trip.

Referring to Reagan's days on the 707, Smith offers an observation that remains true today: "When the president travels, the 'access itch,' the urge to be physically close to the president, becomes acute. The fewer people who can fit into a plane, a helicopter, a presidential limousine, the more competitive the inner circle becomes. . . . Long trips touch off a power scramble for choice seating on *Air Force One*."

AMONG THE MOST frequent of the frequent fliers are the media, specifically the rotating *Air Force One* pool of a dozen reporters and photographers who occupy the rear cabin. As a veteran of some 200 *Air Force One* flights over 17 years of covering the presidency, I can say that it's still a thrill to ride the big plane, but we in the press compartment really have little or no idea what is happening on the aircraft.

George W. Bush, for instance, approved the details of his proposal to create a new Department of Homeland Security, to fight terrorism, on a flight to Berlin in 2002. This would have been a huge story, but the reporters on the plane never had a clue until Bush announced the specifics weeks later. As is described later in this book, Bush also has held at least one Christian prayer service on the plane, opening himself up to charges of crossing the line between church and state—unbeknownst to his traveling press corps.

The biggest problem is that reporters can't leave the press cabin and go forward to the staff areas without an escort. This means the journalists are totally dependent for information on the press secretary and other officials who might come back to the media den. Presidents generally don't bother to talk to reporters on the plane because they could find themselves in an uncontrolled environment. There are exceptions. Now and then, for example, Bill Clinton would make news on the plane. But as a rule, the spoon feedings served to the media from the briefers tend to be totally self-serving and with minimum news value.

SECURITY AND SAFETY MEASURES have always been paramount. Even the initial construction phase of the current 747 was carefully monitored. Security and technical officials patrolled the production lines at Boeing, the manufacturer, to make sure a spy did not imbed explosive devices or listening or jamming devices in the air frame, with the capability of triggering them months or years later.

Maintenance is rigorous. The jet engines are changed much more frequently than those on commercial flights, and fresh tires—not the recaps routinely used by the airlines—are the rule. The crew regularly takes the 747 and its backup on test flights to make sure the planes are in top form and to run through emergency procedures, such as what to do in case of a fire, a blown engine, or a terrorist attack.

Everyday precautions are scrupulous. The planes are guarded around the clock, even in their mammoth hangar at Andrews Air Force Base outside Washington. When the planes are parked in open areas outside Andrews, a roped-off security perimeter is set up around each aircraft, and it is constantly patrolled. Even the fuel is guarded, as are the refueling trucks. In addition, Air Force specialists analyze the fuel before it is pumped into *Air Force One* to check for contaminants and other foreign substances.

Secret Service officials consider takeoffs and landings the most dangerous times because of the risk of shoulder-fired, heat-seeking missiles, or snipers with high-powered rifles. The danger is considered greater now because of suicidal terrorists.

As a result, before takeoffs and landings, a duty officer from base operations and a senior Secret Service agent make a sweep of the runway either on foot or in a van, looking for debris, explosives, or anything suspicious. At Andrews, agents shut the gates to the tarmac when *Air Force One* is about to depart; traffic is stopped in the vicinity of the terminal (and sometimes on the entire base if there is a special alert), and aircraft movement on the field is halted. Security teams with dogs patrol near the taxiways. Officers armed with sniper rifles and other weapons are stationed around the field at predetermined posts. Fire trucks, ambulances, and other rescue equipment stand ready.

The president's routine for reaching the aircraft is firmly established, and it is heavily dictated by security concerns.

He almost always leaves the White House from the South Lawn in his green-and-white *Marine One* helicopter (although a motorcade is used in bad weather), triggering a variety of activities at Andrews, a 10-minute chopper flight away.

As *Marine One* lifts off, a steward aboard *Air Force One* makes an announcement over the onboard public-address system: "We have a departure. The president is ten minutes out." This is a signal for the crew to make final arrangements for the arrival, for the staff to walk down the stairs of the plane to greet their boss, and for the traveling reporters and photographers to stand under the left wing in case he makes remarks or suffers a mishap, such as falling down the stairs (as Gerald Ford did on a trip to Salzburg in 1975).

When *Marine One* touches down about 100 yards from *Air Force One* and begins taxiing up to the president's jet, its engines now roaring, the steward announces, "We have an arrival." The chopper will approach to within about 100 feet of the front of the plane, the door will fly open, and the president will descend a short flight of stairs. He will either salute the Marine guard standing at rigid attention at the base of the small staircase or walk directly to *Air Force One* with an aide or the commander of the air base. This scenario is familiar to anyone who watches television news coverage of the White House.

The president's staff will walk a few discreet steps behind him so they are not shown in photographs. The president, often accompanied by the First Lady, will greet any dignitaries who have shown up, then walk up the long staircase to a small platform at the top, where he will turn and wave. Sometimes this ritual seems bizarre when there is no crowd to watch him depart. In that case, he will gesture happily to the buildings or to the reporters and photographers who record his movements—all to get that familiar wave on the evening news or the front pages.

Secret Service agents are trained to think in terms of providing 360 degrees of protection for the president, creating sectors of increasingly tight security from an outer ring to an inner ring. "It forces the assassin, we hope, to go through a lot of hoops," says retired Secret Service agent Jerry Parr. "That means he's liable to get caught."

The protection extends of course to presidential motorcades. Two or three identical armor-plated black limousines are used, and no outsider can be sure which one the president will enter. The others are used as decoys. Orange masking tape in an *X* is placed on the tarmac precisely where the pilot is supposed to position the nose of *Air Force One*. Agents will then park the primary limousine with its door open near the base of the front stairs so the president can board immediately. The limos are always placed between the president and any crowd, as a buffer in case of attack.

A presidential motorcade can consist of 40 or 50 vehicles, including security cars, staff cars, VIP vehicles, press cars and vans, and an ambulance and local police escorts. Of particular note is a black Suburban with tinted windows called the "war wagon." Inside is a heavily armed counter-assault team of agents, clad in black, trained to "attack and destroy" anyone who tries to harm the president.

As a general rule, other aircraft can't land on or take off from the same runway as *Air Force One* for 15 or 20 minutes before the president's plane arrives or departs, no matter where he is. Sometimes this also applies to adjacent runways or entire airports—a big reason why officials at some large airports don't want the big presidential jet to land there. It's just too disruptive of their normal operations, and his motorcade tends to hopelessly snarl traffic on local roads. Years ago, for example, presidents stopped routinely flying into New York's busy John F. Kennedy Airport for precisely these reasons. Now, when a president goes to New York City, he usually lands in Newark, New Jersey, a short helicopter ride from Manhattan.

Air Force One is never delayed by air traffic; it is always cleared immediately for takeoff and landing because, according to Federal Aviation Administration regulations, the president comes first. Bill Clinton abused this privilege by getting a haircut on the tarmac in Los Angeles early in his first term; and while his aides insist he didn't delay commercial flights (a dubious proposition), he easily could have, and that insensitivity was the problem. The "Haircut Incident" showed how isolating the atmosphere on *Air Force One* can be and how presidents often believe that whatever they do on board is beyond challenge or reproach.

Air Force One also gets cleared more easily to avoid bad weather. When the pilot and his crew detect storms or turbulence, they generally fly around or over them, a luxury that is often not available to commercial jets because their flight paths are more strictly controlled. Still, there are cases when unexpected turbulence shakes the plane and sends the crockery and an unbuckled passenger or two flying; that's a part of air travel that not even a president can avoid.

Sometimes other aircraft go off course and fly too close. This has happened a surprising number of times over the years. Just after midnight on May 27, 1997, for example, a Paris-bound *Air Force One* with President Clinton on board was over the Atlantic, 213 miles west of Shannon, Ireland, when UPS Flight 6080, a 747 cargo jet, came within about two miles horizontally and 1,000 feet vertically of the president's plane. This was too close for comfort and a violation of FAA rules. And on October 12, 1988, *Air Force One* with President Reagan aboard came within 1.58 miles of a Bar Harbor Airlines commuter plane as both were landing at Newark Airport. In each case, pilot error or mistakes by air controllers were blamed. But there apparently has never been a near collision, according to Air Force sources.

Despite the potential for tragedy, the Air Force resists sending fighter escorts with the president's plane wherever he goes. It's very expensive and, more important, it's considered too dangerous on routine flights in the already crowded skies. Escorts are more common in international air space where there is little traffic or in potentially hostile situations.

The plane has a special "skin" designed to harden it against electromagnetic pulses that could knock out its communications and navigational systems in the case of a nuclear attack. And it contains a highly classified system of defensive countermeasures designed to ward off heat-seeking missiles. For example, White House sources say that handheld, portable, shoulder-mounted Stingers and other types of missiles can be deflected by using chaff, flares, and other types of protective systems. This equipment is positioned to face the rear (where incoming missiles would presumably home in on the jet) and mounted above each of the plane's four engines and underneath the plane's fuselage. Apparently, these systems have never been used.

A 747 called the "Doomsday Plane" frequently accompanies *Air Force One* and is often parked near where the president lands, although it is rarely seen. This aircraft is packed with ultrasensitive communications equipment and military hardware and is designed to serve as a mobile command post in case of a catastrophic attack, particularly nuclear war. It can fly for longer periods of time and at higher altitudes than the regular *Air Force One*, and, like the primary 747, can be refueled in the air. Yet it has never been used by a commander in chief during a crisis, and some government officials believe the Doomsday Plane has outlived its usefulness. With the communications and security systems on *Air Force One* being updated continuously, there will come a time in the near future when the Doomsday Plane will not offer anything special to the president that he can't find on his regular aircraft.

Just as important, if the commander in chief ever boarded the Doomsday Plane, it might set off a panic. That was one reason President George W. Bush never flew on it during the crisis of September 11, 2001. The distinctive white Doomsday Plane was, in fact, parked within sight of *Air Force One* at Offutt Air Force Base in Nebraska when Bush landed there on September 11. White House officials considered transferring the president to that plane but nixed the idea. "We were very concerned about how that would have looked to the public," admits a senior White House official. "It might have scared people."

Air Force One has been the target of many bomb threats over the years. But most of them are ignored today because the security procedures—which include checking off each passenger's name on a manifest upon boarding and repeated inspections of baggage—are so thorough that they can't be easily penetrated. At least security officials hope so. Searching all the luggage and other onboard items of passengers is so disruptive and time-consuming that only a severe, credible threat would trigger such a response.

IN A LITTLE-KNOWN episode of the cold war, *Air Force One* was, for a while, equipped as a spy plane. In 1959, Allen Dulles, director of Central Intelligence, ordered his operatives to secretly install extremely sensitive cameras in the wheel wells under the 707's belly, which could be exposed to the ground during flight when doors opened up in the front of the wheel wells. The cameras were capable of photographing points at a great distance with very high clarity. "We could read license plates on the ground from twenty-nine thousand feet," said Ralph Albertazzie, a veteran Air Force aviator who served as Richard Nixon's presidential pilot and is intimately familiar with the plane's history.

Known as Project Lida Rose, the goal was to take photos of military installations, such as missile sites and air-defense bases, during President Dwight Eisenhower's planned trip to the Soviet Union in 1960. It was gamed out to such an extent that the CIA assumed a Soviet navigator would be allowed in the cockpit during Ike's scheduled trip, as a concession to Kremlin security and to help the Americans get where they were going in the super-secret U.S.S.R. As a result of this expectation, the equipment was designed to be operated surreptitiously by the copilot. He would use a false air vent or gasper unit just below waist level near his seat to adjust the cameras, guided by tiny lights on the control panel mounted at such an angle that only the copilot could see them. Using this system, the CIA concluded, thousands of spy photos could be taken during the trip, and the Soviet navigator would be none the wiser.

It was all apparently installed without Eisenhower's knowledge, according to past crew members. Yet the system was never used, says Albertazzie. Eisenhower's trip to the U.S.S.R. was cancelled amid recriminations over the downing of the American U-2 spy plane over the Soviet Union on May 1, 1960.

After President John F. Kennedy took office in January 1961, the reconnaissance cameras were removed. At that point, the spying gambit was considered too risky because the Russians would have been furious if they ever found out, and relations with the Kremlin were bad enough as it was. Yet U.S. officials suspected that the Kremlin had used the same technique on Soviet planes when they traveled in the United States and other Western countries.

For many years, when *Air Force One* flew across the Atlantic or Pacific, the military arranged for Coast Guard or Navy ships to patrol along the route. Vessels were strung along the vast expanse of water at 250-mile intervals in a long picket line, all of them in radio contact with the president's plane in case a rescue was needed. Vessels at coastal bases were alerted in case they had to join a search, and Coast Guard ships transmitted weather data to the *Air Force One* pilot when he approached their sectors.

But this elaborate system of oceanic escorts became obsolete in the late 1970s. Arranging such a huge armada of ships was no longer needed after the Air Force created a fleet of rescue airplanes—called "Duck Butts"—that were specially modified cargo aircraft carrying life rafts, rescue supplies, and medical teams. These planes would either accompany *Air Force One* or be ready to take off from various military bases at a moment's notice. The rescue squads were trained to parachute into the sea to assist survivors if the president's plane had to ditch and as rescue vessels proceeded to the scene.

A form of this system, combining air and sea elements in case of a disaster over the ocean, is still used today.

Finally, U.S. aircraft carriers, battleships, destroyers, and other large ships are often deployed as close to a president's flight path as possible to serve as emergency hospitals. Such vessels have more elaborate medical facilities than *Air Force One*, and the president could be treated on board if circumstances warranted.

JUST AS REMARKABLE as the security setup is the backup system that supports the president in all his travels. He takes with him all his ground vehicles, including two or three armored black limousines and his *Marine One* helicopter if a chopper trip will be necessary. Also accompanying him, in one or more giant Air

Force C-130 cargo planes, are communications gear and other cars, and modified vans and recreational vehicles for the Secret Service.

Service leaders believe this system is more reliable and safer than leasing vehicles and other equipment. As a result, the president generally travels with two or three huge support planes, cargo aircraft, and a press plane.

In addition, a vast network of advance workers supports his travel even before he starts. They visit every place he will visit, and try to trace every step he will take so that all goes smoothly.

SAFETY IS ALSO the first priority in more mundane matters, including food and beverage service. The flight attendants are responsible for making sure that nothing on *Air Force One* will cause a problem, even an upset stomach, for the commander in chief. "We make sure that anything that could be consumed in any way, shape, or fashion has not been tampered with," says former chief steward Howie Franklin. The flight crew receives an itinerary from the White House and determines how many meals or snacks are needed for each day of a trip. Then the flight attendants propose a menu and submit it to the White House Mess, partly to avoid redundancy. "We wouldn't want to serve salmon when the president had salmon the night before," Franklin told me.

The stewards do their shopping in civilian clothes at different markets around the Washington region. "We do it incognito and very low key," Franklin says. "We never want it to be predictable. That's the best security you can get. If they don't know you're coming, they can't prepare for you."

The 747 has brought *Air Force One* into a new world of food service, not a small consideration in an era when the president is airborne so much of the time. Not only are today's two full galleys more sophisticated than the two small kitchens on the 707, allowing more foods to be prepared fresh, but the refrigeration facilities are far more extensive.

In the era of the 707—from 1959 to 1990—the stewards lugged gray ice chests on board containing dry ice for frozen foods. These chests supplemented the two three-foot-by-three-foot refrigerators, one in the front kitchen and one aft. It was a serious challenge to maintain sufficient supplies of dry ice on long foreign trips to places where it was difficult to come by; the crew sometimes obtained supplies from U.S. Embassies and military facilities. "Keeping food on the 707 was an incredible task," Franklin says.

And the food service was a source of constant complaint. When Richard Nixon went to China in 1972, TV personality Barbara Walters flew on *Air Force One* and was not pleased when the stewards served her the dinner of the day—stuffed pork chops, which she spurned as too heavy. A flight attendant returned a few minutes later with a Spam sandwich, and she was so displeased that she complained about the food on television. Franklin recalls the incident with a laugh. The stewards didn't want to buy perishable ingredients in the local Chinese markets because they weren't sure the quality and health criteria were adequate.

Today, the crew can store enough food and beverages on *Air Force One* to serve everyone three full meals a day for two weeks. "It makes a big difference," says Tim Kerwin, the former chief flight steward who designed the 747's food-service system. "We can assure that all the food is from the United States. We don't have to get food in foreign countries," where it might not be up to American standards.

For years, the tradition has been to bill White House staff members—and the president, First Lady, and their families and guests—for their meals on the plane. The cost of an average breakfast is $4 to $6; lunch, $6 to $8; and dinner, $8 to $11. The effort to hold down costs is one reason why the meals aboard *Air Force One* are hardly gourmet fare; no one wants to spend a lot of money on them.

Particularly during the Bush and Clinton eras, the presidents and First Ladies have insisted on more low-fat meals and have preferred bottled water or diet soda rather than sugary soft drinks or alcohol, all for health reasons. Under Ford and Carter, for example, breakfast would often be scrambled eggs with cream cheese, hefty sausages, fried hash brown potatoes, a biscuit or danish, and a small fruit cup. Today, breakfast on board tends toward bran muffins, cereal, fresh fruit, and yogurt.

In President Johnson's day, in the 1960s, the staff would stock up on

Fresca and other soft drinks rather than risk his thundering wrath if they ran out. Still, they sometimes ran dry because the facilities for storage and refrigeration were relatively primitive by twenty-first-century standards. These days, a president can have just about any food or drink he likes, at any time of the day or night.

There is one galley for the president and his staff at midship and another galley for lesser lights in the rear of the plane. The military stewards, chosen for their affability and work ethic, will go to great lengths to please their boss and anticipate his wishes—bringing in Texas barbecue for George W. Bush when he returns to Washington from his ranch in Crawford, just as they stocked jelly beans for Ronald Reagan and juicy steaks for Lyndon Johnson.

In fact, the dining habits of the presidents amount to a rich story in and of itself. George H. W. Bush banned broccoli from *Air Force One* as a sort of late-in-life rebellion because he hated the taste and smell of the mineral-rich vegetable, and his mother used to make him eat it when he was a boy. Bill Clinton started out eating junk food—burgers, fries, tacos, and the like. But because of the advice of his doctors, and because he was concerned about his ballooning weight, by the end of his second term he was quite a healthy eater, consuming lots of chicken, fish, fresh vegetables, and salads. George W. Bush eats anything put before him, but he prefers Tex-Mex items such as burritos and fajitas, and he loves Asian food.

The White House provides a list to the *Air Force One* crew of every new president's likes and dislikes. The list also includes a rundown of the commander in chief's health problems, allergies, and anything else the crew might find helpful in serving him.

"Every president that I worked for was interested in his weight," says Franklin, who served Ford, Carter, Reagan, Bush, and Clinton. "They were all interested in eating low-calorie diets. President Ford's favorite thing was cottage cheese with A-1 steak sauce. It was low-fat and it was considered a dietary thing during that time and he wanted to dress it up a little bit with A-1 sauce. It was also very common for him to have carrot sticks, seedless grapes, celery sticks."

Yet Mike McCurry, former press secretary to President Clinton, says, "Most people would assume that there's a little bit more luxury than there is. . . . People would be surprised at the food. Not to offend the Air Force, but it's basically military chow."

Passengers are expected to eat what they are served. And the stewards are not pleased if a guest rejects a regular meal. That means more work for the galley. When a passenger asks for a substitute, such as a chicken-salad sandwich or similar light fare, the stewards try to handle the requests diplomatically but aren't happy with the disruption of their routine.

FROM TIME TO TIME, someone in Congress or in the media raises questions about whether the cost of transporting the president has become excessive. They have a point.

Operating costs have soared over the years. In the 1950s, it cost $348 per hour to fly Eisenhower's four-engine prop plane. In the mid- and late 1960s, under Lyndon Johnson, the 707 cost $1,995 per hour to fly. By 1976, under Gerald Ford, the cost had edged upward to $2,300 per flying hour. By the late 1970s, under Jimmy Carter, the operating cost for the 707 was about the same, $2,327 per hour.

Since 1991, the Air Force has estimated that it costs more than $40,000 per hour to fly the big 747. But fuel and supply costs fluctuate, and the estimate does not include many related expenses, such as the salaries of the crews or the special hangar that houses the aircraft at Andrews Air Force Base.

In 2000, President Clinton's visit to Asia cost taxpayers an astronomical $63.5 million, which raised eyebrows on Capitol Hill. That included the cost of operating the two 747s, one as the primary presidential aircraft and one as the main backup, and flying other support planes, including a C-20C Gulfstream III in case of an emergency requiring a smaller aircraft, in addition to more than 60 other aircraft to haul personnel and equipment halfway around the world.

Yet the criticism has never caught on with the public. Americans seem to want their leader to travel in style as well as safety. And the amenities keep on proliferating. Under George W. Bush, satellite TV was added, along with a 50-

inch-wide flat screen in the conference room. This gives the senior staff a much wider assortment of programming to watch from all around the world—especially baseball games, the president's favorite TV fare—and breaking news on the networks. It also makes viewing more of a communal experience, because the large screen provides the feeling of a movie theater.

Passengers in each compartment have access to a list of first-run and classic movies in the *Air Force One* library, and they can pick whichever one they prefer on each cabin's screen. Usually it is done by an informal consensus, although in the press cabin the photographers and TV crews often get to the phone first and simply order what they want. That generally means a shoot-em-up cop film or Western, a sci-fi flick, or a racy R-rated selection.

This can lead to bizarre moments. During Clinton's 1996 campaign, the journalists grew fascinated with the movie *Fargo*, a brilliant but violent film about a pregnant cop and a variety of felons. On nearly every leg of every trip, *Fargo* would appear on the screen in the press compartment, and several passengers would recite the lines of each character from memory. This eventually caused a rift in the press corps as some reporters tired of the gambit.

THE 26-PERSON flight crew loves today's plane like a member of the family. To them, the plane is known by its manufacturer's designation, Boeing 747-200B. Actually, there are two identical jets with tail numbers 28000 and 29000; 28000 is the primary aircraft, and its twin, 29000, is the backup, flying almost wherever the primary jet goes, just in case. Whenever the president is aboard either plane—or any other Air Force aircraft, for that matter—the radio call sign is *Air Force One*.

"This is probably the most unique airplane in the world because it carries the most powerful leader in the world," says Mark Rosenker, former director of the White House Military Office, which is responsible for the president's overall transportation. ". . . You sit back and say, 'My Lord, I'm sitting with the president of the United States. That's unique."

"*Air Force One* is adventure, camaraderie, teamwork," says Franklin. ". . . You're with these people for long periods of time. You're putting them to bed, you're waking them up. You're seeing them at their absolute best. You're seeing them when they're absolutely tired. . . . I mean, long days, long hours, you've been over in the Middle East or the Far East, and you're tired, and you've probably got the runs. And they come back on *Air Force One*, a little bit of home. It's America. It's a symbol and it's a comfortable place to be. All the presidents have said they enjoyed *Air Force One*."

THE PRESIDENT'S PLANE is much different from the standard 747 that a commercial traveler might fly. The VC-25A, which is the special model used by the commander in chief, has exotic electronic and communications equipment, relatively plush and spacious accommodations and furnishings, a self-contained baggage loader, front and aft stairs, and the capability for in-flight refueling. Its four General Electric CF6-80C2B1 jet engines can take the aircraft to 701 miles per hour. It stands 63 feet, 5 inches in height; is 231 feet, 10 inches in length; has a wingspan of 195 feet, 8 inches; and has a maximum takeoff weight of 833,000 pounds. It has 4,000 square feet of usable space, twice that of the average single-family American house.

The president's suite would do a luxury hotel proud. It consists of a state-room in the nose of the aircraft, decorated in beige, rust, and brown and featuring a wall mural that resembles a desert sunset. There are two couches, one along each side, that can be converted to beds and, next door, a bathroom with shower. Adjacent to the suite is a mini-clinic with a large cabinet full of medications and a surgical table that pulls out of a wall in case of a health emergency.

Next to this area is a spacious presidential office with a big beige wraparound desk, a first-class-style leather seat directly across from the desk, and two couches. The White House photographer's office keeps the walls of the suite hung with up-to-date photos of the president's journeys.

Behind the president's suite is a senior-staff cabin, a galley, another staff compartment, a large conference room, another cabin for staff with a desk and chairs, a workroom with computers, a guest cabin, a Secret Service compartment, a press cabin, and the rear galley. The two galleys provide up to 100 meals at one sitting. There are six lavatories, which include facilities for the disabled.

Running along the left side of the fuselage is a long, softly lit corridor containing couches, tables, and lamps, like the reception area of a conference center in a big hotel. This "public area" is on the left side for security reasons. *Air Force One* always pulls up to an air terminal or public ceremony with its left side parallel to onlookers. This allows the president, senior staff, and other dignitaries to remain on the far side to lessen the chance of a successful attack.

AIR FORCE COLONEL MARK TILLMAN, the pilot, says the crew members, who are assigned to the 89th Airlift Wing under the Air Mobility Command at Andrews, "spend hours upon hours to make sure we never have a hiccup with it." Still, not everything always goes perfectly.

The communications system, for example, is not what one might expect. Presidents and other passengers are regularly disconnected from secure calls—to foreign leaders, their national-security advisers, or others—and this problem has existed for years. Clinton used to rage about it because he would be embarrassed over frequently losing the connection in mid-sentence.

George W. Bush has endured the same problem, but he deals with it more philosophically. After September 11, the communications systems were upgraded, but White House advisers say it did not make a huge difference. "I can say to you that they're good, they're not great," says a senior Bush adviser. "The not-secure calls are fine—but secure calls just take a while to establish sometimes. It's just the nature of encryption—encryption moving at thirty-five thousand feet, at five hundred to six hundred miles an hour." Mack McLarty, Bill Clinton's former White House chief of staff, points out that a caller has to push a button on the side of the phone to talk when the security system is in use, and this causes a slight but unsettling delay. As a result, people talk over each other and conversations get confused.

And the plane is not immune to pilot foul-ups. Clinton's plane was grounded for more than an hour in January 1998 at the LaCrosse, Wisconsin, airport when it got stuck in the mud. The White House used a smaller 707 instead of the 747 jumbo jet that day because the airstrip was judged too short for the larger plane, but still the pilot accidentally rolled one set of wheels off the runway on preparation for takeoff.

Efforts to extricate the jet using the pull of the engines failed while Clinton played a game of cards on board. Officials considered whether to remove some fuel to make the plane lighter, or to tow it out of the mud with trucks, but a simpler solution was found: A backup Air Force 707—in fact, the one (designated SAM 26000) that had flown John F. Kennedy's body back to Washington from Dallas in 1963—was brought in, and this finally got the president out of town. The 707 pilot who got stuck in the mud never flew Clinton again, according to White House officials.

THERE ARE MANY FOLKWAYS aboard *Air Force One*. All the seats are assigned, regardless of which party is in power. But each White House has its own policy for deciding who goes where. Republican administrations like those of Nixon, Reagan, and the Bushes tend to strictly assign seats based on seniority, with the most important aides getting the first-class chairs and the junior staffers stuck in the *Air Force One* equivalent of steerage.

GOP administrations tend to impose a protocol that no one is allowed to enter the seating areas in front of his or her assigned location. The president himself and the senior staff stay in the forward-most areas, which means the middle-level and junior aides are deeper and deeper into the plane. The most junior aides and a dozen Secret Service agents are in a rear compartment just ahead of the press pool, which fronts the rear galley.

Democratic administrations tend to give the aides the run of the plane. In Clinton's time, everyone on the staff—including the president—mingled freely with everyone else, although no one could just walk in on the president in his bedroom or his office. If it happened by mistake, Clinton would glare at the offender. He would usually be clad in jeans and a T-shirt, and would be reading, watching TV, or listening to jazz turned up very loud to overcome his hearing problem. Some staffers couldn't stand to be in his cabin at these times because it was so noisy.

At the start of each flight, each compartment receives a neatly printed menu of the food to be served and a weather report for the destination. Stewards come by shortly after takeoff to solicit drink orders, much like what happens in the first-class section of major airlines. Food service is prompt and efficient.

At one time, many trinkets and baubles were available on the plane, such as blue or white pads bearing the embossed words "Aboard *Air Force One.*" Also prized were *Air Force One* playing cards, mugs, glasses, and M&M's candies in small boxes bearing a presidential signature. These items are very difficult to find today because the supply of freebies has been cut back drastically. What is still available is an almost unlimited supply of small, white paper napkins bearing the words *Air Force One* in blue. These, of course, have limited utility as gifts compared with the items available in the old days.

Another big change is the placement of the restroom for staff members and guests. Aboard the 707, the president and First Lady had their own lavatory, and nearly everyone else was expected to use the restroom in the rear of the aircraft, just behind the press cabin. This meant that the VIPs had to walk down the aisle past reporters and photographers when nature called. Sometimes it was awkward because the officials, for obvious reasons, had no time for niceties. As they ran the gauntlet, the officials were questioned or badgered by the journalists, who tried to pressure nearly every walk-through into giving a mini-press conference.

The new 747 solved that problem. The aft restroom was given over totally to the press and extra facilities were added in the forward areas to accommodate the staff members and guests.

OVER THE YEARS, there have been many tales of amenity abuse on presidential trips. Some of the rumors are true.

For one thing, 40 years ago, White House staff members could arrange for girlfriends (the staff was virtually all male in those days) to hitch a ride on the plane and be given royal treatment. And while crew members and others say Lyndon Johnson had assignations with female passengers in his cabin, it would have been very difficult for staff members to have the same experience. There was too little privacy, and too little space, for that.

What *has* happened is more mundane, such as abuse of luggage privileges. During Gerald Ford's era, presidential aides arranged for much-coveted Coors beer to be transported on the backup planes, since it was then a rare treat on the East Coast. And at the end of any trip to California, presidential aides and journalists showed up at check-in time with cases of wine to be lugged into the cargo holds of *Air Force One* and the press plane by baggage handlers. There is less of that today, since someone in the media would be sure to blow the whistle on such self-indulgence. Still, staff members, journalists, and guests continue to bring back prize purchases from exotic locales, ranging from rugs to wooden carvings. Once in a while, someone will get caught trying to avoid paying duty on a purchase, but this is rare.

TECHNICALLY, THE WHITE HOUSE and the military consider any aircraft carrying the president to be *Air Force One*, whether it's an executive-style jet or a lumbering C130 cargo plane (and presidents have ridden on both, depending on the size of the airport he is traveling to and other factors). But what most people think of as *Air Force One* is a Boeing 747, the sleek and powerful four-engine transcontinental jet with the bubble top that is the president's customary mode of travel.

The plane was ordered and designed starting in 1985, just after Ronald Reagan won his second term. Pentagon brass had recommended building a special 747 for the commander in chief for years, but no president had dared order it because they feared it would look profligate. In the end, two 747s were produced—one as a primary aircraft for the president and one as a backup—at a cost of more than $660 million. (And contrary to the myth popularized in the movies, the plane does not have an escape pod.)

The new plane was supposed to be on line in November 1988, but it took more than four years to build—a year longer than expected because of complications that arose in installing the sophisticated communications equipment that allows secure phone calls all over the world. Another problem was that the communications system was planned by Boeing for a smaller, less sophisticated model of the 747, and it didn't work properly in the special version that the White House ordered. It took many months to redo it, according to flight personnel.

The VC-25A version of the 747, tail number 28000, first flew as *Air Force One* on September 6, 1990, when George Herbert Walker Bush took it from Washington to Kansas and Florida. Its twin, tail number 29000, was deployed March 26, 1991, according to the Air Force.

Everyone was thrilled, even though it came at a very high cost—an estimated $185 million a year to operate the plane and pay its crew, depending on how actively a president travels.

WILL THERE BE A NEW, twenty-first-century version of *Air Force One*? Flight experts predict that in the not-too-distant future, perhaps in 20 years, the president will routinely fly on a supersonic airplane. It will take that long because there are so few facilities around the world that can accommodate such a jet on a routine basis, and many years will go by before supersonic travel becomes economical. In addition, the supersonic jets now built by the aircraft companies are much smaller than the 747, so they would have limited utility for presidential entourages.

For the foreseeable future, the 747 will remain the president's aircraft. "The president doesn't need a bigger plane," says retired Air Force general Brent Scowcroft, a former pilot and White House national security adviser who once served as head of the White House military office. "And you can upgrade the communications anytime you want. I don't see any need for planning [for a new jet]."

Mark Rosenker, former director of the White House Military Office for George W. Bush, agrees. "There's no plan in this administration to talk about a new transport," he says.

Rosenker adds: "We're always working to make improvements, not only in the operations but certainly any type of hardware improvement as advances come along. We're dealing with an aircraft that is twelve years old, but the 747 [as a type of plane] has been around for twenty-five years. So when we can make technological improvements, we try to do that."

The next improvement, he says, will be the addition of broadband communication, with the ability to get the Internet onto the airplane. This will let the staff shoot video and send it down to an earth station. It also will allow video-telephone calls and video conferencing. Plans are also being considered to upgrade the seats, converting each one into a larger, fully reclinable sleeper.

"It's slowly going to be modified over the years," says *Air Force One* pilot Mark Tillman, "but this plane is going to be around for quite a while."

CHAPTER THREE

FRANKLIN ROOSEVELT, HARRY TRUMAN, AND DWIGHT EISENHOWER: THE FIRST "FLYING PRESIDENTS"

A T THE START OF Franklin Roosevelt's administration, Americans thought it was too dangerous for a president to fly. Besides, they felt that their leader belonged in the White House and should stay there, especially in times of crisis.

No president had traveled abroad until Theodore Roosevelt sailed to Panama in 1906. But he used an American ship and stayed outside U.S. waters for only a few hours, specifically to tamp down criticism at home. Woodrow Wilson wasn't so careful. He traveled by ship to the Paris Peace Conference after World War I, spending several weeks away from Washington, and caused a furor that helped to undermine his leadership. Many Americans thought their president should never stray from the United States, and Wilson's venture—trying to organize a new political order in Europe and create a League of Nations—was not a popular mission to start with.

Franklin Roosevelt changed the whole dynamic. In fact, the act of flying showed Roosevelt to be not only a daring individual, but also a creative and pragmatic thinker, willing to give new things a try, just as he was in so many other areas.

The Depression and World War II had shaken America to its core, and Roosevelt felt he had to project confidence and effectiveness. So he emphasized a spirit of jaunty optimism as much as possible, and flying was part of his mystique. It served notice that the president would do whatever it took to get his job done, and Americans appreciated that.

On January 11, 1943, he became the first chief executive to travel by air when he boarded a hulking, prop-driven Pan Am Dixie Clipper, nicknamed the "Flying Boat," for a secret meeting with Winston Churchill in Casablanca. His mood was upbeat. "He was about to see a new continent, Churchill, combat troops," wrote historian James MacGregor Burns. "And he would travel by plane for the first time since his famous flight to the Democratic convention in Chicago in 1932 [before he was elected]. He would be the first president to fly, the first to leave the United States in wartime, and the first since Lincoln to visit an active theater of war. To take a trip, to enter a war zone, to create precedents—no combination of events could make Roosevelt happier."

Privately, he expressed concern that an airplane moved so fast that he would not be able to enjoy the sojourn at his leisure. "I'm in no hurry," he said. "The sooner I get where I'm going, the sooner people will be wanting something from me." Like so many men and women of wealth and power at this time, he saw travel as a respite, a way to escape the burdens of his job, rather than a way to get things done en route to his destination, which is the way modern workaholic presidents view their time on *Air Force One*.

FDR had an additional problem. Despite his vigorous public persona, his legs were paralyzed from polio, and air travel was a hardship. At 6 feet, 2 inches tall and 188 pounds, he would have been uncomfortable in the relatively small airplane cabins of the day under any circumstances. But he felt doubly confined when he had to spend long periods of time without the opportunity to move around freely by wheelchair or on crutches, as he could on a train or a ship. Roosevelt also found it difficult to conduct his famous monologues above the roar of propellers and engines.

Finally, he never forgot that pre-presidential flight to the Democratic convention in 1932, when storms buffeted the plane and threw a scare into the passengers. For all these reasons, Roosevelt made only three trips by plane during his more than 12 years in office. He used an aircraft only when he considered it absolutely necessary.

But he felt that the Casablanca trip was one of those times. The outcome of World War II was very much in doubt, and Roosevelt believed he needed to sit down face-to-face with Churchill to better understand the British leader and to plan out the long-range Allied campaign in Europe. The military decided that going by ship was too dangerous because German submarines were lurking all across the Atlantic. The brass also concluded that few people expected the president to fly, so FDR would have the element of surprise on his side. And Casablanca was a totally unexpected site.

The trip, described later by pilot Howard Cone, provided a glimpse into FDR's gregarious personality and his everyday challenges as a polio victim. Typically, he made the best of it. Eleanor, his wife, often remarked that Franklin had learned patience and empathy during his grueling struggle against polio, which he contracted as an adult, and these traits were on display during the airborne trip.

First, the president traveled under utmost secrecy from Washington to Miami by train. After takeoff at dawn from Dinner Key in South Florida, Roosevelt changed into an open-collar shirt, a sweater, and baggy slacks, and began eagerly looking out the window at the azure waters off South Florida's Atlantic coast. He kept track of the plane's position with navigation charts that he spread out before him on a small table in the passenger cabin. He called over a steward and pointed out a spot where he had once gone deep-sea fishing during a vacation trip, and reminisced about how much he loved being on the water with friends. He also kept track of the Atlantic Clipper, the Dixie Clipper's sister seaplane, which was flying close by, filled with military and government officials and a contingent of Secret Service agents. As the flight progressed, he remarked on the jungle of what was then Dutch Guiana, the Amazon River, and the merchant ships near the Brazilian port of Belem.

The seaplanes first flew 1,633 miles in 10 hours from the Miami area to Port of Spain, Trinidad, where everyone spent the night ashore. Next morning, the two clippers droned 1,227 miles in eight hours southeast along the coast of

South America to Belem, Brazil. Roosevelt read, napped, and played solitaire. After a three-hour layover to refuel and service the plane at Belem, the Flying Boats swung eastward across the South Atlantic on a 2,500-mile, 15-hour flight to Bathurst in what was then British Gambia, near Dakar. Roosevelt and his entourage then boarded two C-54 prop planes, one of which had been outfitted with ramps so his wheelchair could be pushed easily into the aircraft. They proceeded for another 1,500 miles over nine hours to Casablanca.

Otis F. Bryan, the pilot on the final overland leg, later recalled that Roosevelt asked many questions about the geographical features below as the North African landscape rolled beneath him. "He didn't ask for special privileges," Bryan said. "In fact, we removed several seats to make him a bed, but he preferred to sit up and stay awake because the others in the plane didn't have similar conveniences."

Roosevelt spent 10 days in Casablanca planning the Allied invasion of Europe. He took a few extra days to visit Liberia, home to thousands of former slaves from America, and meet with President Edwin James Barclay. He disembarked in Brazil to see President Getulio Dornelles Vargas and to review U.S. troops at the Natal air base, stopped again at Port of Spain, Trinidad, and flew back to Miami.

For the final leg from Trinidad to Florida, the Dixie Clipper's staff prepared a special meal for the president to celebrate his 61st birthday—caviar, turkey, potatoes, peas, coffee, and a big cake, all brought aboard at Port of Spain. Roosevelt loved being the center of attention, and he cut the cake himself with a small metal spatula as he sat at a cramped table covered with white linen. Fleet Admiral W. D. Leahy sat to his right, adviser Harry Hopkins was directly across from him, and pilot Howard Cone sat across from Leahy. FDR carved big slices with gusto and handed the dessert to each staffer and crew member aboard.

As amazing as it is to ponder today, with our 24-hour news cycles and media ubiquity, the president's trip was kept secret until Roosevelt decided to reveal it at the end of the journey. There were no leaks and no intrusive reporters in tow, only the president and his cast of white, middle-aged, male advisers, assistants, and military and security personnel. (Diversity was not a priority in the America of the 1940s.)

Roosevelt made the trip in what would today be considered an eternity—three days of travel, including 42 hours in the air *each way*. Nowadays it would take about eight hours to fly the 3,875 miles from Washington to Casablanca. And the president was exhausted by the experience. He developed a fever on the way home and, as the engines roared with incessant background noise, wrote his wife, Eleanor, that, "All has gone well though I'm a bit tired—too much plane. It affects my head just as ocean cruising affects yours."

In her memoirs, Eleanor, who loved to fly, wrote, "It was his first long trip by air across the water and I had hoped he would be won over to flying, but instead he disliked it more than ever and much preferred travel by ship. I tried to tell him that the clouds could be as interesting as waves, but he always said: 'You can have your clouds. They bore me after a certain length of time.'"

Still, the first presidential trip by air was liberating. It was all the more impressive to Americans because Roosevelt seemed truly courageous to have made the journey at all. It was, after all, only 16 years since Charles Lindbergh had startled the world with his solo nonstop flight from New York to Paris aboard the *Spirit of St. Louis*.

FDR made two more trips by plane—to Teheran and Yalta—demonstrating that from then on, no president would be limited by the innate slowness of ground or water transportation.

In 1944, Roosevelt had a Douglas C-54 Skymaster four-engine prop plane, later nicknamed the "Sacred Cow" by an irreverent press corps, converted for his exclusive use. The redesign included a wheelchair lift in the belly of the aircraft. The tinny, gray-colored contraption resembled an old-style telephone booth, but it was only four feet tall and could barely accommodate the president in his wheelchair. The lift was raised from the ground into the plane's belly electrically, then a door neatly folded over the opening so that an outsider would never realize the wheelchair compartment existed. Roosevelt didn't want anyone beyond his inner circle to know of his affliction, and he didn't want any spies to figure out which plane he was on.

The Sacred Cow also had a small, rectangular bulletproof window in the president's 7.5-by-12-foot stateroom in the aft compartment, where it was quietest. The room contained a single chair for the commander in chief, a small desk, and a two-seat couch. Across the narrow aisle were seats for seven and a sofa that opened into a bed; a drape could be pulled across the bed for privacy. The plane was furnished with upholstery of blue wool. Draperies at the windows were of blue gabardine, embroidered with the insignia of the Army, Navy, Marine Corps, and Coast Guard.

There was a primitive galley and a crew of seven. The flight attendants were nicknamed "hotcuppers" because they used electric devices to heat coffee, soup, and other beverages in cups, an indication of the basic nature of service by today's standards.

FDR managed to use the Sacred Cow on only one trip before his death. He took an airborne hop from Malta to Yalta after crossing the Atlantic aboard the heavy cruiser *Quincy* in February 1945. At Yalta he met with Soviet leader Josef Stalin and Britain's Churchill to plan the endgame of World War II and consider the shape of the post-war world. Roosevelt then flew on the Sacred Cow from Yalta to Cairo, where he boarded the *Quincy* for his voyage home.

Future presidents would make far more use of the flying White House. Over the next half century, as technology advanced, presidential aircraft progressed with it, extending the reach of the leader of the free world more than anyone imagined was possible when FDR became the first commander in chief to fly.

UNLIKE ROOSEVELT, HARRY Truman loved to travel by air, and the way he did it reflected his feisty personality and his down-to-earth approach to life. Also unlike Roosevelt, whose planes were unadorned and designed not to stand out so spies and other outsiders wouldn't know he was aboard, Truman wanted everyone to know he was there. He and his advisers had the front of his plane, the *Independence*, painted to resemble the head of an eagle, complete with yellow beak (quickly repainted white because the yellow interfered with radio signals and visibility) and blue tail feathers on the rear of the fuselage.

In fact, Truman flew so often that he reassured many Americans that air travel was a safe, convenient way to move around the country. If the president was comfortable doing it, it must be a good thing—and why not the rest of us?

Actually, Truman had not taken to flying naturally. He rode his first airplane in the 1920s in a World War I-era biplane, and when it landed in a farm field, he walked over to a fence and vomited. His mother also had a bit of trouble when Truman sent the Sacred Cow to pick her up, along with his sister, Mary Jane, in Grandview, Missouri, to visit Washington for Mother's Day 1945. It was her first plane trip. "Mama got a great kick out of the trip," Truman recalled in his memoirs. "The only thing she did not like was her experience with the elevator [the one specially installed to accommodate Roosevelt]. When the plane landed and she was being taken down, the elevator stuck. It had to be pulled back to get her out. She turned to Colonel Myers, the pilot, and said: 'I am going to tell Harry that this plane is no good and I could walk just as easily as I could ride.'"

But such glitches aside, Truman picked up where FDR left off, as he did in so many other areas. Truman made his first flight on the Sacred Cow on May 5, 1945, less than a month after taking office upon Roosevelt's death. That day trip from Washington to Kansas City—to visit his home in nearby Independence— was the first domestic flight for any president. And it showed that Truman had no qualms about breaking with tradition if he thought it was appropriate.

Truman was the first president to fly routinely. On June 19, 1945, he traveled to the West Coast and stopped in Olympia, Washington, for some politicking, fishing, and sightseeing. His main goal was to attend a ceremony in San Francisco adopting the United Nations charter. In a letter to his mother and sister on June 22, shortly after he arrived in Olympia, he revealed that the pace was wearing: "Dear Mama & Mary," he wrote, "Well, we arrived safely day before yesterday . . . after twelve-and-a-half hours continuous flying. Rather rough on the last end because of sunshine on plowed fields. Have been going at a terrific gait all the time."

In his memoirs, Truman summed it up:

*I had always been in the habit of making my own traveling arrange-
ments—driving my own car, buying my own railroad tickets, carrying my
own bags—but as President none of these things was possible. I had to do a
great deal of traveling as President, but wherever I went I was accompanied
by at least a part of the executive branch of the government. There was never
a time when I could not be reached immediately by Washington. To facilitate
this, special communications arrangements had to be made, and I always had
to have staff assistants with me.*

*For the Potsdam conference, Cabinet officers, ambassadors, the Chiefs of
Staff, the White House staff, the State Department, the Army, Navy, and
the Air Force, the Treasury and the Secret Service, all had a share in the
working out of arrangements. Many of them had to take part in the work of
the conference. The White House, in a sense, had to be moved to Potsdam for
the duration of the conference.*

*The President of the United States can never escape being a public fig-
ure, and when he travels, Secret Service agents travel ahead of him to inspect
the route that he will follow, the vehicles he is to use, and the buildings he
intends to enter.*

This was a good summary of a president's needs on the road at the time. And the
demands of presidential travel have become far more rigorous and extensive in
the succeeding years.

In July, Truman made his first foreign trip when he visited Germany for the
Potsdam Conference with Stalin and Churchill. He reluctantly agreed to use his
plane only for the final leg from Brussels to Berlin because he wanted the extra
time aboard ship to read his briefing memos and think about the post-war world.
"I decided to make the journey aboard a naval vessel," Truman wrote, "since I
felt I would be better able aboard ship to study the many documents that had
been assembled for my information. There would be an opportunity as well to
consult with my advisers without interference by the usual White House routine.
And I needed to have uninterrupted communications with Washington for trans-
acting government business and to keep in touch with London and Moscow.

Arrangements had to be closely coordinated with the preparations of the British and the Russians, and exchanges of messages were a continuing process."

Today, of course, the president has no such concerns, because *Air Force One* has the latest in communications and there is plenty of room to accommodate the senior staff and scores of other officials. A president also may order use of as many backup planes as he wants, and often hundreds of U.S. officials, aides, guests, and journalists travel with him. But in Truman's time, as for FDR before him and Dwight Eisenhower after him, flying was basically a way to get somewhere as fast as possible, and not yet a full extension of the Oval Office.

Still, Truman made good use of his three-and-a-half-hour flight to Berlin that July. For part of the route from Kassel to Magdeburg, he wrote later, "Those two cities, as viewed from the air, appeared to be completely destroyed. I could not see a single house that was left standing in either town."

No other president had ever experienced this aerial view of the devastation of war—the flattened homes, the destroyed bridges, roads, and railroad lines, the burned-out factories, the craters from months of Allied bombing, all testaments to the misery being felt by desperate people trying to get on with their lives. Truman never forgot it as he pushed for programs to rebuild Germany and Japan after the conflict ended.

For the remainder of his nearly eight years in the White House, Truman flew whenever he could because it made travel so easy. And sometimes he "lent" his plane to other leaders, including Churchill and Madame Chiang Kai-shek, wife of the Chinese leader, and to key advisers such as Secretary of State James F. Byrnes and his successor, Dean Acheson, and General Dwight Eisenhower, then the supreme Allied commander in Europe.

The end of World War II and the onset of the atomic age and the cold war brought a new set of challenges. Europe needed to be reconstructed, Communism contained, and the economy rejuvenated. Underlying all the other problems, there were widespread doubts whether Truman, largely unknown to the public and with a rather ordinary record in the Senate before he was named Roosevelt's vice president, was up to the job. As vice president, he had been kept out of the loop by his boss. He never was told about the development of the atomic bomb until he succeeded to the presidency. Within a year, he had ordered two of the bombs dropped on Hiroshima and Nagasaki. Truman would use the president's aircraft to demonstrate this same kind of decisiveness.

He was, in fact, the first president to use the plane to enhance his stature. He had been sensitive for many years about his unimposing presence; he was 5 feet, 9 inches tall and weighed 167 pounds—by no means a small man—but his thick eyeglasses, slight build, and colloquial way of speaking seemed to minimize him as a public figure. And when he succeeded Roosevelt, he was widely criticized for being an accidental president who could never fill FDR's shoes.

Partly as a way to enhance his image, he publicized his travel schedule as widely as possible—a technique that every one of his successors has used. This guaranteed Truman huge amounts of publicity and built up his image as a hard-working, activist leader who loved to be among the people. His "whistle-stop" train trips during his 1948 campaign have received nearly all the attention from historians but his air travel was also important because it immeasurably expanded his reach. Truman and his advisers were quick to realize that Americans wanted their president to avoid the isolation of Washington once the war was over and pay more attention to their everyday concerns. He also knew that modern leadership required a president to meet with his counterparts around the globe, from Potsdam to the South Pacific. That's what he did.

IN 1946, TRUMAN's advisers told him the Sacred Cow had become outmoded. Military and security officials wanted the president to travel on a new, four-engine, prop-driven Douglas DC-6, with more power, more range, more effective radar and communications, and better amenities than Roosevelt's plane. Truman agreed.

With its four propeller engines, it was capable of a cruising speed of 315 miles per hour and a maximum speed of 358 mph, and had a range of 4,400 miles without refueling. The DC-6 also had a state-of-the-art cabin pressurization system—a big improvement over the oxygen bottles that the crew lugged onto FDR's plane for the first presidential flight in 1943.

Just as impressive, the plane contained a more-spacious presidential suite in its 67-foot cabin, which was decorated in dark brown, dark blue, light gray, and tan. The suite contained a large swivel chair that reclined, a table for eight, three windows, and an elk-hide sofa that converted to a full-sized bed. It could carry 25 passengers and had sleeping berths for 12. As with Roosevelt and, later, Eisenhower, the presidential stateroom was placed at the rear of the aircraft to minimize noise from the four engines (a tradition that lasted until Richard Nixon redesigned *Air Force One* and placed the presidential compartment at the front; by then, the forward section, beyond the jet engines, was quieter and more stable in flight).

Naming the aircraft caused more than a few problems. "Pentagon officials had never liked the name an irreverent press corps had bestowed upon the first presidential plane," wrote authors J. F. terHorst and Ralph Albertazzie. "The brass thought it frivolous for a president of the United States to arrive anywhere, especially a foreign capital, aboard an airplane dubbed the 'Sacred Cow.' . . . Senior Air Force officials wanted to call it the *Flying White House*, the name originally intended for the Sacred Cow. At least it was a dignified name and it expressed the purpose of the craft. But that too ran into resistance from the pragmatists. The *Flying White House* had not caught on with the first presidential airplane; what reason was there to believe it would be acceptable this time?"

In the end, Truman took the suggestion of his pilot, Hank Myers, and christened the DC-6 *Independence*, in honor of his hometown in Missouri and the feeling it gave him when he used it.

Truman took his first flight on the *Independence* in September 1947, for a trip to Rio de Janeiro where he attended an Inter-American Defense Conference. He kept watch on a compass, altimeter, and speedometer installed in the executive cabin to satisfy his curiosity about where he was and how high and fast he was flying. He enjoyed wandering the plane to chat with aides, greet guests, stretch his legs, and schmooze with the crew in the cockpit.

TRUMAN AND HIS advisers were savvy enough to use the plane *itself* as a power tool. Part of that effort was painting the aircraft to resemble the eagle. This would seem cartoonish today but it worked in Truman's era. In effect, he invented the use of the president's plane as a modern spectacle. In nearly every city he visited, Americans would show up at the airport to watch the president arrive, and they loved to read about it in their hometown newspapers. It was front-page news. It still is.

There was a similar awe among foreign leaders, and it continues to this day. Prime ministers and potentates the world over respect and envy the American president's power and prestige, and the airborne White House symbolizes those traits in a vivid way. Truman understood that people loved to come aboard, hoping to bask in the reflected glory, and he brought guests with him whenever possible so they could spread the word about the rare honor of flying with the commander in chief.

And the awe was not just confined to the guests; the president experienced it, too, in those early days of presidential flight. Truman, a prolific and eloquent writer, turned almost poetic when he recalled his flight across the Pacific to confer with General Douglas MacArthur in October 1950: "I had breakfast and then went forward again and sat in the second pilot's seat as we approached the Hawaiian Islands. It was still dark, but at regular intervals the lights of ships could be seen below. These were the destroyers the Navy had stationed along my route—just in case a mishap occurred to the plane. Colonel Williams, the pilot, said that visibility was exceptionally fine that morning; in any case, I had a breath-taking view of the entire chain of islands rising slowly out of the western sky, tiny little dark points in a vastness of blue that I would not have believed if I had not seen it myself. Then slowly the specks of land took shape and were distinct islands. At last the plane passed Diamond Head, circled low over Pearl Harbor, and came in for a landing at Hickam Air Force Base."

Finally, like all his successors, Truman considered his plane a refuge where he could be himself. He sometimes savored a snort or two of bourbon and water, and enjoyed playing poker and other card games with his aides.

He was the first chief executive to watch television aboard the presidential aircraft. It was installed in his quarters in time for his July 25, 1952, flight to the Democratic National Convention in Chicago. He and Mrs. Truman watched his party begin the roll-call vote that nominated Illinois governor Adlai Stevenson as the standard-bearer against Eisenhower that fall.

Truman felt so uninhibited aboard the plane that he indulged his penchant for earthiness and practical jokes. He once told his pilot, Myers, that whenever he flew to Independence, he was to be notified as soon as the plane reached Ohio. This was the home state of Republican senator Robert A. Taft, his political nemesis. When the plane crossed into Ohio, the president would get up from his seat and use the bathroom in the rear of the aircraft, then order Myers over the intercom to release the waste into the air. It was Harry's way of demeaning Taft.

On one occasion, he ordered Myers to buzz the White House, a risk that no president would dare to take today. But Truman couldn't resist. On Sunday, May 19, 1946, he suddenly decided to fly home to Independence again to visit his elderly mother. He departed with only two Secret Service agents and the plane crew, leaving the press behind. As the plane took off, Truman caught a glimpse of an air show featuring new jet aircraft that was going on nearby. Thousands of people were on the ground watching the latest-model P-80 fighter planes maneuver in the skies just outside Washington. The observers included, he realized, his wife, Bess, and daughter, Margaret, who had planned to watch from the White House roof. "Could we dive on them?" the commander in chief asked his pilot playfully. ". . . like a jet fighter? I've always wanted to try something like that."

Pilot Myers agreed, even though it was against air security regulations and common sense. As the president strapped himself into his seat, Myers turned the plane toward the west. With the four engines at full throttle, the Sacred Cow dove straight for the White House and dropped down to 500 feet as it roared over the roof. Truman waved from his window and laughed uproariously. He ordered another run, and the plane circled and swooped down again to 500 feet. At this point, Bess and Margaret recovered from their initial shock at being dive-bombed and realized the president was giving them a special show. They began jumping and waving, and Truman was delighted with himself.

It was no laughing matter for the military, the local police, and the Secret Service. At one point, the Service thought someone had stolen the president's plane, and officials frantically made calls to find out what was happening. Finally, the Air Force reached the Sacred Cow by radio, and Myers explained that the president was aboard and had ordered the stunt. That's where the matter ended. The commander in chief had his prerogatives, after all, and Truman saw nothing wrong with taking advantage of them to make a little mischief.

As his presidency proceeded, Truman spent increasing amounts of time on his plane ruminating about the problems he faced. There was no more important example of this than his setting the groundwork, during a flight in June 1950, for U.S. involvement in the Korean War.

At about 10 P.M. on Saturday, June 24, he was in Independence, Missouri, for a weekend with his family, sitting in the library of their home on North Delaware Street, when Secretary of State Dean Acheson telephoned with news that the North Koreans had invaded South Korea. Acheson suggested asking the United Nations Security Council to immediately declare that the North Koreans had committed an act of aggression, and Truman agreed.

Acheson called again the following morning at about 11:30, "just as we were getting ready to sit down to an early Sunday dinner," Truman recalled in his memoirs. The secretary of state said the situation was increasingly grave; the North Koreans showed no signs of slowing their all-out invasion. Truman decided to fly back to Washington as soon as possible.

The crew of his plane had the aircraft ready in less than an hour, and the president departed so quickly that two of his aides were left behind. Truman observed:

> *The plane left the Kansas City Municipal Airport at two o'clock, and it took just a little over three hours to make the trip to Washington. I had time to think aboard the plane. In my generation, this was not the first occasion when the strong had attacked the weak. I recalled some earlier instances: Manchuria, Ethiopia, Austria. I remembered how each time that the democracies failed to act it had encouraged the aggressors to keep going ahead. Communism was acting in Korea just as Hitler, Mussolini, and the Japanese had acted ten, fifteen, and twenty years earlier. I felt certain that if South*

Korea was allowed to fall, Communist leaders would be emboldened to over-
ride nations closer to our own shores. . . . If this was allowed to go unchal-
lenged it would mean a third world war, just as similar incidents had
brought on the second world war.

This line of thinking became the basis for Truman's intervention in the Korean conflict.

Over the years, he also took some historic actions while airborne. On July 27, 1947, for example, he signed the National Security Act, which created the Department of Defense and the Central Intelligence Agency, and established the Air Force as a separate branch of the military services.

On the lighter side, Truman had no qualms about using the plane for personal trips. He not only would fly to his hometown periodically but would also visit Key West, Florida, for vacations. Sometimes his critics objected but most Americans didn't seem to mind. They gave their industrious leader plenty of slack in those difficult times. Presidents have followed his lead ever since, using *Air Force One* for all manner of R and R. In all, Truman made 61 flights and logged 135,098 air miles as president.

REPUBLICAN DWIGHT EISENHOWER pledged to bring a "new broom" to Washington when he took office in January 1953, and he swept out Truman's *Independence* along with the Democrats who had run the government for 20 years. Ike chose as his regular aircraft a four-engine, prop-driven Lockheed Constellation similar to the C-121 he used as supreme commander of Allied forces in Europe in 1950 and 1951. He called the sturdy silver plane *Columbine II*, for the official flower of Colorado, his wife's home state. (He had first used the nickname "Columbine" for his Lockheed Constellation C-121 transport while he was still an Army general.)

In November 1954, at the end of his second year in the White House, he began using a third Constellation, this time a faster, longer-range, stretch version of the Lockheed 1049C, which became *Columbine III*. The 1049C could cruise at 355 mph, slightly faster than Truman's plane, and had a range of 3,500 miles, less than Truman's, although it could fly at higher altitudes, enabling it to avoid many storms and other turbulent weather patterns, and it was a bit roomier.

In Ike's America, everything was about normalcy after the turmoil and hardship of the Depression and World War II, the divisions and disappointments over the Korean War, and the strains of the cold war. Ike's approach to his plane reflected that attitude.

Eisenhower, like Truman, loved to fly. In addition, he was a pilot during his military career—experienced mostly in light aircraft—and had even more of an appreciation for aircraft than his predecessor. He took a special interest in redesigning the *Columbine II* into the *Columbine III* to meet his needs, complete with a sophisticated display panel of navigational instruments so he could keep track of the plane's progress. He had two clocks installed above his bed, one to show the time in Washington and one at his destination.

The plane, decorated in a drab color scheme of gray, blue, and green, had two couches, two single beds, and a large bathroom/dressing room in the presidential cabin. Eisenhower ordered two big leather easy chairs installed for himself and the First Lady, whom he expected to fly with him as often as possible, even though Mamie did not like air travel at first. This was a dislike she shared with Bess Truman, who preferred to stay home while her husband gallivanted around the world. But Mamie got over her phobia. During the course of traveling 22,000 miles in Eisenhower's first presidential year, she finally came to trust the pilot, Bill Draper, and his crew, who reassured her that flying was safer than car travel.

Ike preferred flying to all other forms of transportation, and flew 308,402 miles during the eight years of his presidency—more than double Truman's total. He saw air travel as the fastest way to get from one point to another, not as a regular extension of the Oval Office, so he rarely made big decisions on the plane. But sometimes it did happen. He finished his "Atoms for Peace" speech to the United Nations, outlining the peaceful uses of nuclear energy, while aboard the plane in December 1953, less than a year after he took office. It was a hectic experience, especially since he had to ask his pilot to circle Manhattan for an extra half hour while copies were mimeographed and stapled together on board. He later told aides he didn't want to leave such things to the last minute again.

True to his military background and the habits of many men of his era, he was a disciplined and compliant passenger. He kept his seat belt fastened throughout every flight and rarely visited the cockpit, as Truman liked to do. Nor did Ike wander the aisles chatting with aides or dignitaries. When he wanted to see someone, the old general sent for him. He didn't drink nearly as much as Truman and didn't like the naughty stories that Truman enjoyed.

Sometimes he slurped his soup directly from the bowl, in his homespun Kansas way, which even his most cultured guests often felt compelled to emulate, giving the crew a good, if private, laugh. Yet Ike never suffered a diminishment in stature over such incidents. He was, after all, the former supreme commander of the Allies in Europe and had led them in the Normandy invasion. At nearly 5 feet, 11 inches and 170 pounds, with the bearing of a general, he had a dignified demeanor that held him in good stead as a public figure.

Befitting a man accustomed to the chain of command, Ike took the pilot's advice almost as a direct order. After all, the captain was in charge, and according to military tradition, his word was law aboard his aircraft. Bill Draper would even tell the president when to go to bed on long flights to keep his body clock in order. Returning to Washington from a Colorado vacation in September 1953 to attend the funeral of Chief Justice Fred Vinson, the pilot told Eisenhower to get some sleep soon after the 9-P.M. takeoff. It was 11 P.M. in Washington, Draper said, and would be a good time for the president to "relax." Without hesitation, the commander in chief replied, "Okay, Bill," and went to sleep.

Also reflecting the formality of the fifties, Ike almost never worked in shirtsleeves. He would remove his business suit coat as soon as he boarded but would quickly don a tweed jacket and rarely loosened his tie.

Under Ike, the president's plane returned to its Roosevelt-era unadorned state. Gone was the eagle motif of Truman's *Independence*, and in its place was a simple gray, utilitarian, military-style aircraft. The only concession to flamboyance was the red, white, and blue stripes on the very end of each propeller blade, and they were mainly designed to make the whirring blades highly visible so no one walked into them.

Ike embodied the no-nonsense spirit of the cold war, and the plane reflected the man and his times. A big, gray safe was added to store secret documents on the plane. Ike allowed virtually no photographs released to the press of him or his staff on the aircraft. He thought this was frivolous and could conceivably reveal something important to the Communists. He ordered a motion-picture projector that contained a small screen placed opposite his desk so he could view Pentagon and State Department briefings on film at his convenience. He had a big radio installed over the pillow in his berth so he could pick up news and occasionally music while he was lying down.

Ike would enjoy a martini or two once he got settled, to relax. He generally did some paperwork and talked policy with aides on board, but sometimes sipped his drinks alone and read the latest Western novels, which the staff stocked in his cabin.

One thing that Ike wouldn't forgo was the use of his plane to take frequent holidays, a tradition that continues to this day with George W. Bush's repeated trips to his ranch in Crawford, Texas. Eisenhower was the subject of criticism for his trips to play golf, fish, or shoot quail at various locations, including Augusta, Newport, Denver, and his farm in Gettysburg. His pleasure jaunts prompted Democratic National Chairman Paul M. Butler to complain that Ike was a "part-time president" who spent too much time away from Washington. This was a delicate matter, since many Americans sympathized with Eisenhower's need to take it easy because of his heart problems. "We say," said Butler, "that aside from his health, aside from his illness, the president has been absent from the White House more than any other president in the last 24 years." The country didn't much care.

IT WAS DURING Ike's era that the name *Air Force One* was first used by the military to identify any Air Force plane carrying the president. It started after a potentially dangerous mixup.

Columbine II, known as Air Force 610, was carrying Eisenhower to Florida when air traffic controllers briefly confused it with Eastern 610, an Eastern Airlines plane on a commercial flight in the same area. Ike was never in danger but Draper, his pilot, decided from then on to call the president's plane *Air Force One*, and the name stuck. No other aircraft has a similar name.

WHAT TRULY GAVE the presidency its global reach was the advent of jet aircraft. Commercial airline companies were already adding jets to their fleets by the late 1950s, and the Pentagon was converting to jets for its fighters, bombers, and transports. The civilian government wanted to do the same. Adding to the sense of urgency, Secretary of State John Foster Dulles told Eisenhower that the prestige of the United States suffered whenever the commander in chief arrived for an international meeting in a prop-driven plane while Soviet officials and other dignitaries were showing up in jets.

Eisenhower didn't need much convincing. He became the first president to travel by jet—a four-engine Boeing 707, known in military parlance as a VC-137A, that was part of the government VIP fleet—on August 26, 1959, about 17 months before he left office. Nicknamed "Queenie," it had a special communications cabin in the forward section, in front of a passenger compartment holding eight seats. Next was a center cabin featuring a table, swivel chairs, divans that converted to beds, and a film projector. The rear compartment had another 14 seats, for a total of 40 passengers.

Ike walked onto what he called "the strange jet airplane" at 3:20 A.M. and showed his wife around "the mammoth machine." He later wrote:

> *Both in size and speed the new airplane completely dwarfed the Columbine, the Super Constellation that we had long considered the last word in luxurious transportation. However, no airplane ever looked attractive to Mamie. . . .*
>
> *I settled back in my compartment with the Secretary of State and underwent an exhilarating experience, that of my first jet flight, with its silent, effortless acceleration and its rapid rate of climb. The deep coloring of the*

sunrise, seen from a height of thirty-five thousand feet, was an unforgettable sight.

After refueling at Newfoundland, he arrived in Bonn, Germany, at 6:30 P.M. and met with Chancellor Konrad Adenauer, then flew to London to chat with British prime minister Harold Macmillan and visit Queen Elizabeth. He moved on to Paris to talk with French president Charles de Gaulle, and finally dropped in at Ayreshire, Scotland, for some golf. He returned to Washington on September 7. Ike loved the experience. He told aides the ride was remarkably smooth and the speed very impressive. He covered 8,711 miles in 19 hours and 27 minutes. As historian Stephen E. Ambrose wrote, "He was hooked."

The jet opened up new vistas for the White House, as it did for a nation in which, during the late 1950s, only one out of 10 Americans had ever been aboard an aircraft. Using prop-driven planes for his first seven years as president, Eisenhower had averaged 120 hours of flying time and traveled 30,000 miles annually. In 1960, using the jet aircraft, Ike flew 193 hours and covered 78,677 miles—spending an additional 73 hours in the air on an annual basis but covering more than two and a half times the distance.

Technology now enabled the president of the United States to become an international traveler without peer, and no spot on the globe would be too far away for him to visit conveniently. This fit perfectly with Eisenhower's own instincts. "Travel, just for its own sake, had always been one of Eisenhower's chief delights," wrote Ambrose. "There were many places he wanted to see— most especially India—and he had been compiling a mental list of the sites he intended to visit after retirement. But how much nicer to visit them while he was still President, and could use *Air Force One*, and—best of all—could use his prestige and position to further the cause of peace, to which he had committed himself and his administration."

Ike showed just how far things had progressed. Starting December 3, 1959, he rode his jet to the Vatican and in nearly three weeks made a world tour that covered Rome; Ankara, Turkey; Karachi, Pakistan; Kabul, Afghanistan; New Delhi, India; Teheran, Iran; Athens, Greece; Tunis, Tunisia; Paris; Madrid; and Casablanca in

Morocco. The extent of the trip was seen as an illustration of Ike's leadership. "The President, who has often said he would go anywhere, any time, and meet anyone if by doing so he could further the cause of honorable world peace, is about to demonstrate this resolve more dramatically and with a greater expenditure of physical effort than ever before since he entered the White House," wrote Arthur Krock in *The New York Times* on November 8, 1959. "Moreover, no Western statesman has embarked on a peace mission of such magnitude, and most nations in this itinerary have never been visited by a United States President in office. His place in history will be importantly determined by any palpable advances the errand may produce either toward a durable peace effected without resort to force, or toward a greater unity among the non-Communist nations."

Eisenhower wrote in his memoirs: "Not for a moment during the earlier years of my administration could such an ambitious trip have been deemed practical. But at the beginning of winter in 1959, with travel by jet becoming commonplace, with the Congress not in session, with the Soviet Premier having just completed a visit to America, and with the world relatively calm, such a journey was clearly feasible."

Not surprisingly, it was a logistical nightmare. Several airports, such as Kabul, didn't have adequate weather forecasts to satisfy the flight crew. Others, like Ankara, didn't have fuel for a Boeing 707. Still others didn't have reliable, safe food supplies. Ike's doctors wanted him to drink only bottled water because of his ileitis. By relying on the U.S. military, all the problems were solved, including the stowing of 12 large cases of Mountain Valley water on *Air Force One*.

Still, there were unforeseen developments. In India, Prime Minister Nehru calmed American security officers when he assured them that the Indian army would keep sacred cows from wandering onto the runway when the president was there. He kept his word.

The 69-year-old Eisenhower returned to Washington, weary but content, just before midnight on December 22.

Ike admitted that there were no "concrete or specific achievements," but he added: "I had no doubt that the trip was worth the effort it required. By no means does such a conclusion imply that an American President should spend a large portion of his time traveling the earth. But when any future Executive may find the circumstances favorable for undertaking a similar journey, then whatever trouble and inconvenience he might be subjected to in visiting the less well-known parts of the world will be repaid many times over. He will be showered with kindnesses and courtesies to the point of exhaustion, but he will be rewarded richly by the eagerness of whole populations to learn about America, and by his better understanding of the peoples he, directly or indirectly, as head of the strongest nation on earth, is destined to serve."

Yet it took Eisenhower's youthful successor, John F. Kennedy, to bring *Air Force One* and presidential travel fully into the modern age.

CHAPTER FOUR

JOHN F. KENNEDY:
THE PRINCE AND THE POWER

A T 43, JOHN FITZGERALD KENNEDY was one of the youngest men ever elected president. In succeeding the 70-year-old Eisenhower, he seemed to represent a break from the somnolent conformism of the fifties and to embody America's desire to, in Kennedy's words, "get the country moving again."

The world was still a dangerous place, with the Soviet Union and Communist China rising like red tidal waves to challenge the West, and it was far from clear who would win the cold war. There were crisis points everywhere, from Europe and the Middle East to South America and Indochina. At home, society was changing. African Americans were demanding their fair share of the nation's bounty in the Civil Rights movement, which was gathering force, and there was rising concern about poverty, injustice, the future of the cities, and the troubled economy.

From the start, Kennedy challenged the country to live up to its potential and promised a new era of government activism. He captured the spirit of the times with his inaugural address as the 35th president on January 20, 1961. "Let the word go forth from this time and place," he said on that frigid afternoon, "to friend and foe alike, that the torch has been passed to a new generation of Americans." He went on to issue a breathtaking pledge: "Let every nation know, whether it wishes us well or ill, that we shall pay any price, bear any burden, meet any hardship, support any friend, oppose any foe, to assure the survival and the success of liberty." And he added an idealistic peroration that still rings through the years: "My fellow Americans, ask not what your country can do for you; ask what you can do for your country."

Kennedy realized the importance of public image, especially on the ever-expanding medium of television. And he made *Air Force One* more important than ever as a link between the president and the people.

At six feet tall and a slim 175 pounds, with a distinctive shock of brown hair over his forehead, the dashing young president had matinee-idol good looks, and he knew it. So he made TV appearances whenever possible. With his keen PR sense, he also realized the symbolic value of his plane.

He was well aware that the Secret Service and the military were using a special code name for any aircraft carrying the president—*Air Force One*. He also knew the brass preferred to keep the name secret as a security precaution. But Kennedy believed *Air Force One* had a certain majesty to it, so he authorized aides to use it in public. That has been the name for the presidential plane ever since.

Adding to the mystique, Kennedy approved another important change. He thought the words "United States Air Force" and "Military Air Transport Service" on the upper fuselage were inadequate in conveying the plane's broader symbolism. Instead, he ordered that "United States of America"—in huge, bold letters—be painted on the fuselage, and he added an American flag to each side of the tail fin. He wanted the president's plane to be known not just as a military aircraft but as a symbol of the presidency as an institution and of the nation as a whole.

The new president meant to signal that America was a superpower and was eager to compete in the struggle against Communism, says Jeffery S. Underwood, historian of the U.S. Air Force Museum at Ohio's Wright-Patterson Air Force Base. "This aircraft told everyone we were a world power—we were here, and we were here to stay," Underwood says. "We were containing Communism and we wanted to be the symbol for the free world to look toward. And this was as good a symbol as any, because this symbol was not in New York Harbor, the Statue of Liberty, this symbol could go around the world."

Kennedy loved to generate excitement by having *Air Force One* pull up to waiting TV news and still photographers, abroad and at home. Unlike the no-nonsense Eisenhower administration, White House press aides would routinely call local news executives with the time and place of the president's arrival, and tell them where to position themselves at the appropriate airport. *Air Force One* would be seen descending majestically from the sky, and it would pull up directly in front of the journalists. The gambit was designed to give the local media fresh footage of his arrival, which often would be carried live, and give the three national broadcast networks of ABC, CBS, and NBC the same opportunity. This tradition has been followed by every succeeding president.

Kennedy inherited Ike's basic-model 707 when he took office in January 1961, and he used it for his historic trip to meet with Soviet leader Nikita Khrushchev that year. But on October 10, 1962, a newer model of the Boeing 707, with the tail number SAM 26000, arrived at Andrews Air Force Base. It would become one of the most famous planes in history.

Faster and with a longer range than Eisenhower's plane, this 707 had upgraded communications systems, enabling the president for the first time to contact people around the world in a secure manner rather than over open channels. This made it much easier for the president to make decisions and coordinate policy while "on the road." In fact it was more of a working environment than ever before, featuring a spacious presidential stateroom containing a desk, two leather-upholstered, high-backed swivel chairs, and two sofas that could be converted to beds; a conference room with two tables, six chairs, and a couch seating another three persons; a special galley with four burners to cook meals; and a main passenger cabin containing 24 reclining seats, two desks, and four sleeping berths. *Air Force One* quickly became one of the perquisites of office that Kennedy most enjoyed.

The sleek plane, like the sleek new president and First Lady, seemed to embody modernity itself. To that end, Kennedy asked his wife, known for her exquisite fashion sense and glamour, to help develop a new color scheme. It was Jackie, with the advice of industrial designer Raymond Loewy (creator of the Ritz cracker logo and the designs for Lucky Strike cigarette packaging), who came up with the blue and white hues still in use today. She also brought fine china aboard and hung oil paintings in the presidential quarters.

Kennedy reveled in the idea that he was only six hours from Europe, and told friends he understood now why President Eisenhower had traveled so much during his final year in office, when he finally had access to a jet. People who thought the presidency was the toughest job in the world had never flown on *Air Force One*, Kennedy observed.

He and Mrs. Kennedy used SAM 26000 for the first time in November 1962, a year before he died, to attend the funeral of Eleanor Roosevelt in New York. He flew on it in June 1963 to Ireland and Germany, where he gave his "Ich Bin Ein Berliner" address. And of course 26000 took Kennedy on his final trip, to Dallas on November 22, 1963.

JFK OFTEN USED the plane to relax in his private compartment. "He had a big bed back there," recalled Vernon "Red" Shell, a flight steward at the time. "On a short trip, say to Cape Cod, a one-hour flight, he'd skim through two or three newspapers real fast, maybe have a cup of fish chowder, then take a little nap."

Contrary to his public image, he was not the perfect husband, nor the perfect host. Members of the *Air Force One* flight crew said he would ignore his wife as she struggled on board with their children. Instead, he would immediately begin reading about himself in the newspapers while the First Lady soldiered on. And he displayed a roving eye when Mrs. Kennedy was not on board, talking openly about other women with his aides and guests.

Kennedy allowed the black Labrador of his brother, Robert, to romp unimpeded throughout the plane until the crew came up with a novel way to control the animal: They mixed a couple of martinis and served them to the dog on a plate, whereupon it promptly fell asleep. That was the tactic they used from then on whenever the canine started to bother passengers.

A scion of privilege, Kennedy loved being pampered, and fawning aides were everywhere. They kept *Air Force One* supplied with a half dozen newspapers at all times so JFK could read his notices, which he did as often as possible. Hot New England seafood chowder was always in stock to indulge his passion for the meal he had enjoyed since boyhood.

He loved to smoke cigars and often had an unfinished one in his mouth when he was ready to exit the plane. Just before stepping out, he would take the cigar in his left hand, put his hand in the left pocket of his suit jacket, and walk down the stairs. He sometimes burned a hole in his clothes, but he could then take a few puffs in his limousine en route to his destination without having to light up another one.

True to his nature, JFK and his inner circle spent hours swapping political stories, sharing gossip, smoking cigars, and enjoying a few drinks. Kennedy favored Beefeater gin, Ballantine's Scotch, and daiquiris, but he rarely consumed alcohol to excess, and when his staff overindulged, he would shake his head and frown but never give orders to refrain. His expression of displeasure usually put a stop to it, at least until he was out of sight. Drinking was a part of life for men of power in those days.

So was sangfroid. Kennedy once recalled that Roosevelt's death was not traumatic for him, even though much of the civilian population in 1945 was grief-stricken upon learning of FDR's passing. For men of Kennedy's age who had served in the armed forces, any display of emotion was disdained. "They had learned to keep themselves to themselves, to avoid getting hurt," wrote author William Manchester in 1962. "Today the President, speaking in the idiom of his time, scorns soul-searching as 'couch talk,' and nearly all those who are close to him hold the world at arm's length. . . . Their strong points are manipulation, expertise, and efficiency, even to the sacrifice of individuality. . . . This is the veteran generation. They were young in the early 1940s, and most of them were very much in the war. Men Eisenhower's age were in charge of the maps, but men Kennedy's age did the actual fighting."

A certain degree of cold-bloodedness was shared by every member of the

World War II–era generation to hold the presidency, from JFK to Lyndon Johnson, Richard Nixon, Gerald Ford, Jimmy Carter, Ronald Reagan, and George H. W. Bush. They refused to—indeed, were unable to—wear their hearts on their sleeves, unlike the baby boomer generation represented by Bill Clinton and George W. Bush. To do otherwise was not considered manly.

Instead, Kennedy became a symbol of energy and style—what Manchester described as "hatless, coatless, on-the-ball vigor." He believed in the power of reason to solve the world's problems—a faith eventually tempered by failures such as the Bay of Pigs invasion of Cuba and the near disaster of the Cuban missile crisis.

"John F. Kennedy was a happy President," wrote Theodore C. Sorensen, one of his senior advisers. "Happiness, he often said, paraphrasing Aristotle, is the full use of one's faculties along lines of excellence, and to him the presidency offered the ideal opportunity to pursue excellence. . . . He liked the job, he thrived on its pressures. Disappointments only made him more determined."

He was a self-starter and a cool pragmatist, and he wanted the country to know that unlike the Eisenhower norm, he and his advisers were working 14-hour days. The contrasts were everywhere. While the former general was spit-and-polish and staid, Kennedy was informal and spirited. While Ike was a countrified Kansan, Kennedy was an urbane Bostonian. While Ike enjoyed simple Westerns, Kennedy was proudly and broadly literate, author of the Pulitzer prize–winning *Profiles in Courage* and an admirer of Churchill's memoirs and modern morality novels such as Harper Lee's *To Kill a Mockingbird.*

One Saturday in October 1963, Kennedy flew to Amherst College in Massachusetts to honor poet Robert Frost. Aboard *Air Force One*, he worked over his speech and revealed his appreciation for the life of the mind when he discussed Frost's poems with adviser and scholar Arthur M. Schlesinger, Jr. He expressed admiration for one line in particular: "I have been one acquainted with the night." Somehow, it had special resonance for him.

But another staffer broke his reverie with the lighthearted warning that a woman he knew, who despised Kennedy, might try to interrupt the ceremony and the president might see his aide "struggling with a woman and rolling on the ground." Kennedy brightened at the thought and added slyly, "We will give you the benefit of the doubt."

Kennedy kept in touch with popular culture, watching movies a few times a month; among his favorites were *Casablanca*, starring Humphrey Bogart, and *Spartacus*, starring Kirk Douglas.

KENNEDY EXPERIENCED HIS SHARE of poignant moments on the plane. In December 1961, less than a year after he took office, his father suffered a stroke in Palm Beach, Florida. The president immediately decided to visit him. During that trip, the president and adviser Sorensen reviewed the legislative agenda for 1962, but his father's condition weighed heavily on him. "It was with difficulty and incredible self-discipline that he engrossed himself in our work on that sorrowful flight," Sorensen recalls. "The mutual bonds of affection and admiration between father and son had not diminished in the White House, and Joseph P. Kennedy's subsequent inability to communicate freely to his son removed a welcomed source of encouragement and cheer for the president."

His journey to the divided city of Berlin on June 26, 1963, was a high point of his presidency, and his life. He received a spectacular reception from the vast, roaring throng that listened to him outside City Hall as he delivered one of his most inspired speeches. "Two thousand years ago the proudest boast was 'Civis Romanus sum,'" he declared. "Today, in the world of freedom, the proudest boast is 'Ich bin ein Berliner.' . . . We . . . look forward to that day when this city will be joined as one—and this country, and this great continent of Europe—in a peaceful and hopeful globe. When that day finally comes, as it will, the people of West Berlin can take sober satisfaction in the fact that they were in the front lines for almost two decades.

"All free men, wherever they may live, are citizens of Berlin, and, therefore, as a free man, I take pride in the words 'Ich bin ein Berliner.'"

As *Air Force One* left Germany for Ireland, Kennedy wandered into the staff cabin, obviously pleased with himself. He said the tumultuous reaction would show Americans that their efforts to defend West Germany from the Communist threat were very much appreciated. He said he would leave a note to his successor, to be opened at a difficult time, that would read: "Go to Germany." Then the president sat down across from Sorensen and said, "We'll never have another day like this one as long as we live."

FOREIGN POLICY WAS the all-important subtext of the Kennedy era. It was a dangerous world. The superpowers were bristling with nuclear weapons and tensions with Moscow were on the rise.

Four months into his term, and not long after the disastrous American-sponsored invasion of Cuba known as the Bay of Pigs, Kennedy flew to Vienna for his first summit meeting with Soviet leader Nikita Khrushchev. It would be a pivotal event, and as so often happens with any president under stressful conditions, there were several key moments aboard *Air Force One*.

On particularly difficult trips, Kennedy would bring a doctor—sometimes more than one—to give him medication that would ease the severe pain in his back, which tended to worsen on long flights and when he was under pressure. This was kept secret so he didn't look weak and vulnerable. His staff installed a very firm horsehair mattress in his cabin, which gave him some relief when he reclined, and he wore a medical corset virtually all the time to ease the pain and give him support.

As luck would have it, he aggravated the problem during a tree-planting ceremony in Ottawa in May 1961, not long before his springtime summit with Khrushchev in Vienna. He arrived on June 3, exhausted and in excruciating pain after three days of intense and pressure-packed meetings with French president Charles de Gaulle in Paris. "His doctors had told him that if he must go to Europe, he should use crutches," reports historian Michael Beschloss. "He had shaken his head: he was 'simply not' going to meet Khrushchev 'as a cripple.' As a congressman in 1949, Kennedy himself had charged that the Kurile Islands and other strategic points had been 'given' to Stalin by a 'sick' Roosevelt at Yalta. He wanted no such talk about his performance at Vienna."

Yet much of Kennedy's public image of good health and vigor was a sham. He suffered from not only chronic back problems but also various other ailments, including Addison's disease, which attacks the adrenal glands and causes weakness and, left untreated, death. Kennedy took cortisone for the Addison's, which stabilized the disease and enhanced his stamina but resulted in bloating, surges in libido, and mood swings. His aides scrupulously kept his Addison's disease and the extent of his other illnesses secret.

All this was a huge gamble. Dr. Kenneth Crispell and author Carlos Gomez argue in their study of hidden presidential illnesses: "One might feel admiration for Kennedy's demonstrable heroism in overcoming his illnesses were it not for the fact that he was gambling not only with his future but with the future of his men in the South Pacific [as a young PT boat captain seeking to make his reputation], the future of his constituents from Charlestown, Massachusetts [as a congressman], and later, the future of the people of the United States and conceivably of the entire world. That Kennedy felt compelled to mislead the public about his illness, then to brand his critics as liars when they correctly charged that he was an ill man, also detracts from the heroic qualities."

Historian Robert Dallek adds: "On one level this secrecy can be taken as another stain on his oft-criticized character," but on another level it revealed "the quiet stoicism of a man struggling to endure extraordinary pain and distress and performing his presidential (and pre-presidential) duties largely undeterred by his physical suffering."

It was the back pain that was his immediate problem during his trip to Europe in the spring of 1961. In Paris, he soaked in a golden bathtub in his suite at the Quai d'Orsay. But what relieved his pain were the injections of procaine, an anesthetic, he received two or three times a day from Dr. Janet Travell, a private physician he brought along to keep him at his best. This was double or triple his normal dose. It helped him for a while, but the pain always returned.

Beschloss cites evidence that Kennedy also received mysterious injections from Max Jacobson, a controversial New York doctor who became known for giving celebrities "vitamin and enzyme shots." These unusual concoctions were never proven medically effective, were dangerous, and could have caused erratic behavior. Jacobson claimed that he joined Kennedy in Paris and flew with him on *Air Force One* to Vienna to assist in his medical treatments, even though there is no White House record of Jacobson on *Air Force One* at this time.

The summit with Khrushchev in Vienna went poorly. The blustery Soviet hardliner took the measure of his American counterpart and judged him shallow and weak. A particularly bitter sticking point was Berlin, divided between East and West. Khrushchev bullied Kennedy, demanding that the West leave Berlin or face a lethal confrontation. Kennedy, startled, did not respond with the same resolve shown by his adversary.

The next stop was London, and the atmosphere on *Air Force One* reflected the American delegation's dejection. Everyone, especially Kennedy, seemed depressed, and there was a grim silence for most of the flight. "Kennedy had never encountered any leader with whom he could not exchange ideas—anyone so impervious to reasoned argument or so apparently indifferent to the prospective obliteration of mankind," wrote Arthur M. Schlesinger. "He himself had indicated flexibility and admitted error, but Khrushchev had remained unmoved and immovable. Apart from Laos, about which Khrushchev evidently cared little, there was no area of accommodation. The test ban seemed dead. Berlin held the threat, if not the certitude, of war. Filled with foreboding, the President flew on to London. It was a silent and gloomy trip."

Observed Godfrey McHugh, Kennedy's Air Force aide: "It was like riding with the losing baseball team after the World Series."

Kennedy called Kenneth O'Donnell, one of his closest confidants, into his stateroom and, as so many presidents have done aboard the plane after a pressure-packed event, began to vent. For an hour, he unburdened himself of his frustrations and anger, condemning Khrushchev as a "bastard" and a "son of a bitch." His self-control, so evident in public, disappeared in the privacy of *Air Force One*, and his real feelings came tumbling out as he expressed his deepest fears about a possible war with Russia.

"We're stuck in a ridiculous situation," he fumed. "It seems silly for us to be facing an atomic war over a treaty preserving Berlin as the future capital of a reunited Germany when all of us know that Germany will probably never be reunited."

Kennedy also said, "All wars start from stupidity. God knows I'm not an isolationist, but it seems particularly stupid to risk killing a million Americans over an argument about access rights on an Autobahn in the Soviet zone of Germany, or because the Germans want Germany reunified. If I'm going to threaten Russia with a nuclear war, it will have to be for much bigger and more important reasons than that. Before I back Khrushchev against the wall and put him to a final test, the freedom of all of Western Europe will have to be at stake."

O'Donnell vividly remembered Kennedy's final remarks as the plane was about to land in London. "If we're going to have to start a nuclear war," the young president said, "we'll have to fix things so it will be started by the president of the United States, and nobody else. Not by a trigger-happy sergeant on a truck convoy at a checkpoint in East Germany." He was clearly worried about pushing Khrushchev into making an impulsive and cataclysmic move, and wanted to bear all that responsibility on his own shoulders.

As O'Donnell later wrote in his memoirs, Kennedy "seldom revealed his deep feelings or talked about them at any length. . . . On the flight from Vienna that Sunday night, however, he was in the mood to talk freely about the many questions and doubts concerning the Berlin crisis that were troubling him, as if talking about them would help him to weigh them and put them into order in his mind."

After meeting in London with British officials and dining with Queen Elizabeth II of England at Buckingham Palace, Kennedy boarded *Air Force One* in his tuxedo and tried to relax on the trip home. After takeoff, he ordered his customary hot soup and read the London newspapers, but he could not stop thinking about the momentous events of the previous week.

He stripped to his boxer shorts and called in Hugh Sidey, a friend and correspondent for *Time* magazine. This may seem strange today—a president in his underwear talking to a journalist on *Air Force One*—but in JFK's day there was a much more trusting and cozy relationship between politicians and the press. A president could be reasonably sure that a reporter would not embarrass him under such circumstances. Sidey recalled later that Kennedy's eyes were "red and watery, dark pockets beneath them." The president said his meetings with Khrushchev were "invaluable" if only because they had given him firsthand knowledge of what he was up against.

Before going to sleep in his private cabin, Kennedy wrote out a Lincoln quotation that gave him solace. "I know there is a God, and I see a storm coming. If he has a place for me, I believe that I am ready."

Over the years, this dynamic of introspection has occurred with extraordinary frequency aboard *Air Force One*. Perhaps it's because presidents so often find themselves on the plane after tense situations or amid crises, and they need to talk about their feelings and their fears. Perhaps *Air Force One* becomes a unique incubator of presidential candor because the chief executive tends to be surrounded by friends and loyalists and he believes no one will talk out of school. Perhaps it's the same dynamic that many air travelers experience as they cruise for hours in the sky, alone with their thoughts. But *Air Force One* definitely encourages presidents to look inward.

Kennedy was ultimately proven wrong about German reunification, of course. But he was correct to worry about misunderstandings between East and West. Even more pertinent to his immediate problems, his youth and inexperience were turning out to be liabilities. The following year, Kennedy and Khrushchev would bring the world to the brink of nuclear annihilation in the Cuban missile crisis.

KENNEDY'S BACK PROBLEM got so bad after he returned from Europe that he flew to Palm Beach, Florida, on Thursday, June 8, 1961, to take a badly needed long weekend at the home of a friend, Charles Wrightsman. He got plenty of sleep, sat around in his pajamas, and used crutches to get to and from the heated pool. "In the evening," Beschloss says, "he entertained friends and several of the White House secretaries with daiquiris and Frank Sinatra records on the phonograph."

When he left for Washington, he was forced to use crutches as a hydraulic lift transported him to the door of *Air Force One* at West Palm Beach airport. Again, this was hidden from the public. At the White House, he was forced to stay in bed with a heating pad.

KENNEDY SEEMED PARTICULARLY somber in November 1963. The Washington weather was gloomy, but the president's mood was shaped more by the continuing tension with Moscow and the deteriorating situation in South Vietnam. He would soon be forced to decide how far the United States should go to bail out its ally in Saigon.

Franklin D. Roosevelt celebrates his 61st birthday aboard a Boeing 314 Dixie Clipper seaplane known as the Flying Boat in early 1943, en route home from Casablanca, where he'd met with Winston Churchill. It was the first airborne trip by any president. Roosevelt sliced the cake and distributed it to everyone aboard

Roosevelt had this four-engine Douglas C-54 Skymaster redesigned specifically for his use in 1944. It was nicknamed the Sacred Cow by an irreverent press corps. Roosevelt's willingness to fly established an important precedent, and since his era air travel has dramatically increased the reach of every president.

Crew members check a special elevator installed for FDR on the Sacred Cow. The contraption was barely big enough to contain Roosevelt's wheelchair and would be retracted into the aircraft and covered by a door so spies wouldn't know the president was on the plane.

Roosevelt and General Dwight Eisenhower travel to Teheran for a summit conference of the Allies in 1943. Conditions were cramped and uncomfortable by today's standards.

Truman grins through a window of the Sacred Cow, which he inherited from FDR. He loved being seen on the plane. It helped certify the former haberdasher's legitimacy as president.

Harry Truman recognized the prestige value of the presidential aircraft upon assuming office after FDR's death in 1945. He traveled far more widely than Roosevelt — demonstrating his activism and vigor.

Truman eventually approved the design of a new, more sophisticated and comfortable aircraft for presidential use, which he named *The Independence*. Hoping to impress Americans with his panache, he had it painted to resemble an eagle, complete with beak and tail feathers.

Dwight Eisenhower brought a more staid style to the White House when he took office in January 1953. He and his First Lady, Mamie, were low-key travelers who weren't very interested in public relations.

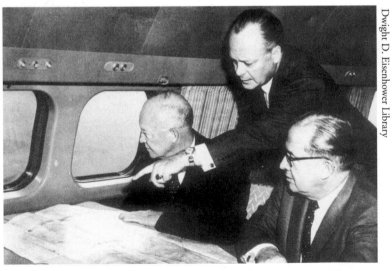

Ike used his plane, *The Columbine*, for many official duties, such as this drought inspection tour in January 1957. Eisenhower didn't want photographs released of the inside of the plane during his eight years in office, worried that it might seem frivolous or, worse, give the Soviets some knowledge of his aircraft.

John F. Kennedy brought a new spirit of excitement to presidential travel. He liked the code name for his 707 jet – *Air Force One* – so much that he allowed his staff to use it publicly. That's been the name used for the president's aircraft ever since.

Unbeknownst to the public, JFK's back often gave him severe pain and debilitated him. On June 12, 1961, in West Palm Beach, FL, his staff arranged for a lift to carry him to the door of *Air Force One* because he could barely walk.

After President Kennedy was assassinated in Dallas on November 22, 1963, his casket was loaded onto *Air Force One* and flown back to Washington, where it was removed under heavy guard at Andrews Air Force Base. It was the saddest day in the aircraft's history.

This is the most famous photo ever taken on *Air Force One*. Lyndon Johnson created enmity with the Kennedy family when he insisted that the distraught Jacqueline Kennedy appear with him as he was sworn in aboard the plane after JFK's death. But Johnson always defended his actions, saying he wanted to signal the world that the Constitution endured and that he would preserve JFK's legacy.

LBJ's ego knew no bounds. He installed a special seat that he could raise at the touch of a button, to reinforce his dominance over everyone around him. Aides called it the "throne" chair.

U.S. Air Force Museum

Johnson's hyperactive personality was evident aboard *Air Force One*. He rarely slowed down, even during meals. Here he meets with Senators Mike Mansfield and J. William Fulbright as he dines and reads paperwork.

Richard Nixon was obsessed with getting credit for his achievements. On his historic trip to China in February 1972, his aides made sure no other senior American official, especially adviser Henry Kissinger, got into the picture when the president disembarked from *Air Force One* and shook hands with Chinese leader Zhou Enlai in Beijing.

Nixon sometimes propped his feet on a big white pillow to relax or to relieve pain in his legs from phlebitis. Yet the duties and burdens of the presidency were never far from his mind. Here he confers with Secretary of State Henry Kissinger on the way to Brussels in 1973.

Gerald Ford's stumble on the steps of *Air Force One* as he arrived in Salzburg, Austria, in June 1975 was a low point in his presidency. It was a rare case where the aircraft was the venue for an incident that hurt rather than helped a president's image.

Ford was a natural athlete but he never conveyed his nimbleness in public. Sometimes he looked silly and "unpresidential," even with *Air Force One* as a backdrop. In this case, he backed into an aide after talking with reporters in San Jose, CA, in 1976.

Behind the scenes, Ford was smart, decent, and hardworking. Here the pipe-smoking president confers with then–White House Chief of Staff Donald Rumsfeld in October 1974, two months after taking office.

He spent another weekend at Palm Beach with friends, then boarded *Air Force One* for the trip back to Washington on Monday, November 18. But even though a regimen of calisthenics had done some good, his back was painful and he spent much of the flight lying in bed in his private cabin. He asked Florida senator George Smathers, a friend who was on the plane, to visit his bedside.

The president's upcoming trip to Texas, it turned out, was weighing heavily on him. Lyndon Johnson, his handpicked vice president, was extremely eager for Kennedy to visit his home state, but the personal conflicts among Democratic leaders were Byzantine and bitter.

"God, I wish you could think of some way of getting me out of going to Texas," Kennedy said. ". . . Look how screwed up it's going to be. You've got Lyndon, who is insisting that Jackie ride with him. You've got [liberal senator] Ralph Yarborough, who hates Lyndon, and Johnson doesn't want Yarborough with him. [John] Connally is the Governor. They're all prima donnas of the biggest order. . . . I just wish to hell I didn't have to go. Can't you think of some emergency we could have?" Kennedy was well aware that Texas was filled with right-wing zealots who hated him, and he felt a sense of foreboding. But he went ahead with the trip anyway.

As the president and his wife flew to Texas on Thursday, November 21, Kennedy thumbed through briefing books on the visit of Chancellor Ludwig Erhard of West Germany, who was to be the guest of honor at a state dinner Monday at the White House. He called aides Kenneth O'Donnell and David Powers into his office and said, "You two guys aren't running out on me and leaving me stranded with poor Jackie at Lyndon's ranch. If I've got to hang around there all day Saturday, wearing one of those big cowboy hats, you've got to be there too."

The ranch visit never came to pass. On Friday, November 22, 1963, John F. Kennedy was assassinated in Dallas.

AS A RESULT OF that shattering event, Kennedy's Boeing 707, SAM 26000, became the most famous of all *Air Force One* aircraft. It was there, in an overheated and cramped staff cabin, that Lyndon Johnson was sworn in, at 2:39 P.M.—

an image immortalized by White House photographer Cecil Stoughton and transmitted around the world. Stoughton's photograph shows a somber Johnson, towering over everyone else, with his right hand raised to take the oath administered by a bespectacled, diminutive federal judge named Sarah Hughes, wearing a polka-dot dress. A stricken Jackie Kennedy, still in her bloodstained pink suit from the fatal motorcade, stood at his left side and a dazed-looking Lady Bird Johnson stood at his right. The cabin was crammed with grim-faced aides.

At first, Kennedy's staff had thought Johnson, for reasons of safety, was going to return to Washington immediately after the shooting, since no one knew if the new president was in imminent danger. The Kennedys expected that the slain president's widow, his body, and his aides would leave for Washington a bit later, after the casket arrived.

When the Kennedy party got on the plane at Love Field, the group was astonished to find Johnson was still there with his own retinue. He said he thought it wise for them all to go back together. Johnson added that he wanted to take the oath of office before departure and he was waiting for federal judge Hughes, his old friend, to administer it. O'Donnell took it upon himself to be Jackie Kennedy's protector at her moment of trauma, and he was very unhappy with the way things were going. Mrs. Kennedy was under extreme strain, and he believed she should get back to Washington as soon as possible. Besides, he felt, taking the oath was just a formality that could wait until later.

Meanwhile, the *Air Force One* crew had to figure out what to do with the casket. It didn't seem proper to place it in the cargo hold with the luggage, and it was too big to fit in the rear compartment, where the Kennedys wanted it. Joe Chappell, the flight engineer and veteran Air Force troubleshooter, hastily removed a bulkhead and two rows of seats just forward of the rear door, which gave him sufficient room to wedge the coffin inside. LBJ helped maneuver it into the compartment, Chappell recalled. They swung it hard to the left at the top of the rear stairs and placed it along the left side of the cabin. Still, the casket barely fit. Someone brought in a chair and placed it next to the casket. That's where a dazed Mrs. Kennedy sat in the ghastly atmosphere, only a few hours after she and her husband had made their triumphant arrival in Dallas.

There was another complication. The Secret Service wanted to move *Air Force One* out of sight to protect the new commander in chief from snipers or other attacks, but there was no secluded spot to park it at Love Field. This made the bodyguards even more nervous.

Amid the confusion, Johnson still insisted on delaying the departure, telling his own aides that he wanted to reassure the country that the continuity of government was being preserved—and he felt that taking the oath aboard *Air Force One* would be a very effective symbol. He also told the Kennedy aides that he wanted Jackie at his side, to certify his own legitimacy. Although numbed by the ordeal, she agreed.

As everyone assembled, Secret Service agents pulled down the shades so snipers couldn't draw a bead on the new president through the windows. After the swearing-in, Johnson offered Mrs. Kennedy the use of the president's lounge in the middle of the plane but she declined. Back in the rear, with the casket two feet away, the Kennedy clan, including the grieving widow, drank several glasses of Scotch apiece. O'Donnell and Kennedy confidant Dave Powers described the atmosphere as "a wall of coldness" between the Kennedy group and the Johnson people.

During the two-hour flight, Jackie Kennedy and her husband's advisers traded warm and funny stories about the slain president in what resembled an Irish wake. Mrs. Kennedy brought up her husband's visit to Ireland, his ancestral homeland, the previous June, where he received a tumultuous reception. "He said it was the most enjoyable experience of his whole life," the widow recalled with a smile. They talked about how proud he had been that his father had actually seen him ascend to the White House, and how, on a sad note, the president had been so deeply hurt by the death of his infant son, Patrick, only a few months earlier.

When *Air Force One* landed, Attorney General Robert Kennedy, the slain president's brother, rushed onto the plane and dashed through each cabin until he found Jackie in the rear compartment with the casket. Johnson later complained that he had extended his hand to Robert Kennedy for a handshake but the attorney general ignored him. Kennedy aides said the brother was just too distraught and emotional to think about such things, and may not have noticed Johnson's offered hand.

In any case, it was the start of a descent into bitterness for all sides, just as Lyndon Johnson's controversial presidency was beginning.

CHAPTER FIVE

LYNDON B. JOHNSON: KING OF THE COWBOYS

LYNDON JOHNSON DIDN'T WASTE ANY time. From the moment of his swearing-in as the 36th president, he moved forcefully to put his imprint on the country.

His first order was short and to the point. "Now let's get airborne," the new president declared over the roar of the idling jet engines on *Air Force One*. And even though his aggressive exercise of his new powers alienated the Kennedy family, in retrospect his actions were the right ones. "He wanted to have a picture taken of the ceremony so it could be flashed around the world when he landed, as a symbol that the Constitution works and that the light in the White House may flicker but it never goes out," recalled Jack Valenti, an LBJ confidant who was on board. "And Johnson wanted Mrs. Kennedy in the photograph with him, to show that the Kennedy legacy was still intact."

While Mrs. Kennedy and the slain president's aides kept vigil with his casket in the rear cabin, Johnson was extremely busy up front. He conferred with Larry O'Brien, Kennedy's chief congressional lobbyist, asking him to stay on the Johnson team, and jumped immediately into legislative strategy. They talked about a pending amendment in the Senate to a foreign-aid bill that Johnson feared would damage the program; Johnson ordered O'Brien to fight the amendment.

Johnson coordinated by phone with Cabinet officers and ordered meetings with the nation's governors, congressional leaders, and former presidents Eisenhower and Truman. He also talked with Rose Kennedy, the slain president's mother, and Robert Kennedy.

This latter phone call caused lasting hard feelings. Johnson expressed his grief, but he also asked Robert Kennedy pointed questions about the legal issues involved in taking power, such as who should administer the oath. This was appropriate in a technical sense, since Kennedy was attorney general, but other officials could easily have handled such matters.

LBJ's insistence that Jackie Kennedy stand next to him during the swearing-in also angered Kennedy associates because they thought it was too much to ask of the obviously distraught widow, according to historian Robert Dallek. Mrs. Kennedy participated willingly, but the episode started Johnson on the wrong track with the Kennedy family.

"Robert Kennedy was less cooperative," Dallek writes. "In a state of profound shock and grief, he was in no mood to indulge anyone's needs beyond those of his immediate family. When *Air Force One* landed at Andrews Field in Maryland, Bobby, 'his face . . . streaked with tears,' hurried by the Johnson party to Jackie's side." Johnson later admitted he felt snubbed: "He ran [past LBJ] so that he would not have to pause and recognize the new president."

The first hours of Johnson's presidency were typical of his entire administration—moments of brilliance, strong leadership, and civic-mindedness mixed with bouts of insensitivity, egotism, pettiness, and insecurity.

JOHNSON BELIEVED THE COUNTRY wanted and needed a larger-than-life leader to guide it through the trauma of the Kennedy assassination and through a period of enormous social change. He felt that his towering personality would naturally fill the bill.

He was only partially correct. The nation was enduring severe turmoil over civil rights, the youth rebellion, the Communist threat, and, of course, the Vietnam War. And Johnson knew only one speed—full throttle—to reach his objectives. He went too far.

LBJ pushed as hard as he could in virtually every category, dubbing his vast network of proposed social programs the "Great Society." A consummate Washington insider after a generation in the Senate, where he had served as majority leader, he hoped the force of his Texas-size personality, reinforced by his physical presence (at a bulky 6 foot 3, he towered over nearly everyone he dealt with), would overcome every objection. But he was on the wrong side of history in fundamental ways.

Scholars have unearthed tapes of Johnson's private White House conversations that show his deep doubts about winning the war—even while he was predicting victory in his public statements. But Vietnam became a matter of honor and machismo, personal and national, to Johnson, so he would not change course.

As the growing casualty toll triggered violent protests and divided the country, Johnson couldn't speak in most major American cities without causing angry demonstrations against the war. On campus, it was even worse; the chant was often "Hey, hey, LBJ—How many kids did you kill today?" During his final years in office, he traveled abroad as often as he could. Sadly for him, for a while he got a better reception there than in his own land.

Air Force One provided glimpses of the unvarnished LBJ as he traveled more extensively than any of his predecessors—523,000 miles over five years in office. And it was not a pretty picture. Those who worked for and with him acknowledged that he was often petty and imperious, and always demanding and unpredictable; they stayed with him, if they did, because they believed in his programs.

"Johnson's all-embracing style was even more evident aboard *Air Force One* than around the White House," wrote authors J. F. terHorst and Ralph Albertazzie (former commander of *Air Force One*). "The magic carpet has a way of intoxicating presidents, imparting a sense of power every bit as real as the jet engines outside the cabin windows. One moment he could be earthy, profane, selfish, devious, or rude, and then polite, considerate, affectionate, and downright charming. Whatever his mood, it was usually excessive."

Added another former White House official who knew Johnson well:

"Southern men from a certain background like to humiliate people they don't like. This was something that Johnson did. There were famous stories about him doing interviews while sitting on the toilet, just to embarrass someone." This pattern intensified on the plane.

Robert MacMillan, a steward, says Johnson made ridiculous demands. Once he ordered a root beer on the way back to Washington from Texas and his staff followed his lead, quickly exhausting the supply of a dozen cans. When Johnson asked for seconds, he flew into a rage when told there was none left and ordered the chief steward to keep several thousand cans on board. The staff ignored him and kept eight cases on hand, but Johnson never mentioned the incident again. Johnson would also throw his glass of Scotch and soda on the floor when stewards didn't mix it the way he liked—strong, with the glass three-quarters full of liquor.

He had a history of overindulging. "He had episodes of getting drunk," said George Reedy, Johnson's former spokesman. "There were times when he would drink day after day. You would think this guy is an alcoholic. Then all of a sudden, it would stop. We could always see the signs when he called for a Scotch and soda, and he would belt it down and call for another one, instead of sipping it."

Johnson's insecurity about Kennedy would surface regularly on even the most mundane matters. "Jack Kennedy always wanted soup," Reedy said. "Johnson really did not like soup, but he finally found a chili soup. It was a diluted chili con carne. And by God, every place we went, we had to load cases of it on the airplane. It was a lousy soup."

MacMillan recalled, "We were serving roast beef one time. He [Johnson] came back in the cabin. Jack Valenti was sitting there. He had just gotten his dinner tray. On it was a beautiful slice of rare roast beef. Johnson grabbed that tray and said, 'You dumb son of a bitch. You are eating raw meat.' He brought it back to the galley and said, 'You two sons of bitches, look at this. This is raw. You gotta cook the meat on my airplane. Don't you serve my people raw meat. Goddamn, if you two boys serve raw meat on my airplane again you'll both end up in Vietnam.' He threw it upside down on the floor. He stormed off."

MacMillan said Johnson also let his hypocritical side show. On one trip, he was discussing his proposed civil rights bill with two governors and said, "I'll have them niggers voting Democratic for two hundred years." The former steward told author Ronald Kessler that he witnessed this scene, and said, "That was the reason he was pushing the bill. Not because he wanted equality for everyone. It was strictly a political ploy for the Democratic party. He was phony from the word go."

Yet historians who have studied Johnson's life, such as Dallek, say Johnson was genuinely committed to civil rights. Their interpretation of such behavior is that he occasionally used offensive language to shock people or to impress other politicians with his tough-mindedness.

JOHNSON SAW THE PLANE as a private preserve and locker room. He had no reluctance to mortify aides and crew members with temper tantrums when something went wrong, such as when his steaks weren't juicy enough or when the plane hit some turbulence. "President Johnson's attitude was: 'I'm from Texas. I'm the bull of the pasture,'" said former steward John Haigh.

"He was like a dog," recalled flight engineer Joe Chappell. "He could sense fear and if he did, he got on your ass." The best way to get respect from President Johnson, Chappell told me, was to "just not be afraid of him." That was easier said than done.

"He had this crude manner to him," said Dallek. "It was a way to get attention and a way of controlling people."

He once demanded that a military attendant wash his feet before he put on new socks; on another occasion, he had an attendant clip his toenails. Former steward Gerald Pisha says LBJ once shoved him and told him to get out of his way when he was in a hurry. And Johnson had no qualms about stripping down to his underwear in front of his staff, including his female aides, when he changed clothes after takeoff and again before landing. "He was totally naked with his daughters, Lady Bird [Mrs. Johnson], and female secretaries," MacMillan said. "He was quite well endowed in his testicles, so everyone started calling him 'Bull Nuts.' He found out about it. He was really upset."

On a trip to Texas, Johnson ordered a new pair of pants and he was eager to try them on. Suddenly he erupted. "I need some more goddamn ball room in these pants!" he shouted, fully aware that everyone near his cabin could hear him.

He made passes at his female guests and ogled them without concern. Some stewards said he would sometimes lock himself in his stateroom with attractive secretaries, and the staff and crew assumed he was, in the words of one, "fooling around."

"Johnson was not a man to sublimate his macho instincts," wrote Reedy, his former press secretary. "They were well developed. I doubt the suggestion of one of his aides during the White House period that he had 'extra glands.' But all of the external evidence suggests that those he had were in good working order and frequently exercised. . . . The reigning queen of any given moment was not announced through newspaper advertisements but, short of that, there was little secrecy." Because the news media in those days left the president's private life alone, it was never a matter of public knowledge.

Six weeks after Kennedy's assassination, Johnson showed up in the press cabin and began to hold forth on a flight from Texas to Washington. "I can't do the job alone," he said earnestly. "I need your help. I'll tell you everything. . . . There won't be any secrets except where the national security is involved. You'll be able to write everything. Of course I may go into a strange bedroom every now and then that I won't want you to write about, but otherwise you can write everything. . . . If you help me, I'll help you. I'll make you-all big men in your profession."

This account, as reported much later in *LBJ, The Way He Was*, by longtime White House correspondent Frank Cormier of the Associated Press, provides remarkable insight into the cozy relationship that existed at the time between the president and the media. The incident reflects the good-old-boy nature of the White House press corps of the sixties, which was almost all male. Johnson could talk candidly about his adulterous ways and count on the media to keep it quiet. This arrangement would be inconceivable today, as Bill Clinton learned to his chagrin.

Johnson's vulgarity seemingly knew no bounds. He once bit down on a piece of gristle in a steak sandwich, spit it into his hand, and threw the offending morsels across the plane. They landed in a bowl of potato chips on a table being used by his wife and a reporter. He made a habit of belching loudly when he ate or drank. Cormier recalled the day when Johnson called reporters to his compartment and gave them an economics lecture while he was naked and toweling off after a sweaty campaign appearance.

On another flight, not long after his smashing reelection victory in 1964, Johnson was drinking highballs with four reporters from the press pool in his suite when he saw fit to expound on all the changes that were occurring in foreign governments. "Look around the world," the president said. "Khrushchev's gone. Macmillan's gone. Adenauer's gone. Segni's gone. Nehru's gone. Who's left—de Gaulle?" Then Johnson leaned back in his huge chair, beat his chest like a gorilla, and shouted, "I am the king!"

Shortly after taking office, he installed a special seat, which his aides called "the throne," that he could raise at the push of a button so he could ascend to a higher, more regal elevation than everyone else. He also had the staff install a similar device in his table, so he could raise and lower it at will. When members of Congress were aboard, he gave them "the treatment"—nose-to-nose lobbying for hour upon hour as he argued his case for Vietnam and the Great Society. As with his predecessors, Johnson regularly flew away on vacation or for long weekends, frequently to his ranch on the Pedernales River in central Texas, where he acted like the lord of the manor.

Yet LBJ was always insecure about his appearance, his big ears, doughy face, and unctuous manner on TV. He had the crew install magnifying mirrors and extra lights in his bathroom so he could get a better idea of how he would look under the television lights with makeup, according to flight engineer Joe Chappell. He was never satisfied with the results.

AS A RULE, Johnson rarely kept to himself aboard *Air Force One*. He hated to be alone, even when he went to sleep. When his wife was not aboard, he insisted that a flight steward or a White House aide stay in his compartment while he slept because he was afraid he might have another heart attack—he had suffered his first one in his forties—and no one would be there to help him.

Johnson was gregarious to the extreme. He made frequent phone calls and mingled freely with staff and guests, chatting about issues, talking about what he expected from them, sometimes showing off his knowledge of their home districts or states and what was important to their constituents.

When he became president, there were seats for 36 passengers aboard, in addition to the 12 crew members. He had the interior reconfigured to accommodate more than 60 passengers, including a dozen Secret Service agents, so he could have more people around.

He also had the passenger seats face to the rear, where the presidential compartment was located in those days, so he could have a commanding view of nearly everyone on "his" plane and so they could see him when he emerged from his stateroom.

Johnson had some cherrywood panels removed between his office and the adjacent cabin, and replaced them with clear plastic dividers so he could dominate virtually the entire aircraft if he wished. If he wanted privacy, stewards could draw the curtains to his office or close the door to his bedroom.

At the start of his presidency, Johnson even tried to do away with the press pool, which had accompanied the president on his airplane since Eisenhower's day. In Johnson's era it consisted of a correspondent each for the Associated Press and United Press International, the main wire services; one reporter for radio and television, and a correspondent for the rest of the press corps, usually a newspaper reporter.

Unlike today's *Air Force One* pool, which is larger and seeks to cover everything the president does, the LBJ-era pool was there "protectively"—and would report to the rest of the press corps or file stories only in case of emergency, such as another assassination attempt or a world crisis. Johnson had other ideas. "He insisted that they were 'spies' (his exact word) whose only purpose was to search out embarrassing secrets," said George Reedy.

At first, Johnson's response was to spend as much time as he could with the reporters on the plane, hoping to divert them, with the force of his own personality, from their supposed game of "gotcha." Predictably, the journalists initially were happy to spend hours in conversation with the president.

But the relationship soured after a few weeks. Trapped with Johnson for hours, the journalists found themselves exhausted by his overbearing manner and endless monologues, and they got little or no news from the arrangement. All in all, they preferred to gossip among themselves or chat informally over drinks. For his part, the president got bored with the journalists and concluded that his news coverage didn't improve.

This led him to abolish the *Air Force One* pool altogether, at least for a while. Again, LBJ had gone too far, and this decision only worsened his relationship with those who covered him.

In an act of pettiness, he wouldn't tell the reporters in advance whether he was going to his Texas ranch for the weekend. Each correspondent would show up at the White House on Friday mornings with a weekend's worth of clothes in a suitcase and wait to find out his plans. Recalled Ron Nessen, a TV reporter who later became Gerald Ford's press secretary: "At four o'clock in the afternoon they'd come on the loudspeaker and either say it's a lid for the weekend, which meant he wasn't going, or 'The press bus leaves the Southwest Gate in fifteen minutes.' You never knew until Friday afternoon whether he was going to fly to Texas."

PERHAPS MORE THAN any other chief executive, Johnson used *Air Force One* as a lobbying tool—not only cajoling, persuading, and bullying other politicians traveling with him, up close and personal, but doing the job long distance. Some of his phone calls involving members of Congress were extremely effective.

Walter Mondale, then a Democratic senator from Minnesota (and later Jimmy Carter's vice president), recalls a fierce controversy over a fair housing bill that had stalled in the Senate when opponents tried to talk it to death through filibuster. Efforts to shut down the debate had failed, and before the fifth attempt to bring the matter to a vote, Mondale feared that he and other supporters were on the verge of defeat. He decided to ask for Johnson's help. Mondale reached LBJ as he was flying to Latin America, and he explained the situation.

"We're one vote short," Mondale said, and he suggested the name of a senator from Alaska who could make the difference. "I believe he'd like a housing project there in Anchorage."

Johnson said, "Okay," and hung up.

In the end, the senator voted with the White House and the fair housing bill passed. The following week, the federal government announced that a new housing project would be built in the Anchorage area.

WHAT HAS NOT been generally known is LBJ's penchant for safety. It went back to an incident just after the election in November 1961, when he won the vice presidency on the Democratic ticket with Kennedy.

Johnson wanted his twin-engine private plane to pick him up at his Texas ranch, but it was a stormy night and the plane crashed, killing the civilian pilot and copilot. From then on, Johnson was a stickler for safety. "We want to be always safe," he told James Cross, his pilot, on many occasions. "You remember, I lost my own airplane one night."

Johnson was also a stickler for details and a notorious micro-manager determined to get his way. "He was a very intimidating fellow," Cross says. "He'd browbeat you—say, 'You're supposed to be the best there is.'"

The pilot got a call one afternoon in December 1967 with a surprise announcement. "You better get my big plane ready," the president drawled. "It looks like we're gonna leave tomorrow to the funeral of Prime Minister Holt." It turned out that Harold Holt of Australia, a friend of LBJ's, had drowned and Johnson wanted to pay his respects.

Cross reminded Johnson that he had approved his request to have the primary 707 overhauled and it was still at a maintenance facility in New York. LBJ had forgotten about the project but had a solution: "Just go up there and tell 'em to put it back together—and we leave tomorrow."

Cross said that wouldn't be possible, but the president persisted. "Well, call 'em up and get 'em to fix it tomorrow," he commanded.

The pilot said there were three other 707s in the presidential fleet as backups, and even though they had a shorter range and weren't as plush as the primary aircraft, each could get the job done.

Finally, Johnson said that would be satisfactory, but he had other concerns: The backup planes were too noisy. "Hell, see if you can put in some sound-proofing—like on my plane," the president said. "I don't like it so noisy—and too much light gets in there through the windows." Even with the curtains drawn, Johnson complained that he couldn't get a decent rest.

Cross said all that could be arranged, and LBJ hung up the phone, placated for the moment.

LBJ'S BEHAVIOR ON THE PLANE revealed that he was not just an egoist but a genuine social reformer. From the start, he wanted Americans to think of him as a benefactor in the same league as Franklin Roosevelt. To that end, he submitted to Congress a vast array of social programs to fight poverty such as legislation to create jobs, provide work training, and set up an Office of Economic Opportunity. Naturally, he pressured his speech writers and senior aides to invent a slogan that would match FDR's "New Deal"—in time for his 1964 election campaign.

He toyed with "a better deal" and "a prudent progressive," but felt, correctly, that these phrases lacked pizzazz. Borrowing ideas from Eric Goldman, a Princeton historian working in LBJ's White House, and speech writer Richard Goodwin, Johnson settled on the "Great Society." He told his staff to build an entire speech around it and he decided to deliver it as the commencement address at the University of Michigan in Ann Arbor on May 22, 1964.

"For a century, we labored to settle and to subdue a continent," Johnson declared to a crowd of 80,000 in the university's football stadium. "For half a century we called upon unbounded invention and untiring industry to create an order of plenty for all of our people. The challenge of the next half century is whether we have the wisdom to use that wealth to enrich and elevate our national life, and to advance the quality of our American civilization. . . . For in your time we have the opportunity to move not only toward the rich society and the powerful society, but upward to the Great Society."

The crowd loved the speech. En route home, he was "manic" and "absolutely euphoric," aides said. He even broke his own rule and treated himself to a Scotch and water in the presence of the reporters whom he allowed to travel with him. The journalists, not wanting to offend their host and genuinely impressed with his ideas, told him how wonderful the speech was. LBJ even read his favorite portions aloud as he stood in the gold-carpeted aisle of *Air Force One* and encouraged the press corps to highlight these sections in their dispatches.

Charles Roberts of *Newsweek*, one of the journalists aboard, wrote that "Lyndon Johnson was as pleased with himself on May 22, 1964, as I have ever seen him. . . . 'How did I do?' he asked eagerly as he hitched up his trousers and moved forward to the press pool table aboard *Air Force One*. He had 'done' well. . . . He had the crowd with him all the way, I ventured."

Roberts said LBJ had been interrupted 12 times by applause. But Johnson disagreed. "There were more than that," the president retorted, and he ordered Valenti to verify this impression. Valenti said there had been 14—Roberts had not counted the applause at the beginning and the end of the commencement address. Johnson was elated. After he settled into his seat and gathered the reporters around him, he said, "We are talking about legislation for the next generation, not just the next election. I'm going to get the best minds in this country to work for me," he added.

It was a moment of insight into the essence of the man. "Johnson's euphoria rested not only on the reception of his speech," writes historian Dallek, "but the sense that he was fully in command of the nation's support—that his appeals for a war on poverty and a Great Society were being met with enthusiastic anticipation of better times and greater achievements for the country." To a large extent, he was fooling himself. Dallek points out that "few Americans took Johnson's rhetoric at face value," and he really had little idea whether his ideas would work. But LBJ wanted to think big and enter the history books as a great achiever, so he set himself up for failure by promising too much.

. . .

HIS TRIP TO ASIA in 1966 crystallized his roller-coaster approach to governing. "While in Asia, Johnson kept an eye on events at home," recalls Joseph Califano, one of LBJ's key domestic policy advisers. "Traveling in very different time zones, he called me at all hours to give instructions and receive reports. During his journey, the president came up with the idea of a triumphal tour of the country to sign major Great Society bills Congress had passed. A whirlwind trip just before the November 8 elections would highlight his accomplishments and give him a chance to help Democratic candidates for Congress and several statehouses. . . . The trip was set to begin on Friday, November 4, two days after he returned to the White House."

After ordering his aides to make the arrangements on the fly, however, Johnson cancelled the campaign trip just before he arrived home. He decided that too many congressional Democrats might lose, and that would tarnish both him and his Great Society programs. When a reporter asked him why he had reversed himself, Johnson claimed that he never had planned to make such a campaign trip in the first place—a lie made all the more ridiculous since at least a score of politicians in 10 states, including Governor Pat Brown of California and Senator Paul Douglas of Illinois, had already changed their schedules to greet LBJ. They were at that moment scrambling to readjust their itineraries because of the president's change of mind.

LBJ's intuition proved correct. In the 1966 midterm elections, Democrats would lose 47 seats in the House of Representatives, 3 in the Senate, and 8 governorships. He was increasingly angry and frustrated that he was not being given credit for his legislative accomplishments.

He was particularly galled during the Asia trip as he contrasted the lack of appreciation he felt at home with the enthusiastic reception he experienced abroad, especially in New Zealand, Australia, the Philippines, South Vietnam, Thailand, Malaysia, and Korea, where 2 million people lined the streets of Seoul to greet him.

At one point, he told aides, "I am willing to let any objective historian look at my record. If I can't do more than any [one else] to help my country, I'll quit.

FDR passed five major bills the first one hundred days. We passed two hundred in the last two years. It is unbelievable." He proceeded to tick off one piece of legislation after another that he had persuaded Congress to approve, including bills on education, medical care, conservation, clean water, and truth in packaging. "There never has been an era in American history when so much has been done for so many in such a short time. . . . We must tell people what we have done."

But LBJ was growing out of touch with Americans' hopes and fears. The nation was being torn apart by a variety of schisms that would make themselves increasingly clear over the next two years: divisions over race, crime, poverty, and civil rights, increasing inflation and economic trouble, and most of all the Vietnam War. By the end of 1966, that conflict had killed 6,500 Americans and wounded 37,000. U.S. troop strength had risen to 385,000, and there was no end in sight. More and more Americans were questioning LBJ's strategy of gradual escalation and the morality of involvement in a civil war where the administration seemed to be supporting the wrong side.

WITHIN A YEAR, as American casualties increased, as U.S. victory seemed more in doubt, and as antiwar protests mounted across the country, Johnson could no longer travel freely, even abroad. American bombing had failed to defeat the North Vietnamese or break their will, and their Viet Cong allies were as dangerous as ever.

In the fall of 1967, even Defense Secretary Robert McNamara, one of the most vehement hawks around Johnson, began to express doubts about continuing the war. Johnson lost faith in him, and McNamara resigned to become president of the World Bank. The administration's war policies were unraveling.

In this context, LBJ decided to attend the funeral of Australian prime minister Holt in December. As he told pilot James Cross, Johnson truly wanted to honor Holt, but he seized on the trip as a way to bolster support for the war. The president secretly called Jack Valenti, by then an executive with the

Motion Picture Association of America, with a special "chore"—to secretly arrange a visit with the Pope on his way back from Asia. "I don't want anybody to know this," Johnson said. "And don't call from your house and don't call from your office."

Valenti dutifully left his home and drove to a pay phone outside a service station. When he reached a friend at the senior level of the Vatican, he spoke in a quasi-code: "My friend wants to meet your friend." The contact, knowing LBJ's inclination toward secrecy, understood immediately. Valenti added: "And my friend said to tell you that he doesn't want you to talk to the American ambassador or anybody." The arrival would be some time on Christmas Eve, Valenti said, and Vatican officials were to work out the details and get back to him.

Why such secrecy? Valenti later told me: "Rather than say, 'I'm going to Italy' and then having masses of protests and that sort of thing, it just made it easy to operate under an aura of secrecy and to be able to have these meetings without being tormented by demonstrations."

From his departure on December 20 to his return late on December 24, the trip was vintage LBJ. "We flew around the world," says Valenti. "We spent fifty-five hours in the air and lived on that airplane." The group spent only one night on the ground, getting a few hours sleep in Australia; the rest of the four days, the president caught catnaps in the bed in his stateroom and the staff slept in their seats and, for the senior advisers, in a handful of pull-down beds.

As *Air Force One* took off in the predawn chill, only LBJ knew for sure the full itinerary. Not even the Secret Service or his traveling staff, and certainly not the press, knew much more than that the president was going to Holt's funeral. (Johnson had secretly told Pentagon officials to have a U.S. military helicopter ready in Rome "just in case" the president landed there, and no one leaked the arrangement.)

As the plane sped to a refueling stop in Hawaii, Valenti and other staffers were furiously making contingency plans after Johnson briefed them, finally, on what he wanted to do: attend the funeral, visit U.S. troops in Vietnam, spend some time with leaders of friendly governments in Thailand and Pakistan. Then he wanted to meet with Pope Paul VI to discuss his war aims in Southeast Asia and ask the pontiff to intercede and gain release of U.S. prisoners of war in North Vietnam. Since he would visit the pontiff, meetings also had to be scheduled with Italian leaders in Rome to avoid any hard feelings in the Italian government, so they were added to the mix. The Americans decided that it would be best to land only at military bases or out-of-the-way airports and to land at night or in the predawn hours whenever possible, all to guarantee maximum security and control.

Unfortunately, nothing much came of the papal visit, which was the key to the trip—and this disappointed everyone. After a few hours at the Vatican, LBJ was airborne again, heading back to Washington.

JOHNSON'S HOPES for a peace settlement in 1968 were to be shattered by the massive Tet offensive by the Communists in late January. On March 12, Minnesota senator Eugene McCarthy, a dove on Vietnam, astounded the nation when he took 42 percent of the vote in the New Hampshire presidential primary. Johnson actually won with 49 percent, but he had been expected to capture more than 70 percent. On March 16, New York senator Robert Kennedy announced his own challenge to Johnson as an antiwar candidate. Johnson's approval ratings continued to drop as Kennedy's surged. Now his party was being torn apart, just as the country was being ripped open by the war.

On March 31, a Sunday evening, Johnson announced that he would not run again.

It was an extraordinary surprise to most Americans and it effectively ended the political career of one of the most remarkable leaders in the country's history.

BUT IT WAS NOT the end of Johnson's experiences on *Air Force One*. He made a few more trips on the plane during his remaining 10 months in office, but the war and the divisions raged on. In fact, things got worse. Both Robert Kennedy and Martin Luther King were assassinated, and the nation seemed to be approaching a nervous breakdown.

When he flew back to his Texas ranch after the inauguration of Richard Nixon as his successor, LBJ had his aides clean out the plane of memorabilia, including cups, silver, china, and playing cards and matchbooks bearing his name—even the "throne chair." It was his final act of megalomania as president.

CHAPTER SIX

RICHARD NIXON: THE SOLITARY BROODER

ICHARD NIXON WAS A WORKAHOLIC and a loner who focused on his job relentlessly and pursued his goals ruthlessly. Eight years after his bitter loss to Kennedy, he was elected in a very close campaign against Democrat Hubert Humphrey in 1968 and quickly began isolating himself. Longtime associates, including aides who had served him during his vice presidency under Eisenhower, say this was a big change, because he was actually quite accessible, even friendly, in the No. 2 job. Yet he allowed his campaign staff to build a wall around him, and he continued the pattern in the White House.

If anything, this isolation intensified on *Air Force One*, where he would spend most of his time in his private cabin with the door closed, either alone or chatting with a handful of aides, especially White House Chief of Staff H. R. "Bob" Haldeman. He allowed Haldeman and other advisers to screen not only his visitors but virtually all his phone calls on the plane; in the end, his contacts with the outside world were minimal.

He was reelected overwhelmingly in 1972 by giving Americans the kind of cultural conservatism and hardline but pragmatic foreign policy they wanted at the time. Even if the country didn't like Nixon's humorless, devious personality—his nickname was "Tricky Dick"—Americans preferred him to George

McGovern, the liberal Democratic challenger whom Nixon managed to pigeon-hole as a dangerous left-wing radical.

In the end, however, Nixon went too far when he covered up White House involvement in the burglary of the Democratic National Committee in Washington's Watergate Hotel and endorsed a range of domestic spying, dirty tricks, and lying to Congress.

Just as important, his escalation of the Vietnam War fractured the country even more than it had been under Lyndon Johnson. Despised by a large segment of the electorate, Nixon made few attempts at healing despite his campaign promise to bring the country together. Instead, he played upon the country's divisions over Vietnam, law and order, race, crime, and other issues, because it gave him and Republican conservatives a political edge. And no detail of his administration was seemingly too small to merit Nixon's attention, resulting in a breathtaking focus on both the profound and the trivial.

He was capable of great decisiveness, and also great vacillation. As usual, these traits became vivid on *Air Force One*. On February 23, 1969, a month after his inauguration, he boarded the plane en route to Brussels for the start of his first foreign trip as president. An hour or so into the flight, Nixon suddenly ordered the bombing of Cambodian sanctuaries outside Vietnam. It had long angered him that North Vietnamese troops were staging attacks from these areas against American forces, and he was determined to stop them. Henry Kissinger, his national security adviser, persuaded him to postpone his order for 48 hours so his advisers could consult with U.S., South Vietnamese, and other officials and develop a diplomatic plan for dealing with possible repercussions. Nixon agreed.

The next morning, Kissinger, Haldeman, and Alexander Haig, Kissinger's deputy, returned to *Air Force One* to work out the bombing plan. It was the only place where they felt sure no one could eavesdrop on them electronically.

But as doubts about the plan rose among his senior advisers, including Defense Secretary Melvin Laird, Nixon reconsidered. Ordering the bombing would only inflame the antiwar movement at home and abroad at the very beginning of Nixon's regime. Nixon cancelled the attacks. He would order them, finally, several weeks later, but this initial episode showed how unsure of himself the new president could be.

Nixon's many quirks were clearly visible on the plane. During the flight from Berlin to Rome on that first foreign visit, Nixon became peeved when William Safire, his speech writer, recalled the first trip he made with Nixon, then vice president, in 1958. Safire related how Nixon and Queen Elizabeth II had listened in historic St. Paul's Church in London as a choir sang the "Battle Hymn of the Republic." Nixon grew angry and interrupted the reverie. Ordering his aides not to mention the incident, he growled, "That's a Kennedy song." It was a manifestation of his resentment toward the man who had defeated him in 1960 and whose charisma he always envied.

As he did at the White House, he hatched many plots to outmaneuver his enemies, and he was obsessed with his news coverage. He believed the Eastern Establishment media, especially *The Washington Post*, *The New York Times*, and the three broadcast networks of ABC, CBS, and NBC, were out to get him, and he fumed to his senior aides, especially White House Chief of Staff Haldeman, about how unfair they were.

Ironically, shortly after he took office, Nixon ordered LBJ's taping system aboard SAM 26000 removed from the aircraft. This primitive system had recorded all incoming and outgoing calls, just as Nixon was to do from the White House. It remains unexplained why Nixon removed the *Air Force One* system but upgraded the one in the White House, which was to provide damning evidence to the Watergate investigators during his second term.

Kissinger said later that Nixon suffered from "a lack of assurance even during his greatest accomplishments," one of the character flaws that led to the paranoia-fed Watergate scandal. And Nixon's vengeful mindset was evident even in his moments of triumph.

His pathbreaking trip to China, for example, started off well. In his departure ceremony on the South Lawn on February 17, 1972, he borrowed from the words of the first astronauts who had landed on the moon in describing what he hoped the trip would be remembered for: "We came in peace for all mankind." It was an elegant way to begin, and everyone seemed to recognize the historic nature of the visit. The networks gave live coverage to *Air Force One*'s takeoff.

Yet Nixon was peeved. For one thing, he wasn't happy that his effort to rename the presidential aircraft *The Spirit of '76* just before the trip was a flop; the media preferred *Air Force One* and would not accept the change. He began going over the manifest naming the 100 journalists traveling with him. "Are there any non-Jews here?" Nixon asked as he scanned the list. His aides (including Kissinger, who was himself Jewish) didn't know whether he was kidding or displaying anti-Semitism, and didn't know how to respond.

Nixon considered himself an expert on the media and was constantly fine-tuning his staff's public-relations plans. For the China trip, he had insisted that the 100-person media contingent, pre-approved by the White House from a list of 2,000 applicants, contain a heavy concentration of television anchors, correspondents, camera personnel, and technicians. Nixon wanted the visit to be a TV spectacular, and he got his wish.

Yet throughout the outbound trip, reports Kissinger in his memoirs, "Nixon oscillated between anxiety that his otherwise competent staff was oblivious to the finer points of public relations and serious, indeed dedicated preparation for his sojourn in China. Having read every briefing book, he plied me with questions on the long hours of that plane ride."

In an astounding departure, Nixon even strolled back to the press compartment on the Boeing 707 on the outbound leg—a first for him as president—and talked with the seven pool reporters and photographers on his plane. (As usual, a separate press charter had gone ahead to land before *Air Force One* and record the arrival.) Nixon awkwardly tried to make small talk, asking his antagonists if they knew how to use chopsticks.

As author Richard Reeves recounts, "One reporter showed him an elaborate China atlas with CENTRAL INTELLIGENCE AGENCY embossed on the cover. 'Do you think they'll let us in with this?' he asked.

"'This will probably show how much we don't know about China,' answered the president."

Nixon returned to his suite at the front of the plane and resumed studying the huge stacks of background briefing books. He memorized hundreds of "talking points" that he wanted to use in his talks with the Chinese leaders.

On the hop from Shanghai to Beijing, Nixon, sitting alone, looked out the window of *Air Force One* and, Reeves says, "thought the villages looked like pictures from the Middle Ages." He felt that he was bridging not only ideological divides but historic ones, and considered this to be one of the most important missions of his presidency. He was right.

His trip was a triumph. Even if there were no huge breakthroughs on policy, it seemed a moment of historic conciliation. To this day, the term "Nixon goes to China" is shorthand for a political leader playing against type and doing what his critics never could have accomplished. Here was the seemingly implacable anti-Communist making overtures to Beijing. It was something a politician with a more lenient attitude toward the Red Menace could never have achieved; conservative leaders, such as Nixon himself, would have pilloried such a politician for naively taking risks with national security. Nobody thought Nixon would ever do that.

And even the seemingly small moments worked to Nixon's advantage. On Nixon's arrival in Beijing, a burly staffer blocked the aisle so aides could not walk off *Air Force One* at the same time as Nixon. Haldeman had given the order, and his goal was to keep everyone else out of the picture—particularly the publicity-hungry Kissinger—when Nixon shook hands with Chinese premier Zhou Enlai with *Air Force One* as a backdrop. This moment ended decades of enmity between Washington and Beijing, and was carried live on prime-time American TV—all to Nixon's credit.

There were other memorable pictures that resonate to this day of his remarkable opening to China. The images, beamed all over the world, showed Nixon on the Great Wall; Nixon meeting with Mao Tse-tung; Nixon strolling in the Forbidden City.

Yet when he began his trip home, he fell into a funk. Nixon spent considerable time complaining to aides that his enemies in the media and in the Democratic party would criticize the trip as an election-year PR ploy, while ultra-conservatives would complain of a sellout. Surrounded by trusted aides who fed his every whim and fueled his bizarre theories, his insecure personality again came to the fore and he fretted that his enemies would twist the meaning of the trip to hurt him.

As Kissinger observed: "Triumph seemed to fill Nixon with a premonition of ephemerality. He was, as he never tired of repeating, at his best under pressure. Indeed, it was sometimes difficult to avoid the impression that he needed crises as a motivating force—and that success became not a goal but an obsession so that once achieved he would not know what to do with it."

ON THE EVENING of Monday, June 19, 1972, en route to Washington after a long weekend in Key Biscayne, Florida, Nixon called Haldeman to the front of *Air Force One* and received what, in his diary, he called a surprise. "On the way back," Nixon wrote, "I got the disturbing news from Bob Haldeman that the break-in of the Democratic National Committee involved someone on the payroll of the Committee to Re-Elect the President." Nixon didn't say whether he knew anything about the burglary in advance. But whether he did or not, his subsequent efforts to cover up the connections to his White House proved his downfall.

ON ELECTION DAY, November 7, 1972, Nixon carried 49 of the 50 states with 60.7 percent of the popular vote, one of the greatest presidential victories in U.S. history. And even though Republicans lost two seats in the Senate, they gained 12 seats in the House. Yet, the next morning, Nixon insisted that Haldeman demand the resignations of his Cabinet and senior staff so he could decide where to install new blood. The president struck his intimates as ungrateful and even angry.

Earlier that morning, November 8, he had reviewed his White House–prepared summary of the day's news—which was dominated by glowing reports of his success. Instead of relishing his triumph, he again saw the downside. He wrote across the news summary: "The opposition line will be: 1. McG's mistakes lost it and not his views and not RN's strength. 2. The low vote proves no one liked either candidate, 3. RN let down his party." He ordered Haldeman to take preemptive action against unnamed Republican officials who he predicted would blame the president for not helping them more. "Cut that off," Nixon said. "Make sure that we start pissing on the party before they begin pissing on me. Blame bad candidates and sloppy organization."

The flight to Key Biscayne on November 8 was supposed to be celebratory. But Nixon's vindictive mood incubated on *Air Force One*. He told Haldeman he understood that 80 of the 89 members of the White House press corps had voted for McGovern (no one was sure where he got that number but no one challenged him on it). And he complained that it was McGovern's campaign that had played dirty, not his.

He vented about the perceived slights, errors, and sins committed against him by *Time, Newsweek, The New York Times*, and *The Washington Post*, and *CBS News*. "Freeze them," he snapped, ordering his staff to keep the offenders out of the loop. As Haldeman reported in his diary, "He wants total discipline on the press, they're to be used as enemies, not played for help." As always, his first response against his perceived adversaries was to declare war. But this generally made matters worse in dealing with the media outlets that he singled out, because they had the last word. He also struck at his purely political adversaries. "He wants to be sure the IRS covers all major Democratic contributors and all backers of the new senators," Haldeman wrote in his diary.

THROUGHOUT HIS PRESIDENCY, Nixon descended into fits of cursing and overall pique, contrary to his carefully cultivated public image of rectitude and calm. This was often exacerbated in the plane, surrounded as he was by obsequious aides and with no public schedule to force him to curb his private emotions. After a rough landing on one of his first flights as president, in 1969, he shouted, "That's it! No more landing at airports." His aides weren't sure what he meant, so they never followed through.

His flight crew was overburdened. There were constant demands: for full meal service on one-hour flights to New York; for more and better trinkets, such as ashtrays and mugs that guests could take home as souvenirs; for upgraded menus and wine selections. At one point, Nixon aide Larry Higby wrote a lengthy memo to the military liaison office at the White House asking why the food service was not comparable to that at Trader Vic's, a posh eatery that Nixon liked near the White House. One problem was that Nixon's aides weren't willing to pay the higher costs out of their own pockets or divert money from other budgets to finance their culinary adventures.

Such things didn't mean much to Nixon personally. He was a Spartan eater, and he showed great discipline. For lunch, he almost always had a pineapple ring and cottage cheese, and he liked Salisbury steak with gravy for dinner. Yet the penchant for perks reflected a pervasive sense of entitlement among Nixon and his men.

"His staff was a buffer between him and everyone else," recalls Jim Bull, retired chief of communications on *Air Force One*. "He didn't even say good morning when he came on board. . . . He was so within himself when I flew with him on the airplane, it was kind of like there was a cloud over his head, like he was brooding." On more than one occasion, Bull and other members of the crew would glimpse Nixon in his cabin when the door was ajar; he would be sitting alone with his hands on his forehead and his head bent toward his desktop, as if he were lost in thought.

While Haldeman filtered the president's incoming communications, Nixon instituted a strangely formal process for making his outgoing phone calls. Instead of just picking up his phone and asking Bull to contact someone, Nixon would write a note, buzz for the chief steward, and hand it to him silently. It would contain the name of the person he wanted to talk to. Bull would then use the White House switchboard to track the person down.

NIXON FOUND SLEEPING on *Air Force One* uncomfortable, despite its amenities; on lengthy trips he would insist that the plane stop for the night so he could stay at a hotel, an ambassador's residence, or a rich friend's house. Ralph Albertazzie, his pilot, says Nixon never traveled overnight on the plane during his entire presidency.

Reflecting the law-and-order mood in the nation and his own austere tastes, he imposed a strong sense of protocol and a dour atmosphere. His only concession to informality was a garish red houndstooth sports jacket that he would slip on after removing his suit coat once he was airborne. He also had identical sports jackets, in gray, blue, and a mustard color, which he would alternate on different flights.

In his stateroom, he would occasionally prop his feet on a white pillow that he carefully placed on a table, still wearing his black wingtip shoes, his tie, and his jacket. Once in a while he would have a Ballantine's Scotch or a martini, but his personality remained austere, belying his public claim that he wanted to inject a spirit of joy into his job.

Nixon often retreated into his own world. "He stayed pretty much in his cabin and the door was usually closed," said Albertazzie. "I don't recall that he ever came up into the cockpit to chat in the five and a half years I was his pilot." Added former White House counsel John Dean: "Nixon typically didn't come out of his cubbyhole."

Nixon insisted that staff members leave him time to read, confer with his inner circle, and nap. But one of the things he valued most aboard *Air Force One* was the chance to think, and there is extensive evidence that he was one of the nation's most introspective chief executives. He would often write memos and notes to himself and would accumulate what Haldeman called "an incredible stack of little white note sheets with an amazing array of trivia," and he would badger his aides to follow up on his every concern.

Yet he could never figure out how to operate the lights and the reclining seats, even the radio, and was forever asking the crew to do it for him, interrupting his reveries. "He was the most unmechanical person I ever knew," recalled retired Air Force general Brent Scowcroft, who was Nixon's military assistant. "He wasn't handy at doing anything. He couldn't pin medals on people, and he used to trip over flecks of dust on the carpet." Albertazzie says gently that he was "mechanically disinclined."

The president's memos to himself, whether handwritten on the white note sheets or a yellow legal pad, or recorded on a Dictaphone and transcribed later, showed not only his introspection but, more ominously, a conspiratorial mind at work. He wrote such notes at the White House, of course. But his musings on *Air Force One*, in the solitude of the presidential cabin at 35,000 feet as his mind played out the events he had just participated in or as he anticipated upcoming events and decisions, were especially revealing. What emerges is the picture of a man who at his best recognized the need for noble ideals but who seemed to profoundly misunderstand his inability to live up to them personally.

After a tumultuous reception in Gulfport, Mississippi, in September 1969, a buoyed Nixon flew back to Washington on *Air Force One* and wrote on his legal pad:

H [shorthand for Haldeman]: Tricia job
K [shorthand for Kissinger]: Hijacking plan for Cuba
Most powerful office
Each day a chance to do something memorable for someone
Need to be good to do good
Need for joy, serenity, confidence, inspirational
Goals: Set example, inspire, instill pride
1. Personal image of Presidency—Strong, compassionate, competent,
   bold—Joy in job
2. Nation is better in spirit at end of term.

Three years later, at the end of that first term, he seemed just as obsessed with his legacy. "On October 10, 1972," writes author Richard Reeves, "as he flew from his Florida home in Key Biscayne back to Washington, he worried, not for the first time, about how he would be remembered after all his elections were over, writing: 'Presidents noted for—F.D.R.—Charm. Truman—Gutsy. Ike—smile, prestige. Kennedy—charm. LBJ—Vitality. RN—?'" He suggested to himself that his legacy might be: "The national conscience." This, of course, looks quite deluded in view of the corruption that would soon be revealed in the Watergate scandal.

NIXON'S HYPOCRITICAL STREAK was strong. On the return trip from China, as *Air Force One* soared toward an overnight stop in Anchorage on February 28, 1972, he told Haldeman that he wanted to reward Kissinger for arranging the trip.

"Then he told me to make a note of the fact that K has worked hard and I'm to call [Nixon friend and businessman Bebe] Rebozo and have him give Henry all of his phone numbers of girls that are not over thirty," Haldeman wrote in his diary. And this from the apostle of family values!

Sometimes he would have a glass of Scotch; a 30-year-old Ballantine's was his favorite, and he had the stewards keep a bottle or two on the aircraft. Occasionally he would share a martini with Rebozo in the presidential conference room, where they would put their feet up. Rebozo was one of his few close friends, and the men had a tradition of making martinis for each other and then evaluating each other's bartending skills. Yet Nixon disdained aides who drank openly. Some of them would secretly defy their boss by pouring whisky into paper coffee cups or coffee mugs so no one was the wiser.

He also didn't like people to curse, even though he often used foul language in the presence of his senior aides.

Pat Nixon had her own secret. She was a chain smoker, and the crew liberally stocked packs of cigarettes in the presidential quarters for the First Lady. Many times, she would sit alone in her cabin and puff on one cigarette after another, even though she was from the era in which "ladies" didn't smoke at all. (Mrs. Nixon would die of lung cancer in June 1993, at age 81.)

The staff was preoccupied with status, even to the point of complaining when one aide was not served miniature candy bars that another aide received. Albertazzie described the overall atmosphere on the plane as "puritanically grim." There was a TV in the conference room, for example, but few people watched it. They were too busy working and plotting.

STILL, THERE WERE HUMANIZING moments that showed Nixon was not a cardboard cutout. When the president flew to Poland, local authorities rolled out a red carpet and lined up some impressively dressed troops and a military band. Trouble was, as *Air Force One* landed, someone noticed that everything was placed on the right-hand side of the aircraft, when the president always exited on the left side. As the 707 taxied to a stop, the troops, the band, and the carpet were all rushed to the proper location, stirring derisive laughter among the

Nixon aides and the president himself as they peered out the windows. What one Nixon aide called "an amazing screwup" became the ultimate Polish joke for the president and his men. Nixon got a big laugh out of it for weeks afterward.

Nixon also enjoyed looking up the skirts of secretaries and other young female passengers on his *Marine One* helicopter. He did it discreetly and never openly ogled the women, but he expressed a certain juvenile satisfaction in this forbidden pleasure.

Former White House counsel John Dean recalls flying from Florida to Washington with his wife, Mo, aboard *Air Force One* in 1972, shortly after Nixon's reelection. At one point Nixon sauntered into the staff compartment and introduced himself to Mrs. Dean, who was thrilled. The president playfully cuffed Dean about the ears and tried to banter with the lovely young wife. "We're going to keep your husband damn busy," he told Mrs. Dean. When she said, "I hope not too busy," the president replied, "You may wish you hadn't married him."

It turned out quite differently. It was Nixon who must have had the second thoughts after Dean's testimony in the Watergate scandal helped bring the president down.

IN FACT, DEAN argues that it was on *Air Force One* that he saw the first link in "the chain of events that destroyed the Nixon presidency." This was on January 14, 1971, well before the fateful burglary at the Watergate Hotel that set in motion the final series of lies and cover-ups. Nixon was en route to the University of Nebraska to deliver a speech far away from the protests that were spreading across other campuses. He sat in front of his IBM dictating machine, pushed the button, and began to speak.

"This for Haldeman," Nixon said. "It would seem that the time is approaching when Larry O'Brien is held accountable for his retainer with [billionaire entrepreneur Howard] Hughes. Bebe [Rebozo] has some information on this although it is, of course, not solid. But there is no question that one of Hughes's people did have O'Brien on a very heavy retainer for 'services rendered' in the past. Perhaps [Chuck] Colson should check on this."

After the message was typed and sent to Haldeman the next day in Washington, the senior aide suggested to the president that Dean, rather than Colson, be given the assignment as a test of his loyalty and ability. As a result, Dean was directed by Haldeman to investigate the relationship between Hughes and O'Brien, who was chairman of the Democratic National Committee with offices in the Watergate Hotel. Dean interpreted the assignment just as Nixon and Haldeman intended it. He was looking for scandal—some juicy episode with which to taint the opposition during that election year. This search was the motivating force behind the Watergate break-in.

WHEN THE NEW *AIR FORCE ONE*, bearing the tail number 27000, arrived at March Air Force Base near Palm Springs, California, in December 1972, the White House staff was abuzz with excitement. It was an updated Boeing 707, but reconfigured on express orders of the president from the way Kennedy had kept his 707, the famous SAM 26000. The cabins had a "new car smell," scented with leather and plastic, an aide recalled, with fresh carpeting and expensive wall panels. Sheets had been placed over the seats so no one could leave a mark or spill a cup of coffee on the upholstery before the president flew on the plane. (He would not inspect it until it reached Washington.)

Actually, Nixon had considered ordering a 747 jumbo jet at the time. He loved the size and amenities of the plane, but was crestfallen to learn that it wasn't practical because so few airports could accommodate the huge jets in the early 1970s. In the end, he went with his second choice of the refurbished 707.

Still, the plane was a big hit. For most of the first official flight, the staff behaved like kids with a room full of toys on Christmas morning. They played with the controls on the seats, tested the in-flight music system, and watched the new television monitors that picked up local stations as *Air Force One* cruised over them. Senior aides such as Haldeman quickly donned their brown leather flight jackets, emblazoned with the words AIR FORCE ONE.

But there was a problem. Mrs. Nixon didn't like the layout. It turned out that the presidential compartment was next to the staff compartment, which was adjacent to the guest cabin. This meant that the First Lady's cabin was far removed from the president's, and she had to go through the staff area to see her husband. Further, the Nixons would have to walk among the staff in order to reach their guests, and they were concerned that their retainers would interfere with their comings and goings. The plane was sent back to the factory for reconfiguration, at a cost of $2 million. Mrs. Nixon's cabin was placed next to her husband's suite.

Nixon rearranged the presidential quarters to give him even more privacy, creating four rooms end to end: a presidential office, decorated with the gold-and-blue presidential seal and containing two leather swivel chairs across from a desk and a three-person sofa on the right wall that could be converted to a single bed; a sitting room with a couch that could be converted to another bed for the First Lady; a lavatory; and a conference room or lounge. There was a white telephone to the right of the desk, and a panel to the right of the presidential chair containing switches to control the room's lighting, and another panel to operate the stereo system, although Nixon never quite figured out how to use either one. A corridor was built along the left side of the aircraft so aides would not trouble the president inside his suite when the doors to the hallway were closed.

ON FEBRUARY 8, 1973, as pressure was building on him because of the Watergate scandal and public unrest about the war in Vietnam, Nixon flew to his San Clemente estate for another of his increasingly common "working vacations." On the flight, he told aides he had read stories that he might be nominated for a Nobel Peace Prize but he wanted any nomination withdrawn. There would simply be too much embarrassment if he lost the prize; instead, he decided to take the public position that no leader should receive such honors just for doing his job, and making peace was his duty.

It was clear that he wanted to avoid more embarrassment at all costs and to wall himself off from his problems. He told Haldeman he wanted even more time alone in the coming months, now that the campaign was over. For the record, he wanted all trips to begin in Florida or California, where he had vacation homes, rather than Washington, so he could avoid the custom of inviting members of Congress to join him on *Air Force One* when he left the capital. The members pestered him too much with their demands and what he considered their petty concerns. He wanted no visitors whatsoever at Aspen Lodge at Camp David. He wanted to end state arrival ceremonies and embassy lunches—they were now too trivial for him—and he wanted no more Friday-afternoon meetings, so he could get away early each weekend for relaxation and reflection.

As his presidency wore on and his unpopularity grew, he followed LBJ's pattern of traveling extensively abroad to escape hostile crowds at home. This meant that *Air Force One* was, more than ever, his refuge.

But even here he was not immune from the larger world. He learned this in dramatic fashion in June 1974, two months before he was forced to resign amid the Watergate scandal, when he visited the Middle East and the Soviet Union. En route from Saudi Arabia to Syria, an insulated, autocratic nation that no American president had visited before, a Syrian jet fighter—a Soviet-made MiG—suddenly appeared off *Air Force One*'s right wing, and another Syrian MiG zoomed in on the left wing. *Air Force One* pilot Ralph Albertazzie, not sure what was going on, suddenly popped the speed brakes, causing the MiGs to zoom ahead of the big jet. Albertazzie then put the 707 into a steep dive and took other evasive maneuvers. David Gergen, a Nixon adviser who was aboard, recalls being thrown roughly to the floor along with other passengers in his cabin and wondering if anyone would survive.

"Within minutes—or was it seconds?—word came to our pilots that there had been a huge mix-up on the ground," Gergen says. "[Syrian ruler Hafez al-] Assad had dispatched his jets as a welcoming committee to escort us into Damascus but apparently failed to tell our advance party of his plans. . . . *Air Force One* leveled off and we proceeded smoothly to the red carpet down below, but I always look back on our journey as a lasting symbol of that summer of '74. For the next several weeks, Richard Nixon twisted, turned, and tried to evade his pursuers until he crashed on August Ninth."

In any case, Nixon never mentioned the incident to the pilot or crew, but confided to a friend later that he was stunned and scared.

. . .

WHEN HE ANNOUNCED on August 8, 1974, that he would resign from office rather than face impeachment and removal, Nixon was a bitter man who had retreated almost totally into a shell. His final flight on *Air Force One* to San Clemente, California, the next day, August 9, when he actually left office, was a bizarre wake.

There were 34 passengers aboard, but Nixon ordered that there be no press pool to harass or further embarrass him. More important, there was also no "football" or "black box," containing the secret codes that would launch American nuclear retaliation in case of a surprise attack. When a president travels it is kept in a safe in the communications section of *Air Force One*, and whenever the president leaves the plane, a military aide is assigned to make sure it is never far from the commander in chief. This time, it stayed at the White House with Nixon's successor, the 38th president, Gerald Ford.

Shortly after takeoff, Nixon asked Master Sergeant Lee Simmons, his personal steward, for a martini, which was unusual. He was a light drinker on *Air Force One* and rarely had alcohol at all in the morning. But on this day, he was, understandably, deviating from his routine.

When Ford took the oath of office in the East Room just after noon, Nixon's plane was flying at 39,000 feet over a point 13 miles southwest of Jefferson City, Missouri. Albertazzie spoke to ground control.

"Kansas City," he said. "This was *Air Force One*. Will you change our call sign to SAM [Special Air Mission] 27000?"

"Roger, SAM 27000," came the reply. "Good luck to the president."

Nixon was out of office.

He and Press Secretary Ron Ziegler sipped martinis in the president's cabin, and ate a lunch of shrimp cocktail, prime rib, baked potato, green beans, salad, rolls, and cheesecake. Mrs. Nixon and daughter Tricia were alone in the First Lady's compartment.

As the plane flew over the Midwest, Nixon got up from his seat, still wearing his blue suit and tie, and walked down its length, his face crinkled in a strained smile, thanking crew members and aides for their help over the years. Just remember, he told Simmons, that tomorrow is a new day. You can't let things get you down. You can't stay down, you have to pick yourself up and keep going. Life goes on.

At one point, he came upon a somber group in the conference room and got flustered. Rolling his hands in front of his chest, as he did when he was uncomfortable, he blurted out, "Is everybody enjoying the flight?" No one said a word as they looked at him in shock. Of course no one was enjoying the flight. He walked over to Albertazzie, who had left the cockpit to see how things were going, and said wistfully, "We traveled so many miles together." Then he said he'd like the White House photographer to take a few pictures of them when they landed (which he did) and moved on.

When he got to the rear of the aircraft, Nixon saw that Secret Service agents were seated in the press section, since no journalists were allowed aboard. "Well," Nixon said jovially. "It certainly smells better back here." Everyone laughed nervously.

Then he returned to his private cabin, where he shut the door and remained alone for the rest of the flight.

CHAPTER SEVEN

GERALD FORD: EVERYMAN

VICE PRESIDENT JERRY FORD GOT the top job by succession after Nixon left office on August 9, 1974. The former congressman from Grand Rapids, Michigan, inherited a terrible mess—an angry, bitter, and divided country, residual hatred for Nixon, the tragic endgame of the Vietnam War, and a very weak economy. He did the best he could during his two and a half years in office, one of the shortest terms in American history, but it wasn't enough.

Yet, again and again, those who worked most closely with Ford and saw him in all his moods—the stewards and crew members of *Air Force One*—expressed admiration for him. They said he was a decent man and a hard worker who deserved better than the hand Fortune dealt him. "He was a homespun family guy," recalls Howie Franklin, a retired chief steward. "He was friendly and he interacted with the crew very well. President Ford was like a crew member. It was like we were on a baseball team and we were teammates."

Adds Charles Palmer, another former chief steward who served Nixon, Ford, Carter, and Reagan: "President Ford probably treated the whole crew better than any other president"—always inquiring about their families, and even inviting them to the White House for presidential birthday parties or to social occasions at his Palm Springs, California, home.

James Cannon, a senior Ford domestic policy adviser, made a broader point: "Gerald R. Ford was an ordinary man called to serve America in extraordinary circumstances. In his plain ways and plain speaking, in his forthrightness and genial nature, in his trust in others and their trust in him, Ford was Everyman become president."

Yet Americans wanted a leader they could be proud of after the Nixon scandals, and Ford carried too much baggage, especially after September 8, 1974, when he pardoned his predecessor of any crimes he may have committed as president. This outraged many voters, who suspected a corrupt deal that traded Nixon's resignation and Ford's elevation to the presidency in exchange for the pardon. Others simply felt that Nixon deserved to be prosecuted for his transgressions.

But history has been kind to Ford. Presidential scholars today give him high marks for this attempt at national reconciliation. In 2001, in fact, Senator Edward Kennedy and members of his family presented Ford with the John F. Kennedy Profile in Courage Award in recognition of the pardon, even though Edward Kennedy had criticized Ford vigorously for it over the years. Ford told me in a 2002 interview that this was one of the most important events of his life. He felt vindicated.

AT FIRST, FORD benefited from the contrast to his predecessor, and he played upon it. "Nixon, by nature, was a recluse who preferred to deal with problems through paperwork rather than through people," Ford wrote in his autobiography. "I don't do business that way. From the first I sought an 'open' Administration. One thing I wanted to do right away was to eliminate the trappings of an 'imperial' Presidency, so even before being sworn in, I asked Al Haig to tell the Marine band that I didn't want to hear 'Hail to the Chief' or 'Ruffles and Flourishes'; the 'Michigan Fight Song' would suffice. I also asked Haig to make sure that the Oval Office was swept clean of all electronic listening devices—there would be no bugging or taping during my Administration." One of his first acts was to formally change the name of the presidential aircraft from Nixon's grandiose *Spirit of '76* back to *Air Force One*. "Everyone knew it as *Air Force One*, and I decided that was the name it should have," Ford recalls.

Added Ron Nessen, who was Ford's White House press secretary: "Ford wanted to be Speaker of the House and he realized the Republicans were never going to take control of the House in his time, so he told Betty he was going to run one more time and retire. And then the next thing you know, he's vice president and president, without ever running for it. These guys who spend twenty years of their life lusting after the presidency, their personalities get distorted. Whatever they need to say, they say. Ford never went through that."

"The other thing was, Ford was one of life's winners," Nessen argued. "You know the joke that if Nixon had only made the Whittier College football team, he never would have turned out that way. But Ford did make the football team. He was a high-school football hero, a college football hero. He got into Yale Law School when he really didn't think he would. And he married the woman he loved and stayed married to her his whole life. All this gave him an inner self-esteem, self-confidence. He didn't have to prove anything to anybody."

Ford's normalcy was not an inconsequential trait after the strangeness of Richard Nixon. He even enjoyed the company of his wife, Betty, who would ride with him in the presidential compartment, where Nixon had operated alone. He just wanted her near him. His tastes in food were ordinary, even bland. He liked cottage cheese with A.1. Steak Sauce or ketchup for lunch, pork chops or stuffed cabbage and navy-bean soup for dinner, and he had a sweet tooth. Ford loved lemon sponge pudding and chocolate angel food cake.

He was also normal in not trying to shut himself off from human contact. On *Air Force One*, he didn't want only the chief steward serving as his personal attendant in his stateroom, preferring to rotate that duty around the stewards, so he could get to know them all better. Ford also directed the flight crew to leave the door to his stateroom open. This order wasn't long-lived, however, because too many aides kept walking in on him and he didn't have enough time to himself. He enjoyed quiet contemplation, reading, or talking with key aides as he smoked his pipe. About a month after taking office, he began to close the door.

Likewise, Ford didn't mind people calling him "Jerry" at first, especially his longtime friends and advisers. But within a few weeks, as he realized the importance of sustaining a level of dignity, it was "Mr. President."

What didn't change was Ford's gregarious nature. He made a habit of wandering through the plane, chatting with staff members and guests—something Nixon had rarely done. He would stop in the cockpit and venture into the crew's areas, just to say hello at the start of every flight.

Ford also asked the stewards to place a Bible on the desk in his stateroom whenever he was aboard so he could read a passage and find a bit of solace in times of stress. It is a tradition that continues to this day.

FORD MADE SOME solid decisions as president. He helped persuade the nation that Vietnamese refugees should be welcomed in the United States, not kept out. He continued Nixon's policies of rapprochement with Moscow. And he made progress on arms control. "Ford was President for 895 days," wrote James Cannon. "At the beginning he was such a welcome relief from his predecessor that popular opinion rated him better than he was. Inevitably, as with all new Presidents his popularity declined as he confronted and dealt with the real world."

The Vietnam War was ending badly, resulting in a humiliating evacuation of all Americans and as many South Vietnamese loyalists as possible from a besieged Saigon. Inflation was rampant, unemployment was up, energy shortages were on the rise, and national confidence was ebbing. As Ford wrote in his memoirs, "The years of suspicion and scandal that had culminated in Nixon's resignation had demoralized our people. They had lost faith in their elected leaders and in their institutions. I knew that unless I did something to restore their trust, I couldn't win their consent to do anything else."

But his connections to the hated Nixon, and his image as a plodding, old-style politician in the television age were huge drawbacks.

HIS ADVISERS TRIED their best to use *Air Force One* as a political tool. For one thing, they arranged for the plane to make a pass over just about every major airport before landing, to give TV reporters and photographers some extra pictures of the plane in flight.

At the start of the 1976 Republican National Convention in Kansas City, the race was up for grabs between Ford and conservative challenger Ronald Reagan for the GOP nomination. The night before the opening, Reagan was scheduled to speak at a rally just before the prime-time TV shows and Ford was scheduled to arrive at about the same time. But Ford and his aides had *Air Force One* circle the airfield and land three minutes after the newscasts began. The networks cut away from the Reagan rally to show *Air Force One* swooping into Kansas City on arrival—a bit of one-upmanship that delighted Ford and his staff, and may even have helped burnish his image a bit.

But overall, these gambits weren't enough.

In fact, Ford's image was badly hurt by a mishap that occurred as he was disembarking from *Air Force One*, which had done so much to boost the reputations and enhance the dignity of his predecessors. The problem came when he stumbled on rain-slick stairs as he got off the plane in Salzburg, Austria, in June 1975. He landed awkwardly on one knee with both hands planted on the ground, while ubiquitous news cameras recorded the embarrassing fall for all to see. He didn't think the incident would amount to much at the moment it happened, and even came up with a quip when he recovered and turned to his host. "Thank you for your gracious welcome to Salzburg," Ford said, "and I'm sorry that I tumbled in."

Ford recalled it this way: "What happened was this: Betty and I were descending the steps. I had my right arm around her waist to help her, and I was carrying an umbrella in my left hand. Two or three steps from the bottom of the ramp, the heel of my shoe caught on something. I had no free hand to grab the rail, so I took a tumble to the tarmac below.

"I jumped to my feet, unhurt, and thought nothing of the fall. So I was quite surprised when Ron Nessen told me later that reporters covering my trip were bombarding him with questions about my 'missteps.' . . . I told him not to worry about them. . . . I was wrong. From that moment on, every time I stumbled or bumped my head or fell in the snow, reporters zeroed in on that to the exclusion of almost everything else."

Ironically, flight steward Charles Palmer had offered to hold the umbrella for Mrs. Ford just as the couple walked out onto the steps, but the president brushed him off. "No thanks," he said gallantly. "I'll hold the umbrella for Betty." It was a mistake.

Nessen, Ford's press secretary, exited the plane from the rear stairs and never saw his boss take the spill. Moments after he stepped onto the tarmac, reporters began asking, "What's wrong with Ford?" That question was on everyone's mind within a couple of hours, as the TV image of the fall spread around the world. "I mean, it was the most embarrassing thing you can think of—with the TV of the world focused on you," Nessen said, "so all day long there were questions: What's wrong with Ford? What's wrong with Ford?"

That evening, Ford and his confidants felt compelled to send the White House doctor to meet the press and explain that nothing was wrong with the president except for an old knee ailment. But the damage to his image was done.

That moment, more than any other, gave Ford the image of a clumsy oaf, a national embarrassment—and it was driven into the popular consciousness by frequent skits on *Saturday Night Live* in which comedian Chevy Chase brilliantly portrayed Ford as a nincompoop. It didn't help that he beaned an onlooker with a golf ball on the links one afternoon. This also became part of White House lore.

It was unfair, since Ford, who was 6 feet tall and weighed a trim 195 pounds, had been a gifted football player in his youth, remained a lifelong athlete, and was a bright man who had graduated from Yale Law School. But Ford blamed no one but himself, not even his tormentors in the media. "He was very mad at himself for doing that," Nessen recalls. "He just wanted to be sure that nobody thought there was anything more to it than that he had slipped on the step."

Ford maintained what Nessen calls "a very placid disposition" even amid other cases of media overkill. Once, when he was on a ski holiday at Vail, Colorado, the cameras caught him in a spill and again broadcast his image around the world. Nessen joined him for a drink that evening, and Ford's reaction was mild. "You know, those reporters get most of their exercise on the barstools," the president said ruefully—and left it at that.

Recalls David Gergen, a Ford adviser at the time: ". . . [T]he press turned on him with ridicule that was severe and merciless. Now he was the man who played too many football games without his helmet, the president who bumped his head when he turned to wave from his helicopter.

"Those images of bumbling shadowed Ford for the duration of his presidency," Gergen writes. "Throughout 1975, the press seized upon every verbal or physical miscue and magnified it beyond all bounds. . . . The fact that an aide left behind Ford's tuxedo and the President showed up at a dinner in Tokyo with trousers two inches too short caused merriment as well, as did his occasional falls on the ski slopes of Colorado."

Yet Ford retained his sense of humor. Once, a prankster in the press corps dressed up in a chicken suit and showed up at a Ford news conference at the base of *Air Force One* in San Diego, where a man in a chicken costume had become the local mascot. As reporters shouted their questions, Ford (who had been tipped off to the prank) paused and said seriously, "Next question—let's see—from that chicken there in the back."

Nessen says the most revealing anecdote he knows about Ford's character took place one Christmas while the president and his family were vacationing in Vail, Colorado. They were eating dinner in their rented chalet and one of their dogs messed on the floor. A White House steward started to clean up, but Ford took the rag away and did the job himself. "No man should have to clean up after another man's dog," the president told the steward. But such everyday decency was lost on the American public.

THERE ALSO WERE the dark moments that reflected the nation's overall social troubles. On September 6, 1975, Ford left the Senator Hotel in Sacramento, where he had spent the night after addressing the California Legislature, and walked across the capitol grounds to meet with Governor Jerry Brown. He started shaking hands with spectators across a rope line and spotted a woman (subsequently identified as Lynette Alice "Squeaky" Fromme, a young disciple of mass murderer Charles Manson) wearing a red dress in the second or third row. When he slowed down, she moved closer, and pointed a .45 caliber pistol directly at him, The weapon failed to fire, and Secret Service agents wrestled her to the ground and hustled Ford away from the scene.

Amazingly, there was another assassination attempt two weeks later, on September 22. Heading for his limousine, Ford left a downtown San Francisco hotel and, as he waved to thousands of bystanders lining the sidewalks and across the street in Union Square, he heard a shot. For a moment he froze in place, a stricken look on his face. But he wasn't hit. As they had done in Sacramento, his bodyguards hustled him away, this time pushing him into his limousine, jumping on top of him, and ordering the vehicle to speed to the airport and the safety of *Air Force One*. It turned out that a political radical named Sara Jane Moore had pulled out a .38 caliber revolver and fired at him from 40 feet away, but missed when a bystander pushed her at the last moment.

His Secret Service agents wanted to hustle him onto the plane immediately, but Ford insisted on shaking hands with the cops who had escorted his motorcade and others who were guarding his plane and were standing dutifully on the tarmac. As soon as he boarded, the president walked into his compartment with a handful of aides and ordered a tall drink. He took a large swallow, then he and his staff, with drinks in hand, waited until Mrs. Ford arrived from a separate series of events in the Monterey area.

When the First Lady stepped into the presidential cabin, which was by then crammed with senior advisers, she smiled sweetly and asked, "How did they treat you in San Francisco, dear?"

Clearly, no one had told the First Lady about the assassination attempt, and the president's aides began looking nervously at each other, hemming and hawing. Meanwhile, a steward brought Mrs. Ford a drink.

The president broke the silence. "You mean, you haven't heard?"

"Heard what?" she replied.

More awkward silence.

Finally, White House Chief of Staff Donald Rumsfeld blurted out, "Don't you know that someone took a shot at the president?"

Mrs. Ford was surprised but could see immediately that her husband was fine—he was, after all, sitting right in front of her. Dazed, she took a sip from her tall glass and said nothing.

The tension broke during the five-hour flight back to Andrews Air Force Base. It featured a large dose of gallows humor—including the half-serious question that aides kept asking each other: whether the president's life insurance was paid up. And there was joking that the two attempted assassinations, both by females, represented the next phase of the "women's lib" movement.

More than anything, there was the consumption of a considerable amount of alcohol, to the point where some staffers got tipsy. Ford had a couple of martinis, extra dry, and Mrs. Ford had vodka tonic on ice as everyone tried to relax and count their blessings. President Ford, never much of a worrier, phoned his children to tell them he was all right, ate a big steak dinner, and went to sleep.

But the assassination attempts had serious repercussions. The country's jitters got worse, with fears multiplying that a rancid strain of the American character was reemerging, as it had in the assassinations of John F. Kennedy, Robert Kennedy, and Martin Luther King in the 1960s. From then on, the Secret Service strongly urged the president to wear a bulletproof vest whenever he was in close proximity to the public, a practice that Ford followed for the remainder of his time in office.

ONE EMBARRASSMENT that was kept quiet was his wife's drinking.

The first couple were devoted to each other, but the president could do nothing to help his wife end her addiction to alcohol, which they managed to keep secret throughout his presidency. After their White House years, she admitted she was an alcoholic and also suffered from an addiction to arthritis medication.

Air Force One stewards and presidential staff members say Betty Ford enjoyed vodka tonic on ice at all hours of the day or night, even in the morning as a trip began. Sometimes she got soused on the plane, they say.

In the evening, particularly with dinner or after the last stop of the day, the president joined her with his own Gilbey's martini, extra dry. Steward Charles Palmer said he saw President Ford get tipsy only once, on a trip to the Soviet

Union. He had consumed a few drinks before boarding the plane and didn't stop there. "He was meeting with the Russian premier," Palmer said. "We got away at seven or eight at night. We gave him two or three martinis flying home. We put him to bed. In the middle of the flight, he came out in his underwear and said, 'Where is the head?' Normally, he knew where the head is. He could walk. He was slurring his words. It was the one time he overindulged and was tipsy."

Another mishap involving *Air Force One* was also publicly revealed only years later. It was when a military aide misplaced what military advisers call the football—the locked briefcase containing the codes the president would use to launch a nuclear strike. It is supposed to be near the commander in chief at all times in case of a surprise attack.

But during a trip to Paris in November 1975, the aide left the football on *Air Force One*. He realized his mistake as soon as he boarded the motorcade, and was about to contact the plane when a crew member radioed him and asked discreetly if something important was missing. Relieved, he said something important most certainly *was* missing, and the crew member rushed to the motorcade and passed the briefcase to him before he left the airport. It was a horrible breach of security, but there was no harm done.

THINGS GOT WORSE. Late in his 1976 reelection campaign, Ford was deeply embarrassed during an October 6 debate in San Francisco with Democratic challenger Jimmy Carter when he misstated his views about Eastern Europe. "There is no Soviet domination of Eastern Europe, and there never will be under a Ford administration," the president declared. This was an obvious misstatement, since the U.S.S.R. had dominated Eastern Europe for a generation; this was taught in every high-school history class. The incident made him seem ignorant and fed the notion that he was too dumb to be president.

The next day, as *Air Force One* was flying to Los Angeles, some of Ford's loyalists, including National Security Adviser Scowcroft and Press Secretary Nessen, decided that the president needed to make a "clarifying statement." By then, U.S. representatives of Polish-American and other Eastern European groups were up in arms, fearing that Ford was signaling an abandonment of support for democratic movements in the region. The media also were in full frenzy, and Ford needed to stop the hemorrhaging.

Then–White House Chief of Staff Dick Cheney privately agreed with the need for a statement, and told Ford so on this flight, but Cheney refused to allow Scowcroft or others to make their case directly with the president. This was done out of deference, because Cheney knew how upset and angry Ford was with himself. What he *meant* to say, he told Cheney, was that although the Soviet Union dominated the territory of Eastern Europe by stationing troops there, it didn't dominate the heart, soul, and spirit of the people in those countries. The president just hoped the whole issue would blow over, and he shut himself in his private cabin for the flight.

"I can be very stubborn when I think I'm right, and I just didn't want to apologize for something that was a minor mistake," Ford recalled in his autobiography.

When Nessen and Cheney finally said bluntly that he should admit the mistake, Ford said, "I'm not inclined to do that."

It wasn't until two days after the debate that he agreed to explain himself and admit his error, but by then the harm was irreparable. If he had taken the advice of his aides on *Air Force One* and admitted his gaffe immediately, he might have greatly limited the damage. "He made it sound like he didn't know that Poland was dominated by the Soviet Union," Scowcroft recalls, "and what he really meant to say was, the Polish spirit was undaunted and unconquerable. And if he said that right away it might have been different." Adds Nessen: "It reinforced the bumbler image, that Ford was a guy who couldn't think straight, who couldn't walk and chew gum at the same time."

FORD'S FINAL FLIGHT on *Air Force One* at the end of his 1976 campaign was a wake. En route back to Washington from Colorado, Ford was told by his pollster that he would lose. The exit polls showed that he could not quite overtake Jimmy Carter's lead, and the atmosphere was somber.

Howie Franklin, the flight steward, came into the presidential stateroom to pass along the crew's best wishes. "He was crying and she was crying and I was crying," Franklin recalls. "This had nothing to do with politics. It was on a personal basis. We were sad to see him leave because we enjoyed the camaraderie with him."

Even later, after Carter's inauguration, Ford would phone the plane, say hello to the pilot, and inquire about the flight crew, "How are the boys doing?"

CHAPTER EIGHT

JIMMY CARTER:
THE PARSIMONIOUS PREACHER

WHEN JIMMY CARTER, A BORN-AGAIN Christian and former governor of Georgia, defeated Ford in 1976, Americans seemed eager for a new spirit of rectitude and competence in the White House.

Carter gave it to them—at first. A frequent Bible studies teacher and devout Baptist, he was one of America's most moralistic presidents, and tried to shape his policies according to a strict code.

He was independent to a fault. Carter told me that he relished his role as a maverick even after he was nominated by the Democratic party as "a lonely peanut farmer who promised not to tell a lie." He knew that this outsider's image appealed to independent voters. Likewise, his status as a former governor untainted by scandal had considerable allure in the wake of Watergate and the Nixon pardon. And Carter seemed to be a brilliant thinker, especially when compared with the lightweight image of his predecessor. During his early months he proposed a vast array of initiatives and displayed a mastery of each one.

Throughout his four turbulent years in the White House, he tried to remain true to his inaugural address, when he said, "Our commitment to human rights must be absolute, our laws fair, our national beauty preserved; the powerful must not persecute the weak, and human dignity must be enhanced. . . . We have learned that 'more' is not necessarily 'better,' that even our great nation has its recognized limits, and that we can neither answer all questions nor solve all problems . . . we must simply do our best."

His conquest of the political Establishment with a brilliant grass-roots campaign surprised even the new president himself. On his first flight aboard *Air Force One*, he turned to Press Secretary Jody Powell and said in wonderment: "Three years ago, I was flat broke, and now we're flying on the president's airplane!" But that sense of joy was short-lived.

In an ironic twist on his 1976 campaign song, "Why Not the Best?" Carter's best wasn't enough, and he was quickly consumed by the nation's problems. "We had some very dangerous times when I was president," Carter recalls. "We tried to bring peace to other people as much as we possibly could, and human rights was a basic foundation of our entire foreign policy. . . . We never found a need to drop a bomb or launch a missile. . . . Peace and human rights and democracy and freedom and environmental quality and alleviation of suffering—those are the measures in my opinion of a great nation."

These were grand goals. But Carter could never deliver much in the way of results on the issues Americans cared most about. Specifically, he could not discourage the Soviet Union's militaristic adventures. He failed to project U.S. strength around the world. And he could not stop the deterioration of the domestic economy amid severe oil shortages, high unemployment, and rampant inflation. At one point, he suggested that the nation's biggest problem was a vague, soul-destroying sense of malaise. His pessimistic outlook lent credence to the idea, then popular among some intellectuals, that America's best days were behind her. But many everyday voters came to believe he was making excuses for his own lack of leadership.

AT FIRST, RELATIONS WITH MOSCOW dominated foreign policy. "That's an interesting fulcrum to divide our times," says Jody Powell. "Our main concern was that some series of miscalculations would lead to us and the Russians blowing up the goddamn world. Now the concern is that some religious fanatic is going to crash a Piper Cub into something, or is going to blow up a truck."

The U.S.S.R.'s invasion of Afghanistan was bad enough, taking Carter by surprise and making him seem hopelessly naïve. Even worse was the fact that 52 Americans were taken hostage in Iran, and Carter was unable to free them for the final year of his presidency.

Carter's relations with the news media also deteriorated. "Obviously, Watergate made a profound change in the attitude of reporters toward the presidency," he said in our interview. "When I got there, there was an extreme degree of inquisitiveness. A lot of the reporters felt that something in my background was worthy of revelation and they were going to replace Bernstein and Woodward [Carl Bernstein and Bob Woodward, who broke the Watergate story in *The Washington Post*]. They never found anything, as a matter of fact, but they were constantly searching. So there was more of a deep inquiry into the personal affairs and a more confrontational relationship than maybe in the past."

CARTER'S BEHAVIOR on *Air Force One* illustrated his problems. He worked very hard and traveled widely, and he did achieve a breakthrough in the Middle East by brokering a historic peace agreement between Egypt and Israel that culminated in a dramatic signing by Anwar Sadat and Menachim Begin at the White House. But he became preoccupied with micro-management, and delved into areas he should have delegated to subordinates, such as deciding who should use the White House tennis courts, sometimes making the assignments from *Air Force One*.

He was often aloof and moody, but at other times he could be friendly and gregarious—altogether unpredictable. One flight steward said it was often difficult for Carter to put himself into the toothy, grinning persona that he cultivated as his public image. Aboard *Air Force One*, he would frequently lose his gregariousness and retreat to his stateroom, as if he were a windup doll whose spring had wound down. Before Carter boarded the plane, Powell and other senior aides would warn the flight crew if he was in a snit. That meant they should keep him at arm's length. Carter would make that clear as soon as he entered his stateroom. If he was in a dark mood, the president would tell a steward, "I won't need anything," and close the door. Message: Do not disturb.

Flight steward John Haigh said, "Carter was kind of an introvert, really. He didn't come to the back of the airplane very often. And he didn't like a lot of extra faces coming into his cabin," so he ordered that only the head steward and his deputy serve him.

"The public was the opposite from the private," said Haigh. "He stayed pretty much to himself. Most politicians are, 'Hi, how are you!' Not him. He didn't talk to many people. I was on the plane a year and he never talked to me."

This is much the same impression offered by Zbigniew Brzezinski, Carter's national security adviser, who traveled regularly with him: "I never doubted that I was dealing with a shrewd, rather deliberate yet fundamentally very decent and engaging person who combined high intelligence with occasionally surprising naiveté, genuine dedication to principle with sometimes excessive tactical flexibility. . . . He was generally very serene, and this helped to maintain a stable relationship—but one could also sense within that relationship major shifts from genuine warmth to sudden distance. The latter was especially the case when events, and perhaps my persuasion, made him do things that instinctively he would have preferred not to do."

AFTER BOARDING THE PLANE, Carter would immediately enter his compartment, then reemerge an hour later, dressed in shirtsleeves and holding a handful of thank-you notes he had written for his staff to copy and send out. He would bring stacks of individually typed letters into his airborne office and sign them one by one. Aides marveled at his discipline.

He and the First Lady would chat briefly with the staff and guests, and on rare occasions he would wander to the rear of the plane, or have reporters join him in a forward cabin, to make remarks to the press pool. In such media encounters, he showed he was smart and intimately familiar with the details of policy.

Then he would return to his compartment to study his ever-present briefing books, sometimes correcting errors he found in the appendices. He liked to talk policy with advisers and occasionally gossip about other politicians or world leaders. He deeply admired Egyptian leader Sadat for his bold ideas and his courage in trying to make peace with Israel. He respected France's Valery Giscard d'Estaing for his brilliant analytical mind, which was in some ways like Carter's own, and Chinese leader Deng Xiaoping for his cold appreciation of the use of power and his sense of global politics. But he disliked Chancellor Helmut Schmidt of Germany, above all, for what he considered a patronizing attitude. At home, he never got along well with Senate Majority Leader Howard Baker of Tennessee, even though Baker was the most gracious of men. No one around Carter was quite sure why this was so, but some of his associates speculated that he envied Baker's way of ingratiating himself with people.

A formal man who learned many of his straitlaced habits in the Navy, he would take his jacket and tie off, but would not change into casual clothes except on very long trips or when he was heading for a vacation at his family farm in Plains, Georgia, or elsewhere. He drank alcohol only rarely.

"His memory was phenomenal, his reading voracious, and his thirst for more knowledge unquenchable," recalls Brzezinski. "At times, Carter could also be extremely pedantic. Memos addressed to him would come back with penciled corrections of spelling mistakes or grammatical improvements. He also delighted in giving me lists of security violations committed by my staff (such as leaving a safe unlocked) that had been brought to his attention by the security office. . . . I found the whole thing amusing, for it showed the extent to which he was still a Navy lieutenant who very much enjoyed keeping the ship in trim and proper shape."

Typical of his micro-management was his order to severely limit the supply of trinkets that passengers could take home, such as *Air Force One*-inscribed matchbooks, decks of playing cards, coffee mugs, and notepads. He stopped the practice of carrying cigarettes on the plane altogether as a health measure—a wise move in itself but ahead of its time, so it made him seem prudish and petty.

"I tried to cut down the waste of money and the ostentatious nature of the presidency," Carter said. "Some of my predecessors (and I say this without any criticism) had given quite expensive gifts, for instance, to everyone who came on board *Air Force One*—kind of like it was a mercantile establishment where people would carry away mementos quite costly to the American public. It was just contrary to my nature and so we did away with that element of *Air Force One*."

However, he did arrange for the flight crew to keep a supply of expensive, leather-bound Bibles on board. He would autograph them and give them to religious leaders and special dignitaries who traveled with him—all paid for by the Air Force.

He made a dramatic point of carrying his luggage, at least a bag or two, onto *Air Force One* rather than have the stewards or baggage handlers do it for him. This was more of a problem than it seemed. The flight attendants were offended because, as one told me, "that was my job, and he had better things to do. It was kind of disappointing."

It turned out that Carter would generally bring only one extra suit, two shirts, and a couple of changes of underwear, no matter where he was going and no matter how long he would be away. This meant that his traveling valet (a perquisite he never gave up, along with First Lady Rosalynn Carter's traveling hairdresser) would have to wash and iron a shirt for him every night. Given that his two suits also needed frequent pressing, the president would often look the worse for wear.

Starting with Carter, the *Air Force One* crew took it upon themselves to keep an entire change of clothes aboard for every president, just in case. "They weren't always aware of this," recalls former chief flight steward Charles Palmer. And Carter stopped routinely carrying his bags eventually.

Carter also wanted it known that he was a man of simple Southern tastes in many ways, as illustrated by his preference for grits and buttermilk at breakfast, simple sandwiches for lunch, and for dinner, lentil-and-franks soup, country ham with redeye gravy, fried chicken, and again, grits. He famously preferred cardigan sweaters to business suits. And he would sometimes make fishing flies on *Air Force One* for catching trout.

His cost cutting extended to *Air Force One* personnel, much to the consternation of the crew. He wanted to reduce the number of stewards from seven to five because commercial airliners had only five flight attendants on their 707s. But he didn't realize that the *Air Force One* stewards had many more duties than normal flight attendants, such as helping to maintain and clean the aircraft once the president departed and going to the store to purchase food for the aircraft. Carter was finally talked out of this idea.

He also wanted to transport the vehicles for presidential motorcades by truck rather than by plane, assuming it would save money. It didn't. Carter hadn't reckoned on the need for Secret Service agents, maintenance people, and others to travel with the vehicles, adding hotel rooms, food, and other costs to their trips. In the end, he backed off this cost-saving scheme, too.

Carter ordered that the *Air Force One* crew stop accepting free drinks and snacks—items donated by private businesses—for the plane's larder. He thought it was a conflict of interest. He soon found that this austerity program cost the taxpayers thousands of dollars on an annual basis because those items now had to be bought at commercial rates, but he continued the program because he felt it was the right thing to do.

HIS MANAGEMENT PROBLEMS extended to his immediate family. Neither the president nor the First Lady could adequately control their adolescent daughter, Amy, whom many of the stewards on *Air Force One* considered spoiled. She would play loud rock music in her mother's cabin, annoying everyone in the vicinity, including her mom. Rather than tell her to quit making such a racket, the long-suffering First Lady sometimes slept on the floor of her husband's stateroom. Amy Carter would also crush soda crackers and scatter them around her, just to make mischief, according to former steward Gerald Pisha. Carter has denied the story, but Pisha says, "Guess who had to vacuum it up?" Former *Air Force One* chief of communications Jim Bull, whose console was close to the presidential quarters, adds: "Her greatest thrill was coloring with crayon on the walls of the airplane," which the crew considered insulting. "We were very proud of that airplane," Bull says.

For her part, Rosalynn Carter could be aloof and brittle, just like her husband. The first couple showed affection for each other, occasionally holding hands or kissing in the president's stateroom, but they mostly spent time in separate rooms and they were often unfriendly to those around them. "It took a year and a half for Rosalynn Carter to realize we were there for them and were not against them," says former chief steward Palmer. "I think at first she thought we were the enemy. Maybe she felt a little inferior, a little insecure."

Palmer adds: "The Carters sometimes got mad at each other over Amy. It depended on what she was doing. There was a spanking or two [administered by the First Lady]. She needed it. Maybe thirty or forty minutes from landing, she was told to get ready and change clothes. She would listen to her music. She [Rosalynn] slapped her hand. Maybe they were meeting a foreign head of state. There are a lot of tensions involved in those things. It was not an everyday occurrence. I never witnessed Jimmy spank her. Sometimes there was control, sometimes they let her go. It was inconsistent."

CARTER COULD BE remarkably inconsiderate of those around him. During a trip to the Middle East, he told Colonel Lester McClelland, his pilot, that he wanted to fly over the Aswan Dam, which required a last-minute change in the flight plan. Carter told an aide to make sure McClelland knew that the president sat on the right side of the plane, so the pilot could provide him with the best view possible. That reminder was unnecessary and offensive, since no one knew the layout of the aircraft better than the pilot.

When Mount St. Helens erupted, Carter decided he wanted to tour the disaster site in Washington State immediately. A White House telephone operator reached Bob Ruddick, the *Air Force One* pilot who succeeded McClelland, on the racquetball court and said the president wanted to take off in less than four hours. Ruddick rushed back to Andrews Air Force Base to make the preparations.

As the plane flew over the volcano, Carter took over the jumpseat behind the pilot to get a better view, and he spouted facts and figures about volcanoes in general and this volcano in particular. He was, in part, showing off, but everyone was impressed with his retentive powers. "He was a very intelligent man," Ruddick says.

LATE IN CARTER's third year, on November 4, 1979, a mob of Iranian students stormed the U.S. Embassy in Teheran and took 52 Americans hostage. This proved to be the defining crisis of the Carter administration, and for more than a year, Carter worked doggedly to free them. In fact, he became so obsessed with the crisis that he declared a near-moratorium on his own travel so he could devote full time to liberating them. For much of 1980, until the fall campaign against Ronald Reagan, *Air Force One* was rarely used.

This made the president a prisoner in the White House, and the TV networks began using logos on their nightly newscasts keeping count of each day the hostage crisis dragged on. It made matters worse when the zealots paraded the blindfolded hostages before screaming, threatening crowds in Teheran, all before the television cameras. America seemed helpless.

In April 1980, Carter ordered a military mission to free them, but it failed miserably when a U.S. helicopter collided with a C-130 aircraft in the Iranian desert, killing several American troops. This only deepened the public's sense that he was in over his head. Secretary of State Cyrus Vance, who resigned after Carter overruled his opposition to the rescue mission, said it was a unique folly. "The decision," Vance wrote in his memoirs, "to attempt to extract the hostages by force from the center of a city of over five million, more than six thousand miles from the United States, and which could be reached only by flying over difficult terrain, was different: I was convinced that the decision was wrong and that it carried great risks for the hostages and our national interests."

THE CRISIS DRAGGED on interminably. Then, at 3:45 A.M. on November 2, 1980, two days before the election, Carter got a call during a campaign trip from Deputy Secretary of State Warren Christopher with what seemed to be good news: The Iranian leaders had moved toward an agreement to free the hostages. Nothing was final, but things looked promising. Carter cancelled his campaign schedule for that Sunday and flew back to Washington to work on the deal.

"I will never forget the flight back to Washington, heading eastward into the rising sun," he would write later. "I was in the cockpit of *Air Force One* talking to the flight crew, and through the towering clouds we watched one of the most beautiful sunrises I have ever seen. My prayer was that the Iranian nightmare would soon be over, and that my judgment and my decisions might be wise ones.

In a strange way, I felt relieved. It was out of my hands. Now my political future might well be determined by irrational people on the other side of the world over whom I had no control. If the hostages were released, I was convinced my reelection would be assured; if the expectations of the American people were dashed again, there was little chance that I could win."

The deal fell through.

THE MONDAY BEFORE Election Day, Carter's last stop was a 9-P.M. rally at an airplane hangar in Seattle. As the presidential party was disembarking, a steward collared Jody Powell and said a phone call had just arrived. It was Democratic pollster Pat Caddell and White House Chief of Staff Hamilton Jordan, back at the White House. They wanted to pass along the final poll results, and as soon as Powell got on the line he could hear the disappointment in their voices.

The news was disastrous: The tide had shifted dramatically at the very end, and it was running strongly toward Republican challenger Ronald Reagan. Carter would lose, big time.

Powell turned protective. "We don't need to tell the president *that* before he makes the last speech of the campaign," he said to Caddell.

The three aides agreed not to inform the president until after his remarks.

Once back on the plane, Powell again fretted about breaking the news to his boss, for whom he had worked for many years. Before he could take the president aside, Carter began chatting with the traveling press. Powell took a call from Washington, where Caddell and Jordan wanted to know if he had broken the news. As Powell explained that he hadn't had a chance, Carter suddenly appeared in the staff compartment and leaned on the back of Powell's chair. Drinks were ordered, and the president began to reminisce about the previous four years and what they had accomplished. It was a warm and chummy moment, and Powell didn't want to interrupt.

Air Force One continued its cruise to Carter's hometown of Plains, Georgia, where he wanted to receive the returns, and at 2 A.M. Eastern time, Caddell and Jordan called the plane again. This time, Carter excused himself and went to his private cabin. Informed how badly he would be defeated, his reaction was typically matter of fact. "Oh, really?" he said to Caddell.

He ordered his advisers to keep the information to themselves because a premature leak could depress Democratic turnout in the Western time zones and cost congressional Democrats much-needed votes. Carter then calmly instructed his staff to draft a statement he could deliver in Plains that might at least help bring Democrats back to the ticket and save Democratic candidates in other races.

Most of his aides were disconsolate at the political humiliation that was taking shape. Senior adviser Stu Eizenstat came into the president's cabin and, as Carter later recalled in his diary, "burst into tears. I put my arms around him to comfort him. It was hard for us to believe the dimensions of what Pat was telling us, but it later proved to be accurate."

THE MOST MEMORABLE MOMENTS aboard the presidential aircraft for Carter came on January 21, 1981, the day after he left office. The Iranian hostages were released shortly after Ronald Reagan was sworn in, and the new president immediately asked Carter to fly over on his 707 and welcome the Americans to freedom in Germany. Carter was grateful for the chance. He wrote later: "It is impossible for me to put into words how much the hostages had come to mean to me."

Phil Wise, Carter's chief scheduler who traveled with him from August 1977 to the end of his presidency, was on that trip. "It was very emotional," Wise recalls. "It seems today like such a negative in history for Carter and the rest of us. We were so caught up in it our last year in the White House. To see every hostage come out of there alive was really a victory, but bittersweet."

Carter, chatting with aides on the eight-hour trip to Wiesbaden, revealed his fears that the hostages might not respond positively to him since he had been unable to secure their release for so long. The reality turned out to be mixed. Upon meeting him, many of the former captives expressed gratitude that Carter had not done anything rash that would have resulted in their execution. Others kept their distance, blaming their former commander in chief for getting them into their predicament and failing to extricate them for a year. Still others felt Carter could have gotten them killed with his failed rescue mission in the desert.

Carter defused the situation by acknowledging that the former hostages had mixed feelings toward him but he wanted to say welcome and explain that nothing had been more important to him than getting them home safely and with honor. After his remarks, the atmosphere turned friendly, and many of the hostages gathered around Carter to shake his hand and have their pictures taken with him.

On the way home, Carter and his senior staff were reunited one last time. "Usually after a foreign trip there was a general release of pent-up tensions on the journey back to the States," said Hamilton Jordan. "The speechwriters had no more speeches or welcoming remarks or toasts to write, the advance staff could forget about the president's schedule and who would sit where at each meeting, the Secret Service agents could relax and play cards, and, for better or worse, the work of the chief executive and his advisers was done. So, when everyone climbed back on *Air Force One*, there was usually a joyous mood, if not to celebrate the results of the trip, at least to toast its conclusion."

This flight was different. Carter spent the first couple of hours writing a report to Reagan about the condition of the hostages and the agreement that he had negotiated to win their freedom. He also wrote thank-you notes to officials who were instrumental in the final talks with Iran. Outside his cabin, there was a bittersweet atmosphere, and after a private dinner, the former peanut farmer from Plains joined his aides to share recollections about the Carter years.

At one point, Carter broke out the champagne and raised his glass: "To freedom." These two words seemed to mark for the president and his entourage not only the release of the hostages but the personal liberation they felt now that their White House years were over.

CHAPTER NINE

RONALD REAGAN:
AMERICA'S LEADING MAN

PROPELLED BY HIS BELIEF THAT the country wanted drastic change, Ronald Reagan reversed virtually everything Carter did. Especially important was the new president's sunny optimism, which gave America a welcome lift after the depressing failures and self-doubt of the Carter years.

When the former California governor and movie actor took over in January 1981, things seemed bleak, with the economy reeling and America seemingly in retreat around the world. But Reagan insisted that the country's best days as a "shining city on a hill" were still ahead. When he was shot on March 30, 1981, by a deranged drifter named John Hinckley, Jr., the new president impressed the country with his grace and steadiness. At the hospital, he jokingly asked the doctors if they were Republicans, and he told his wife, "Honey, I forgot to duck." He recovered from the assassination attempt quickly and told friends he felt that God had spared his life for a purpose—to pursue his conservative agenda and roll back what he called the "evil empire" of Communism.

Riding a wave of admiration, Reagan won passage of a series of massive tax cuts and reductions in the growth of government. His hardline policies toward the Soviet Union initially caused consternation and fear, both in the United States and abroad. But in the end they paid off when Soviet leader Mikhail Gorbachev rose to power and entered into a remarkable partnership with his American counterpart. The four Reagan-Gorbachev summit meetings, in Geneva, Reykjavik, Washington, and Moscow, were benchmarks in East-West relations.

As the nation's condition and mood improved, voters gave Reagan the benefit of the doubt even though the septuagenarian president often seemed disengaged and ignorant of his own administration's policies. Time and again, he would be caught in errors of fact at his news conferences and in his off-the-cuff remarks; but the country seemed on the upswing so Reagan didn't pay much of a price for his lapses.

Then came the Iran-Contra scandal, midway through his second term. It turned out that overzealous aides had traded arms for hostages in Iran and then used financial proceeds from the arms sales to help anti-Marxist Contra rebels in Nicaragua, which was against the law. Reagan said he never knew the details of what was going on around him—contributing to his reputation for disengagement. And for a while, it seemed as if his presidency was in jeopardy. But the country tired of the controversy after saturation coverage by the media for many months, and his popularity rebounded.

For much of his second term, Reagan devoted himself to improving relations with Moscow and building on his relationship with Gorbachev. It was a bizarre turn of events, because Reagan had been such a hardline cold warrior for so many years. But Americans supported his efforts.

In sum, Reagan's eight years in office represented a historic era when American exceptionalism—the notion that the United States has a special destiny for greatness, different from any other nation—became generally accepted once again by U.S. citizens and by many around the world. Within two years of Reagan's departure, the U.S.S.R. unraveled, just as Reagan said it would after he applied unrelenting diplomatic, military, and political pressure.

REAGAN BROUGHT HOLLYWOOD to the presidency, using all his skills as a former film star and TV performer. He was perhaps the most scripted of all our presidents. Everything was stage-managed, from how he entered a room (head up,

Jimmy Carter exits *Air Force One* with his wife, Rosalynn, and daughter, Amy, in Caracas, Venezuela, in March 1978. He was a micromanager who sometimes used his time on the plane to decide who should play on the White House tennis court.

Carter occasionally invited journalists to his cabin, especially during lengthy foreign trips when he wanted to explain his version of events. He meets with reporters en route home from Europe in January 1978 as the weary First Lady sits at his side.

Ronald Reagan was more disciplined than the public and
the media realized. He would
carefully prepare for events,
and spent many hours alone
in his suite writing in his diary
before emerging just after
touchdown.

Reagan's first summit
meeting with Soviet leader
Mikhail Gorbachev was
pressure-packed. En route
to Geneva in November
1985, the president had
detailed discussions with
Secretary of State George
Shultz, Chief of Staff
Donald Regan, and
National Security Adviser
Bud McFarlane.

Like all presidents, Reagan let his guard down on *Air Force One*, and
often would unwind by telling stories about his days as a Hollywood
actor. Although formal in public, he changed into sweatpants on
long flights to keep his suit trousers unwrinkled.

Every president enjoys showing off *Air Force One*, and Reagan was no exception when he gave Britain's Queen Elizabeth II a tour.

Reagan loved to travel with his wife, Nancy, and he often seemed a bit unsettled when she stayed home. Once aboard, they would sit contentedly in the president's cabin, reading, chatting, dining, and resting.

George Herbert Walker Bush enjoyed stopping by the press cabin – at first. But as his popularity declined, he limited his contact with reporters, whom he felt didn't treat him fairly.

Bush and his wife, Barbara, were popular with the flight crew aboard *Air Force One*. "He'd give you the shirt off his back," said one steward.

As the first baby boomer president, Bill Clinton brought a new level of informality to *Air Force One,* reflecting his overall management style. Here he lobbies a member of Congress by phone on gun-control legislation while traveling to Europe in June 1999.

Clinton was the most traveled president, and he used not only the big 747 familiar to most Americans but also smaller jets like this executive-style aircraft when he had to land at smaller airports. In this case, he is at Santa Fe, NM, in September 2000.

All presidents love to fly on *Air Force One*, even after leaving office, and they hitch a ride whenever it's appropriate. Former President Bush flew with then-President Clinton and First Lady Hillary Rodham Clinton to the funeral of the King of Morocco in July 1999. Bush introduced the Clintons to the welcoming delegation in Rabat.

Clinton frequently used the time-tested gambit of deploying the plane as a backdrop to enhance his stature. Even standing in front of the aircraft is considered a big advantage because *Air Force One* has such symbolic power.

George W. Bush's decisions aboard *Air Force One* in response to the terrorist attacks of Sept. 11, 2001, marked the most dramatic episode in the aircraft's history, demonstrating the plane's value as a secure crisis-management center. Here Bush coordinates with Vice President Cheney on that fateful day.

A rare photograph showing the spaciousness of the airborne office, which includes a big wraparound desk.

Bush admits he is an impatient traveler. He often paces just behind the door as the big plane rolls to a stop, then bounds onto the stairs to give his famous wave.

Air Force One can reinforce the solitary nature of the presidency. As Harry Truman said about his desk in the Oval Office, the buck stops here.

Reuters NewMedia Inc./CORBIS

Most Americans consider *Air Force One* an icon that symbolizes their country's power, prestige, and technological prowess. The plane is shown flying over Mount Rushmore in South Dakota.

shoulders back, walking jauntily), to where he stood (at spots marked with masking tape to give him the best camera angles).

And of course he brought Hollywood to *Air Force One*. At the end of his successful reelection campaign, in 1984, he even took Frank Sinatra, Charlton Heston, and other legends of Hollywood with him while he stumped through California. They spent time swapping stories, reminiscing, and discussing how well the campaign was going, according to Tim Kerwin, one of the senior stewards.

Heston recalled the hop from San Diego to Los Angeles on the day before the balloting. Nancy had invited him aboard, and Heston said: "That's an offer one doesn't turn down. Virtually everyone on the plane looked exhausted: Jim Baker, Ed Meese, Mike Deaver, even Nancy. The only one in high spirits was the president. He was older than anyone else aboard, but his eyes were shining and he made sure he talked with everyone on the plane.

"Champagne was being poured and I asked Jim Baker what the outcome looked like for the next day. He said we'd probably lose Minnesota and the District of Columbia, but win everything else. I had thought it would be closer, but he said, 'It's a lock, an absolute lock.' And, as it turned out, he was right.

"What I remember most is not that he had won by so much, but that to be successful in politics at that level you have to really love it—and Ronald Reagan did. . . . In fact, when we got off the plane that day in November 1984, he looked as if he could have started the whole thing over again."

Heston's observation is widely shared by Reagan's confidants. One reason for his staying power was his ability to pace himself. Observes David Gergen, one of Reagan's senior advisers: "He was extremely disciplined as a person and that was not well understood." But it manifested itself in many ways.

For one thing, he would say and do exactly what he wanted regardless of how much pressure he was under to go "off message." Whether in public encounters or in private interviews, he could almost never be cajoled, bullied, or sweet-talked by the media into departing from his script. His press secretary went to elaborate lengths to determine the reporters he would call on at East Room news conferences. Reagan would be shown their names and photographs in advance, then a government camera in the East Room would pan the journalists waiting in their seats as Reagan watched a screen in a private room in the West Wing— all so the president could easily recognize them during the questioning. Finally, their names were highlighted on a seating chart hidden in the president's podium.

All this enabled Reagan to give the impression that he was accessible and knew the press corps well, which was far from the truth. He never thought it was necessary to know them very well as individuals, as long as he knew his lines. And he was an excellent salesman for his policies, especially in the all-important medium of television, where he had once hosted *General Electric Theater* and *Death Valley Days*. He was so genial it was hard for even his opponents to dislike him.

This discipline was evident on *Air Force One*. A day or two before departing for some faraway place, he would start eating his meals as if he were already in the time zone he would be visiting, even if that meant having dinner at breakfast time in Washington. When he got on the plane, he did the same thing, to the consternation of aides whose metabolism could not easily adjust to meat loaf at 9 A.M. And Reagan rarely drank alcohol, even wine or beer, aboard the plane, telling aides it sapped his energy. Instead, he consumed quarts of water and cups of decaffeinated coffee, and he nibbled between meals on grapes, apples, plums, and other fresh fruit (with an occasional jelly bean). Reagan always believed this regimen kept him healthy and minimized jet lag.

IN KEEPING WITH his emphasis on stagecraft, *Air Force One* became a fabulous prop. Reagan understood the airplane's power as a symbol and he used it as a backdrop whenever he could, just as other presidents had done. But Reagan perfected some new techniques. One was the "Walk," a carefully choreographed, dignified march from his limousine or helicopter up the stairs and into the magnificent blue-and-white 707. Aides were not allowed near him lest they get into the camera frame. This was a moment for the commander in chief, alone, to stride purposefully into his plane—all for TV. In fact, just about everything was done by the Reagan White House for the three broadcast networks of ABC, CBS, and NBC in those years. That's where most Americans got their news in the era before the broadcast networks lost much of their audience and influence, and before the 24-hour cable networks (CNN was then in its infancy) set the pace.

"*Air Force One* became a symbol of American strength and prestige and power, maybe unlike it was used in the past," former Reagan aide Fred Ryan told me. "We noticed that more and more there was just this awe of *Air Force One*. People felt it was better than any other aircraft. . . . It's not just because it's the president's plane. It's also because so few people have been aboard it. People can go on a White House tour but the general public doesn't tour *Air Force One*." Reagan understood this.

INSIDE *AIR FORCE ONE*, Reagan could be himself. He was a 9-to-5 manager who set his administration on a conservative course and left the details to his aides. It was a popular business model at the time, but it had its drawbacks—especially because it fostered distance between the chief executive and his own policies and personnel.

Reagan's behavior on the plane represented his presidency in microcosm. He would drop by the senior-staff cabin shortly after takeoff to say hello, then return to his compartment to read or relax. His confidants say he was far more devoted to his work than his critics gave him credit for, and always tried to act the role of president. Except on long flights, he surprised guests by continuing to wear his jacket and tie because he thought it was more dignified. On long flights, he resorted to a technique from his days on the road as a pitchman for General Electric: He would take off his suit pants and have a steward hang them up while he changed into velour sweatpants. That way, his trousers would never lose their creases and he would always look immaculately groomed.

"People would come up to see him and he would be happy to have meetings," said David Gergen. "But beneath that affability was a reserve and a discipline that allowed him to get things done."

Adds Ken Duberstein, Reagan's last White House chief of staff: "In many ways, Reagan was a loner. He was from a more formal era. He would socialize, but he was never one of the boys." He believed in wrapping himself in a cloak of mystery, always holding something back. He learned this as a performer, when he was told to leave the stage while the audience still wanted more. That way, the crowd would look forward to seeing him again. Somehow, it worked. "When he walked into a room, he was larger than life," Duberstein recalls.

The flight crew, which got to know him well, respected him immensely. "He was already a public person before he took office," said steward John Haigh. "He didn't have anything to prove. He always was a gentleman and thanked you when you did something for him. And the mark of a good leader is that he inspires people to do their best. That's what he did. President Reagan came in with an optimism about the country and he left with that same optimism. Whenever he got on the plane, there was an aura around him."

Time and again, members of his *Air Force One* crew and his White House aides told me that Reagan somehow made them feel better about themselves, with a joke, an attaboy, or a wink and a pat on the back. "He always had a smile on his face, and he always had a good word for you," says Jim Bull. "He was always 'up.' "

He liked to keep track of the plane's arrivals, and he told crew members how much he appreciated the way they respected his schedule. As the plane pulled to a stop precisely on time, as it almost always did, Reagan would theatrically check his watch and congratulate whichever crew member was nearby. "You did it again," he would say with a grin.

Once, when Reagan noticed the hardworking Bull at his console, sweating heavily under his earphones, he made a jocular reference to his plight. "You look like you're ready for a dip in the pool," Reagan quipped. Bull said, "He just had a way of making you feel better."

Occasionally, the president would walk into the staff conference room, just aft from his quarters, lean on the back of a chair, and tell stories about his life as a politician or an actor, and perhaps offer his impressions of the place he was going. Word would spread that the president was holding forth and, within minutes, the conference room would be crammed with 20 or 30 aides and guests.

It was another performance, and Reagan loved it. At 6 foot, 1 inch and 185 pounds, with thick, dark brown hair that belied his 70-plus years and the fact that he was the oldest man ever elected president, he cut a striking figure. Reagan loved always to look the part of the president. During these airborne sessions, he rarely talked policy or provided any new insight into his thinking; instead, he would retell stories from his speeches and anecdotes that his veteran advisers had heard many times before. Like all good performers, he made his lines seem fresh every time he spoke them. On such occasions, Reagan managed to establish a personal connection to those around him. This was one of his gifts.

Sometimes his listeners would be amazed at his down-home anecdotes, because he had been criticized so often as an elitist. He liked to describe his favorite way of making sure the jeans he wore on his ranch fit properly. He would wade into a lake wearing the new jeans and leave them on until they dried. The result: a comfortable, formfitting pair of pants. He said it was a method he learned in his younger days as an actor who loved the outdoors but always wanted to look good, even sexy.

Veteran flight steward Howie Franklin says Reagan didn't associate with the staff very much, "but he would always come in and say hello. . . . If I went in to give him a glass of water while he was doing presidential work, he did something non-verbally or verbally to raise my self-esteem. I mean, I tried to catch this guy being a phony politician for eight years, and I couldn't do it. He was the same guy all the time."

One homey touch was that Reagan insisted that the crew always have a birthday cake on board. That way, when he found out a staff member or guest was celebrating a birthday, he could hold an impromptu celebration, which he enjoyed. Sometimes he got more than he bargained for. When a Secret Service agent puffed out his candles once, he blew chocolate chips from the top of his cake all over the president.

BUT REAGAN WAS not always a happy flier. He confessed to senior advisers: "I long for the days when the president never left the continental United States, when it was traditional that he never traveled abroad."

Larry Speakes, his first-term White House spokesman, recalled that, "The far-ther away he had to go, the less he cared about going. He [liked] to be at home in the White House, or at Camp David, or, most of all, at the ranch."

Marlin Fitzwater, who replaced Speakes as spokesman in February 1987, added: "He didn't like to travel. For a politician as successful as he was and as popular with the masses, he didn't really enjoy any of the politician's stereotypes, such as rope lines and handshakes, receptions and greetings—or travel. . . . I would guess that we probably traveled less than any other modern president. If he didn't have to go, he didn't want to go. And I remember him talking about not liking to go on foreign trips; they were just too long.

"My speculation was that this was one of the areas where age came into play," Fitzwater told me. "We always had to keep in mind that this fellow was seventy-seven years old and he had traveled a lot, and there were few places he hadn't seen. . . . It was kind of like, 'Been there, done that.' . . . Reagan didn't have a tourist impulse in him."

A man of the old school, he much preferred the train trips he had taken as a corporate spokesman for General Electric. Like Franklin Roosevelt, his boyhood hero, Reagan enjoyed the slower pace of first-class rail travel because it allowed him to relax and ruminate. There was also a fear factor; for years, Reagan and his wife, Nancy, were distressed whenever they read about plane crashes.

In the end, though, they realized that traveling by air would be required if he was to be a successful candidate and governor of California, and they accepted it. Still, as governor, he and his wife made a habit of flying separately as often as they could. That way, both of them would not be killed in a crash, leaving their children as orphans.

But President Reagan tried to replicate the leisurely routine of his younger days. This extended to developing his travel schedule, which would be decided weeks in advance and almost never changed. There was rarely any frenetic activity in Reagan's *Air Force One*. "By the time he got on that plane," says Fitzwater, "the speeches were written and approved, the advance texts were printed, and we knew exactly what was going to be said and when. Basically, we even knew the outcome of the meetings that the president was going to hold."

This allowed the president to have as carefree a trip as possible.

AS PRESIDENT, he enjoyed flying over the United States, especially en route to California. He loved to look out the small oval windows of his cabin, and he would frequently leave his compartment and excitedly tell aides when the Rocky Mountains rolled by; that meant he was nearing his home state. He had more of an eye for geography than most people realized, and could name cities and towns as *Air Force One* passed over. He would ask the crew to verify them, and he was almost always right.

Reagan was at heart a nostalgist who believed in the idealized America that he celebrated in his speeches, a place where middle-class families lived the good life in solid little houses behind white fences with a car in the driveway and maybe a dot of aquamarine in the backyard signifying a swimming pool. He loved to watch such scenes as *Air Force One* flew over the endless suburbs of America. In many cases, the real lives below bore no resemblance to his idealized vision; America was, after all, mired in a deep recession during much of his first term and he seemed to give little thought to the millions left out of the American Dream.

But he remarked to aides that he would love to take the leader of the Soviet Union on a flying tour of America, to prove once and for all that capitalism and democracy worked. Even his aides thought he was naïve to think it would make much difference but Reagan had a simple faith in the goodness of the United States that he believed would triumph. In his mind, this nostalgic vision was always crystal clear. The irony was that George Herbert Walker Bush, Reagan's successor, was able to show Mikhail Gorbachev parts of America from the air, and the Soviet leader *was* impressed, just as Reagan predicted he would be.

IF HIS WIFE, Nancy, was aboard, he would closet himself with her in the front cabin, chatting, dining, checking his briefing books and his speech texts, or reading biographies and history. This was the president's pattern in everything he did: Nancy came first, and he was perfectly content to isolate himself for long hours with her. There were many little touches indicating his affection. He would put his hand protectively on the small of her back as they climbed the stairs, and they would hold hands in the president's stateroom. He had the towels in the bathroom changed from green and white to red, which was her favorite color.

He loved to eat foods from his youth, such as meat loaf and macaroni and cheese but would relent when Nancy was with him. At her request, he would have a bowl of vegetable soup and an avocado-and-shrimp salad, or a plate of fruit and vegetables. "All she wanted was for him to stay alive for a long, long time," says chief communicator Jim Bull, whose console was only a few feet from the president's suite.

But when he was not traveling with her, nutrition would go out the window, at least at his main meals, and his preferred menu would reappear. In addition to the meat loaf and macaroni and cheese, the stewards would serve him lemon meringue pie or chocolate chip cookies, some of his favorites. And he looked forward to seeing Bavarian cream apple pie on the printed menu. When that happened, he would ask the stewards to give him a light portion of the main course so he could indulge himself with a big slice of the creamy dessert. If Nancy was aboard and saw the item, she would tell him, "You're not having any of that," and he would meekly acquiesce.

At a basic level, Reagan was at peace when his wife was at his side and unsettled when she wasn't. "The main difference was his personality," recalls Marlin Fitzwater. "When she was on the plane, he was a more relaxed, contented fellow. When she wasn't on the plane, he was always anxious to get home, less communicative. It *is* amazing, the way people talk about their love story, but his home was wherever she was, and you could see a kind of definition of his life in her circle. If she was with him it didn't matter where we were going or when we got back. He was always comfortable. But he was always a little anxious, a little more on edge and everybody could tell that he was a different personality when they weren't together. He didn't like to travel without her."

For her part, Mrs. Reagan was her husband's protector. When she felt that his aides weren't serving him well, she stepped in to correct the situation. She was a big reason that White House Chief of Staff Donald Regan was ousted during Reagan's second term.

And her influence extended beyond personnel. After Reagan's disastrous first debate with Democratic challenger Walter Mondale in 1984, Nancy sat glumly in the president's cabin on *Air Force One* with her husband and speech writer Ken Khachigian. "Ken," she asked, "why isn't Ronnie mentioning Walter Mondale in his speeches?" Khachigian hemmed and hawed. He didn't want to create a fuss by explaining that senior White House strategist James Baker had ordered a ban on references to the Democratic nominee so Reagan could remain "above the fray."

When Nancy persisted, arguing that Mondale's daily attacks were undermining Reagan's popularity, Khachigian told her about Baker's directive. The First Lady immediately summoned Baker to the cabin and confronted him. "Jim, no more white picket fences," she declared. "From now on, Ronnie has to respond." Baker was angry, but agreed to the new terms of engagement.

All the while, President Reagan sat quietly and doodled on the text of a TV ad that Khachigian had prepared. Nancy was the confrontationalist in the family; but everyone around the first couple knew that the president's silence meant he was giving tacit approval to her demands. And her strategy worked. Reagan went on the offensive and his public standing improved.

REAGAN'S HABITS ABOARD the plane revealed traits that the public never knew about.

In addition to his disciplined style, which went counter to the stereotype of him as lazy, he was more of a general-interest reader than anyone suspected, favoring biographies and Western novels. But he wouldn't allow his staff to leak the information to the media because he didn't want journalists to psychoanalyze him or mock his choices. He was a disciplined reader of his briefing memos, although he preferred them to be concise and got bored with long-winded analyses. He enjoyed reading the comic strips in the Sunday newspapers, and would sometimes chuckle out loud.

He was devoted to updating his diary. He would use the long hours aboard *Air Force One* to jot down his thoughts in a book bound in red leather, with each paragraph carefully written in flowing longhand. He later used these jottings as the basis for his presidential memoirs.

Contrary to his public image of eternal good cheer, Reagan sometimes had a bite to his humor. Once his staff was engaging in chitchat as he did his paperwork, and the talk turned to Hollywood. Someone mentioned a rumor that a film might be made of the life story of pint-size actor Mickey Rooney, whom Reagan had known during his Hollywood days. The speculation turned to who would play Rooney in the movie, and an aide suggested that the actor simply play himself. Reagan, who had been listening to every word, interjected, "He's too short."

Reagan was something of a practical joker. A favorite trick was to prowl the staff cabin and find someone who was sleeping, preferably with his mouth open and in an awkward position. The president would motion for a White House photographer to come forward and he would stand in the aisle, grimace or frown, and wave his arms silently as if he were very upset, all while the photographer snapped pictures.

A week or so later, a manila envelope would arrive on the victim's desk containing photos of the scene, with the president's signature and a handwritten reminder of the trip. Among his favorite targets were Press Secretary Fitzwater and Secretary of State George Shultz. After catching Shultz asleep during a trip home from Latin America, a photo arrived showing the secretary unconscious and the president standing next to his seat in an imploring pose. Reagan's handwritten note said: "George, wake up! The Soviets are coming!"

At first, the gambit caused a good deal of embarrassment, but eventually the pictures became prized possessions.

Reagan rarely showed any temper. One of the rare cases came on a campaign stop in 1984 when the mobile staircase wasn't working and he had to exit the plane through an enclosed jetway. This meant that hundreds of people who had been waiting to see him on the tarmac wouldn't get the chance. Reagan upbraided his staff. "All these people got up early on a Sunday morning to shake my hand," he said sharply, "and they couldn't do that. Make sure it never happens again."

REAGAN WAS MORE SUPERSTITIOUS than most Americans suspected. His wife shared that trait, especially after the assassination attempt in March 1981. Nancy Reagan eventually enlisted the services of an astrologer named Joan Quigley, who would determine when the stars were aligned for good or ill, and Nancy would try to shape her husband's schedule accordingly. Virtually no one at the White House knew about the astrologer, but many suspected that something weird was going on.

Fitzwater recalled proposing a press conference for a Tuesday at 11 A.M., but Reagan sent back a note saying he wanted to do it Thursday at 3 P.M. The press secretary went into the Oval Office seeking an explanation. "What is this?" Fitzwater asked with a laugh. "Why this time? It's kind of strange."

The president replied mysteriously, "Don't ask, Marlin." So they proceeded with the Thurday timing.

It still isn't clear how much the Reagans altered the president's travel schedule according to astrological charts, but several senior aides say Quigley's influence was substantial. For example, Reagan's meetings with Soviet leader Mikhail Gorbachev apparently were scheduled in accord with the movement of the planets and the stars.

Once the staff arranged for Reagan to attend a Baltimore Orioles baseball game on a day the astrologer considered inauspicious. "Nothing better happen to Ronnie today," Nancy warned a senior aide, "because he was not supposed to be gone" from the White House. She would review her husband's schedule in advance, consult with Quigley by phone, sometimes for hours, and send back changes such as when press conferences should or should not be held, when trips should be arranged—even the precise times when the president's *Marine One* helicopter and *Air Force One* should lift off and land.

"My control over the departure times of *Air Force One* when the President was aboard was absolute," Quigley recalls. "This was a matter of safety, first and foremost, both at home and abroad. . . . The original departure time is the most important factor for general safety on a trip. But I never took chances. I cast a chart for both Reagans for the various locations during the times they would be away. In addition, I cast the charts for the countries and cities, when available, for the time of the Reagans' visits, as well as the mundane material for the proposed location, which included the solar ingresses, lunar cycles and cycle charts of the planets Mars, Jupiter, Saturn, Uranus, and Neptune."

Under the astrologer's guidance, Mrs. Reagan set the moment that her husband and Gorbachev, then attending a summit meeting in Washington, needed to sign an important agreement limiting intermediate-range missiles, which both sides had negotiated for many months. It had to be done on a Monday at 2 P.M., the First Lady declared. "Pens had to hit paper then," recalled a senior White House adviser who was familiar with the incident. That's when they signed it, too, although only a handful of White House aides knew why the Reagans were so adamant about the timing.

After former White House Chief of Staff Donald Regan (still bitter over his ouster) disclosed the astrologer's role in his book late in Reagan's second term, it became an open joke in the West Wing. Communications Director Tom Griscom would note the arrival of Nancy's recommended changes in the president's schedule with the line: "Let's go check the bones out" or "Let's read the bones, and see what they're telling us today"—a reference to sorcerers consulting chicken bones to predict the future. Griscom recalled thinking at the time: "It's a heckuva way to control a schedule."

Yet the White House was receiving many death threats against the president, and Mrs. Reagan repeatedly told friends she was worried about a second assassination attempt. This intensified her protective instincts, and she turned to the astrologer for emotional support.

For his part, Reagan had some peculiar superstitions of his own. He would wear the same suit and tie for his summit meetings with Gorbachev and for other important events if things had gone well when he wore those clothes before. He was religious about wearing what he called the "good-luck cuff links," which Nancy had given him many years earlier. Each one contained a calendar of the month of March, with a tiny gemstone marking March 4, their wedding date. Shortly after boarding *Air Force One*, recalls former aide Fred Ryan, "he would flash the cuff links to show he had them on. He felt that things would be safe if those lucky cuff links were on."

He would bow his head and say a prayer before each takeoff. When Michael Deaver, his longtime confidant and media adviser, asked him about the habit, Reagan said he was just asking "the Lord" to take care of Nancy in case anything happened to him.

HE COULD BE remarkably naïve. During one California trip, a member of Congress arrived very late for the flight home; Reagan had invited him as a guest. But the Secret Service was not pleased when the legislator rushed up the stairs carrying a big hunting rifle in a leather case. When Reagan came back to say hello after takeoff, the congressman had a bright idea.

"I know you like guns," he said to the president. "Let me show you this beautiful rifle I've got."

"Really?" Reagan said politely. "I'd love to see it."

The congressman unsheathed the weapon and pointed out the scope along the barrel. "You can pick up something at three hundred yards with this," he said proudly.

At this point, the Secret Service agents and staff were getting nervous.

"Mr. President," the legislator said. "Pick it up. Try it."

Reagan grabbed the rifle, raised it to his shoulder, put his hand around the stock and heard an agent shout, "Don't pull the trigger!"—just as Reagan did just that. The loud click startled everyone, despite the background roar of the 707's engines.

Fortunately, the rifle was not loaded. But the chagrined congressman quietly put the weapon back in its case and changed the subject. Reagan acted as if nothing unusual had happened.

· · ·

ANOTHER QUIRK centered on Reagan's sleeping habits—or lack of them. It was never widely known that he couldn't sleep on airplanes. That's one reason his trips seemed so leisurely.

Most presidents will depart in the evening for a lengthy foreign trip and get at least a partial night's sleep on *Air Force One*, then start the next day with a full schedule at the point of destination. Not Reagan. His staff would make sure the septuagenarian president flew during the daytime, and not for too long at a stretch. He would arrive in time to sleep in a bed at his destination. Nancy, however, could sleep on the plane, and Reagan would often slip out of their cabin to let her rest while he schmoozed and told stories to aides and guests.

Ensuring that the president was well rested became a constant preoccupation, and with good reason. After a long day of meetings in Brazilia during a trip to Brazil, Reagan was barely awake at a late-night banquet given in his honor. At the end of his ceremonial toast, he told his hosts how wonderful it was to be with them in "Bolivia." The news media barraged him with criticism the next morning for not knowing what country he was in, and as *Air Force One* descended into São Paolo, Reagan noticed a banner near the tarmac held by some local citizens: "The people of Bolivia welcome the President of Canada." He pointed it out to aides, and had a good laugh at his own expense.

IN MOST CASES, he left the heavy lifting to his aides. On nearly every flight, the White House staff would be hard at work completing his speeches and policy pronouncements and in general running the government while the president kicked back. His critics called it laziness, or lack of intellectual capacity. Reagan called it delegation of responsibility.

This dynamic was clear in the run-up to his first summit with Gorbachev on November 19–21, 1985, in Geneva. It would be Reagan's first meeting with a Soviet leader, and tensions were high. "There was palpable electricity," says former adviser Duberstein. "It was high-stakes poker."

Flying to Geneva on November 16, Reagan learned that Defense Secretary

Caspar Weinberger, a hardliner toward the Kremlin, had written him a letter urging a firm stand against the Soviets on arms control. The letter, however, had been leaked to *The New York Times* for that morning's editions, and moderate administration officials thought the leak was aimed at ruining the summit. In any case, the incident showed how divided Reagan's advisers were, and how he had been unable to unite them behind a single policy.

On the first afternoon of the summit, he and Gorbachev held a one-on-one meeting for 49 minutes at the pool house of the Chateau Fleur D'Eau overlooking Lake Geneva, and it went well. Even though nothing much was accomplished in concrete terms, the two men agreed to meet again. Reagan was pleased. He believed he had established a rapport with his Communist counterpart.

As he flew home on *Air Force One*, Reagan began to decompress, as so many presidents had done before him under similar high-pressure circumstances. He told his staff: "We've seen what the new Russian looks like. Now maybe we can figure out how to deal with him." He said he had told Gorbachev that the two of them could bring peace for generations to come, and they should work hard to "erase these things that have made us suspicious of each other." It was a heartfelt testimonial to Reagan's optimism and a clear statement of what he hoped to accomplish, but some of his hawkish advisers feared he might have been gulled into a false sense of hope.

Their next summit, at Reykjavik, Iceland, on October 11–12, 1986, was even more dramatic. Gorbachev had asked for the meeting on short notice, and there was little time for Reagan and his staff to prepare. After agreeing in principle on one proposal for arms control after another, Reagan and Gorbachev were on the verge of accepting an extraordinary pact to eliminate all the superpowers' nuclear weapons, which would have been a stunning move. But the deal fell apart when Gorbachev demanded that Reagan give up research and development for a futuristic, space-based "shield"—formally called the Strategic Defense Initiative and nicknamed "Star Wars"—to shoot down nuclear missiles. Reagan said no, and the summit meeting collapsed.

The problem for Reagan and his aides was how to put the best face on what had happened. The first news reports by the wire services and on the television networks indicated that a deal of historic proportions had been within grasp, and Reagan let it slip away. As Speakes tells the story, the counter-spin was largely formulated by key Reagan aides during the four-hour *Air Force One* flight from Reykjavik to Washington.

It happened while Reagan quietly nursed his wounds over the messy outcome. He closed the door to his cabin, causing aides and stewards to fret that he was more upset than they had ever seen him. Yet he bounced back after a couple of hours alone reviewing the events of the previous two days. By the time *Air Force One* was making its descent into Washington, his optimism had returned and he was talking to aides about his desire to meet with Gorbachev again soon. "I'm okay now," he told his senior staff in the conference room. "I know that I made the right decision. It was the right thing to do. We couldn't give up America's insurance policy." He was talking about SDI.

Meanwhile, the PR campaign had moved into high gear. First, White House National Security Adviser John Poindexter gave an on-the-record, 80-minute briefing to the reporters in the media cabin. This was transmitted to the rest of the press corps. Poindexter blamed Moscow for the summit's failure. "Soviet rhetoric was far out in front of what they were actually willing to do," Poindexter said as he puffed on his pipe, at one point dropping wearily to his knees in the aisle so his arms and elbows rested on the press table.

Speakes took a sheet of *Air Force One* stationery and outlined what he called "an unprecedented news blitz that would begin when we got back to Washington." The exhaustive script called for Secretary of State George Shultz to meet with the editorial boards of major newspapers such as the *The New York Times* and *The Wall Street Journal* and decision makers at ABC, CBS, and NBC. Other senior officials, such as White House Chief of Staff Donald Regan, would make the administration's case in separate briefings and interviews with other major news outlets, including the *The Washington Post*, *The Los Angeles Times*, *Newsweek*, *Time*, and *U.S. News & World Report*. Still other officials would appear on the network morning shows, write op-ed articles for newspapers, and give more interviews. Monday night, the day after he returned, Reagan himself would address the nation at 8 P.M. and argue that he had presented the Soviets with the "most sweeping and generous arms control proposal in history."

The remarkable thing is that Reagan had virtually nothing to do with the development of this plan on which so much was riding. He approved an outline of it before he landed, and then went to the residence to rest. More to the point, the plan worked, and the media portrayed Reykjavik much the way the White House wanted.

YET HIS DISENGAGEMENT was also at the heart of the Iran-Contra affair, the worst scandal of his presidency. The episode was politically devastating to Reagan for two reasons: He had promised never to negotiate for hostages, and financing the Contras was against the law.

"Iran-Contra was a very discouraging period for him because he always felt if he was right about something he could go to the American people and persuade them," says former secretary of state Shultz. "He thought he was right in this case because he was trying to free the hostages, and he found that he couldn't convince the American people."

Reagan struggled for many months to clear himself and reestablish his credibility, and he finally came to terms with the fact that some of his aides had deceived him. In the end, the public lost interest after no one could prove that he had direct knowledge of any wrongdoing.

It turns out that Reagan could have seen signs of trouble if he had paid attention to what was going on around him aboard his plane. Jim Bull, the military official who was responsible for all communications to and from *Air Force One*, says he got suspicious because there were so many secure phone calls between Oliver North, a National Security Council operative who turned out to be a key figure in the Iran-Contra transactions, and Bud MacFarlane, the president's national security adviser. MacFarlane generally accompanied Reagan on *Air Force One*. "It seemed to be trouble," Bull says, but he remains certain that Reagan knew little or nothing about what was going on.

·   ·   ·

HISTORIANS WILL SPEND YEARS debating whether President Reagan was lucky or smart, but his admirers say he always had an intuition that the Communist empire could not stand. When he gave his dramatic speech at the Berlin Wall on June 12, 1987—declaring, "Mr. Gorbachev, tear down this wall"—few thought such a thing was possible in their lifetimes. But the wall came down not long after Reagan left office.

Why was he so right about such a fundamental question when so many of the "experts" were wrong? "It came from a depth of conviction about what worked and what didn't work," Shultz told me. "He believed that when something is really wrong it is not going to survive." Communism was in that category. It was not only evil, he believed, it ran counter to human nature and was unworkable.

His visit to Moscow for his final summit with Gorbachev in May and June 1988 brought all these issues to the fore. First of all, *Air Force One* had to fly through Soviet air space—reminding the Americans of the fact that the Soviets had shot down a Korean airliner in 1983 and killed 269 people, including 63 Americans, provoking angry denunciations from Reagan.

The atmosphere aboard *Air Force One* was a mixture of anticipation and trepidation as the president and his staff pressed their faces to the windows, wondering what might happen next. "You had a sense of the vulnerability of the plane and a sense of the history of the shootdown," Fitzwater says. "There was a strong feeling of, 'We're flying into an unknown land and unknown circumstances,' and that was without regard to the unknown issues we were going to have to deal with.

"Reagan was going finally to see the evil empire," recalls Fitzwater. "And we were all part of this phenomenon, and that was kind of magnified by the fact that one of the purposes of this trip was to put an end to the evil empire view of the world."

The trip was a success. Reagan walked with Gorbachev through Red Square and proclaimed that the two nations were now partners, not enemies. It was a remarkable about-face for the quintessential cold warrior.

Yet the moment could not completely erase all those years of superpower tension. "After spending five days in Moscow, feeling like you were bugged everyplace . . . wondering if the maids in the hotel and the drivers assigned to us were all KGB," says Fitzwater, "there was this overwhelming sense of being watched and a kind of paranoia set in about everything. . . . By the time we got back on that plane it was like climbing back into the womb of mother America, and I remember going up the steps and thinking, 'God, let me get up those last six steps and inside the door. When I'm inside the door I know I'm safe. Just let me get on that plane.' It was an incredible feeling. And to a greater or lesser degree, I think the president's staff and the president have that feeling every time they get on that plane."

Minutes after *Air Force One* lifted off from Moscow and began the long flight home, someone started to sing "God Bless America" and the entire staff quickly joined in. Soon after, the stewards began serving the famished staff hamburgers and Cokes—American comfort food—that they had been saving for this moment.

THE EIGHTIES WERE years of public preoccupation with fame, wealth, and glamour. The hot television shows were *Dallas* and *Dynasty*, which celebrated those qualities. Reagan did the same. If the poor were getting lost in the shuffle, so be it. That seemed to be the administration's attitude, or so Reagan's critics said. In any case, the perks returned to the White House and *Air Force One*, where passengers still loved to snitch the plastic cups, napkins, pads, matchbooks, and boxes of candy, all bearing an *Air Force One* logo.

Under Reagan, the pecking order was all-important—to some members of his staff. "By protocol, only the President and Mrs. Reagan were to use the front exit; everyone else was to use the rear exit," recalls journalist Hedrick Smith. "But the TV cameras and welcoming parties were at the front, and the most perk-and-publicity-conscious officials—press spokesman Larry Speakes; Dick Darman, a top presidential aide; national security adviser Bill Clark—would violate protocol and get off at the front, ahead of the president, rather than exit from the rear." Reagan, who hated confrontation and exhibited surprisingly little ego about such matters, let it go.

This easygoing manner helped him in many ways. People believed he was genuine. Even his long vacations at his Santa Barbara estate, *Rancho del Cielo*, didn't hurt his image very much. Americans felt that the septuagenarian president had placed the country on a proper course and he deserved his time off. Not that public opinion seemed to matter to him when it came to his beloved ranch. He told aides he would not forgo traveling there because it refreshed and invigorated him. He told one aide that the more time he spent at *Rancho del Cielo,* the longer he would live and the happier he would be; it was hard to argue with the boss when he put things in such personal terms. After a few months, his staff rarely second-guessed his vacation time, and he ended up spending the equivalent of a full year of his eight-year presidency at the ranch.

In fact, after the Soviets shot down the Korean airliner in August 1983, Reagan was reluctant to leave his cowboy paradise, arguing that he could handle any decisions from there. But his aides insisted that he would look too detached and lazy if he didn't return to Washington, and he did so reluctantly. Still, he seethed. "I want you to know," he told Fred Ryan aboard *Air Force One* as they flew eastward, "the trip got cut short three days. You owe me three days."

Ryan laughed it off, but not long after they got back, he got a note in Reagan's distinctive scrawl. "Remember," the president wrote, "you owe me the three days." Of course he got them.

En route to California, as he anticipated the joys of riding horses, clearing brush, and chopping wood at the ranch, Reagan would loosen up remarkably and so would those around him. During a 1983 flight from Washington to Santa Barbara for the July Fourth holiday, George Skelton of *The Los Angeles Times* pulled a surprise on the president during an interview in his private cabin. A few weeks earlier, Reagan had spoken to a group of young people at a drug and alcohol rehabilitation center in Houston and seemed to counsel them, with a sly smile, to take care of their health so they could enjoy vigorous activities later in life; many in the audience, including several Reagan aides, thought he was referring to sex. Skelton decided to follow up on it when the opportunity arose.

He managed to schedule an interview aboard *Air Force One* about Reagan's overall health at age 72, which was sure to be an issue in the following year's reelection campaign. Skelton took an expansive view of the health issue and asked the president what he had meant in Houston. Reagan denied that he had been referring to sex, insisting that he was talking about riding horses and other outdoor activities. Then, as he sat across a small table from the commander in chief, Skelton dropped the bombshell. "Well, I'm on shaky ground here, okay," the reporter said nervously, "but I've got to ask a seventy-two-year-old president if you still have an active sex life."

Reagan broke into a grin and laughed. "I don't think, no, George, and I'm remembering things like Mr. Carter in Playhouse and so forth [a mangled reference to candidate Jimmy Carter's much-derided admission in a 1976 *Playboy* interview that he felt lust in his heart toward some women]. No, this is a subject I think I'll stay away from."

Reagan took it all in stride, and never held the question against Skelton, whom he had known for many years. Reagan's aides, however, were nonplussed at Skelton's audacity and the president's nonchalant but savvy decision to stay mum.

AS WITH MOST PRESIDENCIES, staff members were eager to travel on the plane as a demonstration of their importance. One aide, who had worked for Reagan while he was governor of California, was known not only to enjoy the perks of the executive branch but also to drink too much. On one trip, he had done his customary imbibing, and then, as *Air Force One* rolled to a stop on the tarmac during the evening he rushed to the front door to supervise the president's arrival. The man hastily stepped out as the door opened, only to find that the outside stairs had not been fully deployed. He fell more than 20 feet to the ground, sustaining severe injuries. He left White House service soon thereafter.

THERE HAVE LONG been rumors about what guests and staff bring home on *Air Force One*, especially during the high-living Reagan days. "Well, everybody brought back mementos and gifts," Fitzwater says. "And generally speaking it was reasonable. It was stuff you could put in your luggage. The only kind of single item that was always talked about and outside the 'too big for luggage' [standard] were rugs, because so many of the government trips were to Middle Eastern countries or even Russia and China, and rugs were one of the things that you could always get cheaper there than you could in America. They could fold them up pretty small but they were still bulky and heavy, and there's no way you could put them on the plane without being seen and being obvious about it."

Each individual was still responsible for paying customs fees on purchases, Fitzwater says, adding, "It was just a convenience." But not a small one, because the buyer didn't have to carry the rugs and check them in himself; government workers would simply pick up the purchases along with other baggage outside staffers' rooms in their hotels and everything would magically show up on the tarmac of Andrews Air Force Base, at the base of the plane, or back at the White House. Someone else did the heavy lifting.

The real problem apparently was caused by journalists traveling on the press plane. "The worst offenders were members of the press corps on return trips from California, who had the travel office staff and the flight crew stock cases of wine in the luggage or cargo holds," says a White House official from those days. Staff people would bring back a bottle or two, but most were afraid to abuse the privilege. "I don't think it was corrupt, just self-indulgent," says the official.

REAGAN'S LAST trip aboard *Air Force One*, on January 20, 1989, provided final insight into the man and his era. Instead of the sadness and recriminations that marked the last flights of Nixon, Ford, and Carter—who all left office as defeated men—Reagan's trip was celebratory.

As is customary, he boarded *Marine One* on the morning of the inauguration of his successor, George H. W. Bush, and was taken on a quick tour of the capital. When the helicopter swung around for a final look at the White House, he said to Nancy, "Look, dear, there's our little shack," bringing her to tears.

The presidential couple kept to themselves for a while on *Air Force One*, but eventually they came out into the main cabin area to thank the staff and crew for their help over the previous eight years. At one point, Mrs. Reagan asked the pilot, Bob Ruddick, "Do you think it would be okay if Ronnie came to the cockpit and watched the landing?" This is something the commander in chief had rarely done since LBJ's day, preferring not to distract the pilot. Ruddick agreed.

As the plane approached the outskirts of Los Angeles, a steward peeked into the presidential stateroom and saw Reagan with Nancy on his lap. They were looking out the window and pointing out landmarks to each other. After a few moments, they got up and stopped in the staff cabin as the big aircraft soared over posh Orange County, part of Reagan's conservative base for many years. "You want to see where all the Republicans live?" Reagan told aides who had gathered around him as he pointed to the suburban tracts sweeping by. "You see all those swimming pools down there?"

Reagan then made his way to the cockpit and took the observer's jumpseat behind the pilot. As other aides and crew members wandered in and out, he pointed out some of the sights he knew so well from his days as California governor and all his trips back to the Golden State.

Suddenly he turned nostalgic, with his particular homespun flair. "What time is it in Washington?" he asked.

"Sir, it's five o'clock in Washington," replied chief steward Howie Franklin.

"Hey, boys, just think," Reagan exclaimed. "George Bush has put his clothes in my closet."

ONE OF REAGAN's many legacies was the 747 jumbo jet that he left to his successors. After he was elected to a second term in 1984, his staff, his military advisers, and the Secret Service all recommended that he order a more advanced plane to replace the then-outmoded 707. The critique was compelling: The 707 was too noisy, generated too much pollution, couldn't fly far enough or fast enough, and was limited in its communications systems and other equipment. "The airplane was an antique," said pilot Ruddick, "and the president's aircraft needed to accommodate a larger number of staff people than the 707 could handle."

Reagan, like Eisenhower under similar circumstances three decades earlier, had another reason to order the new plane. When he attended international conferences, he noticed the leaders of smaller and less consequential countries arriving in 747s, which outclassed his 707.

The president, the First Lady, and their advisers pored over plans and, in the end, ordered not one but two souped-up 747s. This was a security precaution. One would serve as the main *Air Force One* and the other as a backup that would be ready at all times in case the first plane went out of service—at a total cost of more than half a billion dollars.

The aircraft were supposed to arrive in 1988, the final year of Reagan's term. But serious problems developed in the manufacturing process, and the new planes weren't delivered until Reagan had left office. He never set foot on "his" new plane.

It was left to George Herbert Walker Bush, his successor, to take the saga of *Air Force One* to the next level. Beyond that, Reagan's 707 is being kept near his presidential library and museum outside Los Angeles, where it will become the centerpiece of a permanent exhibit on presidential travel.

CHAPTER TEN

GEORGE HERBERT WALKER BUSH:
THE FOREIGN-POLICY PRESIDENT

A s Reagan's loyal vice president, George Bush campaigned as the heir to the "Great Communicator." He was elected to continue Reagan's policies, but with what Bush called a "kinder and gentler" attitude. Mostly he did so, but without his predecessor's charisma.

Bush deftly presided over the demise of the Soviet empire and orchestrated the Persian Gulf War, which pushed Iraq out of Kuwait with a massive air, land, and sea campaign. For a while, his popularity soared, and it looked like he would be unbeatable in 1992. But his public standing was ravaged by the recession of the early 1990s, when he seemed too preoccupied with foreign affairs, too much a scion of privilege, and unconcerned about everyday people's problems.

Bush was more vigorous than most Americans remember him. His first extended foreign trip aboard *Air Force One* was a visit to Japan, Korea, and China during February 1989—in only five days. This set the pace.

Bush also tried to be accessible, as had Gerald Ford. In fact, he was more open to people than Reagan had ever been, contrary to the impression left by Reagan's careful stage management. Bush knew his staff far better than his predecessor did, would keep track of their birthdays so he could send them handwritten notes, and showed an interest in their family situations. He would even visit the press cabin on *Air Force One* during nearly every trip, to talk policy or say hello. Occasionally, it resulted in the TV cameras capturing him swaying awkwardly or losing his balance momentarily as he chatted with reporters during periods of turbulence, adding to his goofy image.

At his core, Bush loved tradition and decorum, and these traits permeated everything he did as chief executive. "George Bush was in awe of the presidency," says David Valdez, his White House photographer.

Valdez recalled a story about Lyndon Johnson: A young military officer once pointed to the presidential 707 in the distance and said, "There's your plane, sir." Whereupon Johnson supposedly replied, "Boy, they're *all* my planes." Bush would never think that way. To him, the presidency was an honor bestowed by the country temporarily on a series of fortunate men, and he would never presume to "own" anything connected with it.

Bush instilled in his staff his own sense of honor about riding *Air Force One*. "That airplane is the greatest plane in the world," says Valdez, who traveled with Bush for 10 years during his vice presidency and presidency. ". . . When you fly on that plane, you are representing the United States, and when you land, that huge 747 sits there as the flying embassy of the United States of America." This was the common view in Bush's White House.

The flight crew respected Reagan but they *liked* George Herbert Walker Bush. They admired his golden resume—former vice president, director of Central Intelligence, ambassador to the United Nations, envoy to Beijing, chairman of the Republican National Committee, congressman from Texas, oilman, and World War II hero. But they liked his genuine affinity for people, and were perplexed and disappointed that he could never convey this quality to the country.

Bush heard that John Haigh, chief flight steward on *Air Force One*, was a whiz at horseshoes—a Bush family pastime—and the president invited him to participate in the first White House horseshoe tournament, in 1989. Haigh won, and from then on Bush would call him "champ" and kid him about it in front of guests, even heads of state. For the son of a Pennsylvania coal miner, this was heady stuff, and Haigh considered it typical of Bush's generosity and consideration.

"He'd give you the shirt off his back," says former flight steward Tim Kerwin. "He was always wanting to do nice things for people." On vacations at his estate in Kennebunkport, Maine, for Thanksgiving and July Fourth, Bush would realize he was keeping crew members away from home, so he would call their hotel and invite them to his home for dinner or a barbecue.

One of the most vivid public impressions of Bush came in an *Air Force One* moment, when he banned broccoli from the plane. He had hated the vegetable since childhood, when his mother made him eat it, and now he was president and he wasn't going to take it anymore. White House officials thought the incident made him look decisive but I had a different view after I broke the story in *U.S. News & World Report*. He looked out of touch to be absorbed with such a silly issue.

While the president banned broccoli, Barbara Bush reaffirmed an earlier ban on smoking aboard the plane. She considered it a dirty, unhealthy habit, and the commander in chief went along with her. But some aides and crew members couldn't call it quits, especially on long flights when the urge to smoke got overpowering. They learned that they could slip into a lavatory, light up and puff into the toilet or the sink, then pull the flush lever or release the plunger. The smoky air would get sucked down the commode or the washbasin, and no one would be the wiser. Of course it was against federal regulations to smoke in the lavatories, but mostly the offenders were worried that if Barbara found out, they would be cashiered. She never did.

WHEN BUSH BECAME the first president to ride the big 747, his eyes widened in awe. His first concern was that voters would think it was extravagant. "I'm glad this was ordered up on Ronald Reagan's watch," he told an aide as he eyed the spacious presidential office. But Bush thought so much of the plane that he wrote an article about it for *Forbes* magazine on November 18, 1996, four years after leaving office.

"History will remember me as the first president to fly on *Air Force One* Tail No. 28000," he wrote.

"Everyone says, 'What's it really like?'"

"Well, let me tell you: it's grand. It's not fancy, with gold bathroom fittings and plush carpets like those G-IV's that fly celebrities. No mirrors on the ceiling, no circular beds, no Jacuzzis, no bidets even. But man oh man, is it comfortable."

He went on to describe the big presidential stateroom that takes up the front end of the aircraft with two couches that convert into beds; an adjacent bathroom with shower; the presidential office next door, decorated in muted brown and beige tones, that features a wraparound desk in one corner, and a medical room with operating table and a cabinet full of medications.

Bush wrote of the senior-staff quarters: "There are three comfortable chairs there, but best of all there are two full-length, double-decker beds tucked into one side of the room, on the left as you enter the door. People would pull rank to get into those bunks on the long flights."

Bush also related a bizarre moment that occurred when he flew aboard *Air Force One*, at President Clinton's request, to the funeral of assassinated Israeli leader Yitzhak Rabin. He was assigned to the four-person senior-staff cabin along with former President Jimmy Carter, Secretary of State Warren Christopher, and White House Chief of Staff Leon Panetta. Bush liked to sleep stretched out, so he eased himself to the floor and began to doze as his cabin mates relaxed in their first-class leather chairs.

"Jimmy Carter must have been thinking 'presidential' too, for when I awakened after a nice four-hour sleep, there he was on the floor, his face but a few inches from my face," Bush wrote. "Scary? No, but different. What would his precinct chairman in Plains say? What would mine in Houston say? AF1 makes the strangest of bedfellows."

The 747 also gave a president rare luxury. The jumbo jet let the commander in chief take a shower on board, and Bush frequently availed himself of this opportunity. Sometimes he would appear before the press immediately after washing his hair, making him look like a wet puppy. (He didn't blow dry.) When he realized there was room for a massage table, he had a military nurse give him rubdowns to relax him, although this was not revealed to the media because it might seem too posh.

He liked to watch an occasional movie but found many modern films too raw. On one flight, the president, the First Lady, and a handful of aides were watching an R-rated film provided by a Washington-area video rental chain when suddenly two large breasts appeared on screen. Everyone froze in embarrassment until Barbara blurted out, "Who picked this movie?" No one spoke up until the president responded meekly, "Well, *I* didn't." In any case, he preferred to read books or listen to country music; the Oak Ridge Boys and Alabama were among his favorites.

Like most other presidents, Bush was concerned about overeating, a worry intensified by his desire to remain in athletic trim but complicated by his love of fattening foods. When the staff found out that he liked rich seafood soups from Bookbinder's restaurant in Philadelphia, they arranged for regular supplies to be delivered to Andrews Air Force Base and they would stock them on the plane. He also was an obsessive user of artificial sweetener for his coffee. Yet, in addition to high-calorie Tex-Mex food and barbecue, he would indulge his sweet tooth on long flights with Eskimo Pies, Baby Ruth bars, and Blue Belle ice cream from Texas.

BUSH WAS A HANDS-ON manager, a smart policy analyst, and a man who genuinely tried to reach out to his adversaries, even the news media. For his first three years in office, he visited the press cabin routinely, which was rare in the Reagan era. In fact, he showed up so often that he wore out his welcome. After a while, some journalists would feign sleep and wear Lone Ranger-style black sleep masks to discourage the president from making news at the end of a long day. On such occasions he would slip into the press cabin, survey the "sleeping" reporters, shake his head at their lethargy, and return to his quarters.

BUSH'S EXPERIENCES ON *Air Force One* reflected his foreign-policy preoccupation. Nearly all his important moments aboard the plane concerned international affairs, and Bush never hesitated to make decisions there. He felt, with considerable justification, that he was a foreign-policy expert in his own right.

One example of Bush's sangfroid came en route to Malta in December 1989 for his first summit meeting with Soviet leader Gorbachev. In the middle of the night, as Bush slept, there was a coup attempt in the Philippines.

Senior officials in Washington called an emergency meeting to discuss what should be done. But there was a major dilemma: Should they awaken the commander in chief? He was, after all, heading for a very important summit, and he needed his rest. Yet a crucial decision had to be made that could affect whether Filipino leader Cory Aquino, a solid American ally, would remain in power.

The question was whether to authorize the Pentagon to intervene militarily. "We were all huddled down in the Situation Room [of the White House]," recalled Andrew Card, who was then Bush's deputy White House chief of staff. Also in the Situation Room, participating via videoconference, were Vice President Dan Quayle, Defense Secretary Dick Cheney, and General Colin Powell, chairman of the Joint Chiefs of Staff.

"We were trying to agonize, do we call the president on *Air Force One,* who we knew was sound asleep?" Card said. Instead, they funneled the information to an airborne Brent Scowcroft, the White House national security adviser, whom they *did* wake up. The rebels had seized an airfield near Manila and were using it to bomb government facilities, and Aquino wanted the Americans to strafe the airfield to stop the bombing runs. There was another complication: Vice President Quayle and Defense Secretary Cheney were squabbling. Quayle had called a meeting of senior foreign-policy advisers in Bush's absence, and he was labeling it a National Security Council meeting, which would have given it decision-making authority. His goal, as a possible presidential candidate in the future, was to burnish his credentials as a decisive leader and he wanted to take command of the NSC apparatus. But Cheney said that since the president wasn't there, there could be no NSC meeting, and he refused to attend. Quayle and Cheney began to call Scowcroft every few minutes, each trying to feed him recommendations that were sometimes at odds.

Scowcroft contacted General Powell and they worked out a plan: American aircraft would fly menacingly over the rebel-held airfield and prevent planes from taking off, but would not strafe it. Bush was awakened, listened to Scowcroft's recommendation, asked a few questions, and gave his approval. Then the president went back to sleep. The flyovers worked, and the crisis was defused.

ONE REASON FOR BUSH's refusal to get worked up about the attempted coup in the Philippines was that he was so focused on the Gorbachev meeting that would begin almost as soon as he landed. He didn't want any distractions.

When he got up, he called in his senior advisers and began to finalize the proposals he would make to Gorbachev in Malta, including measures to increase trade and grant economic assistance as a reward if the Kremlin implemented the democratic and economic reforms it was promising. As aides took notes, Bush summed up the plan and came up with 17 points.

Bush then asked aides who was supposed to start the discussion. Secretary of State James Baker said it would be Gorbachev because he would be hosting the event on a Russian cruise ship, the *Gorki*; the Soviet leader would be expecting to make welcoming remarks and then would segue into substantive issues. Bush wanted a change in the protocol. "I want him to see this package and to hear my proposal before he says anything," the president said, "so that whatever he has to say is reflective of this proposal and not reflective of the past."

It was decided that Bush would let Gorbachev make his welcoming comments, and then interrupt him and outline his plan. "The whole package was put together on *Air Force One*. . . . Actually it was almost the same agenda that Clinton adopted ten years later. It held up a long time," according to Marlin Fitzwater, press secretary to Bush and Reagan.

When the summit meeting started, Bush followed the plan. He interrupted Gorbachev and said. "I know this may violate protocol, but there is something I'd like to say." Then he presented his ideas.

Gorbachev had a three-by-five spiral notebook in which he had jotted his own thoughts about improving the East-West relationship. He flipped the pages as Bush addressed the points he was about to make, one by one. He was obviously taken by surprise. But Gorbachev was delighted, because he hadn't thought he would get this kind of firm personal commitment to U.S. assistance from the president. The summit was a success.

In fact, the superpower relationship had eased so much, and the U.S.S.R. was changing so fast, that the Berlin Wall would come down in only a few months. When it did, Bush was criticized for showing too little emotion at the West's victory, which had been so long in the making.

He later visited the remnants of the wall in Berlin, and on the way back to Washington got into a discussion with aides about why he hadn't climbed on top of the symbolic structure to make a point about the triumph of freedom. He was miffed that anyone would suggest such a thing, adding: "It's up to those people [in Germany] to sort it all out." His objective was not to embarrass the Russians, whose empire was splitting apart and whose reaction might be unpredictable if they felt offended or threatened, but to show sensitivity to a fallen adversary. He talked as if he had just won a friendly tennis match with a chum at the country club. He may have been wise to put future relations with Moscow ahead of a temporary sense of elation, but he came across as distant and bloodless.

ANOTHER REVEALING MOMENT came as he was flying to the Middle East to visit U.S. troops for Thanksgiving in November 1990. He had deployed hundreds of thousands of U.S. soldiers in the Persian Gulf area for the war against Iraq that would begin the following January, and he was, on this occasion, steeped in emotion. These were the young men and women he was about to send into harm's way.

He consoled himself by reading Scripture in his private cabin, and at one point wrote a note to himself on a yellow pad. It read: "This will not be another Vietnam." He placed it in his desk drawer as a reminder. And he was true to his word. He ended the Persian Gulf War after a 100-hour ground attack that routed Saddam Hussein's forces. Yet President Bush would face considerable criticism in later years for failing to pursue the campaign and force Saddam from power.

. . .

ON *AIR FORCE ONE*, Bush loved to wear a bizarre white jacket depicting a map of the world. Completing his ensemble would be white socks and slippers with the presidential seal on each toe. Aides thought he wore the outfit for shock value, just to see people's reactions to the idea that the prim and proper Brahmin from Yale would have such an awful sense of fashion. Mostly he would wear a dark blue jogging suit on the plane, or, on short flights, switch to a blue windbreaker bearing his name and the words *AIR FORCE ONE*.

The informality and the close quarters helped create an atmosphere of familiarity that was important in developing staff cohesion. "Pretty soon everyone is running around in gym suits and shorts and T-shirts and stuff," recalls Fitzwater, "so all the constraints of a tie and a suit kind of fall away and it tends to lead to great camaraderie, great familiarity."

Bush mostly worked at his desk, and he would invite people in as he did at the Oval Office. "He was always doing business," Fitzwater says. He resisted having most of his speeches done in advance, as Reagan had done, preferring to finalize his addresses on board. This was harder on the staff than during the Reagan days, when things were precooked, because once Bush signed off on a text, it would have to be typed up and distributed to the news media while *Air Force One* was airborne, or rushed to the press corps once *Air Force One* landed.

He made an extraordinary number of phone calls to foreign leaders and other government officials, and he liked to have members of Congress along for the ride. Bush also liked big meetings in the conference room, where officials would give briefings on policy, on the logistics of trips, on media coverage, and so forth. "He would actually change agendas and reassign people to attend different meetings, so it was very much a working atmosphere for him on the plane," says a senior aide.

"The presidents clearly feel like it's their world and they're in control of it," Fitzwater told me. "They know the people on there and they trust them. There's a feeling that the information is trapped in the plane. You don't fear all the normal leaks that you do in the White House. It's an interesting phenomenon."

· · ·

BUSH FELT SUCH control over *Air Force One* that he could defy his own non-confrontational nature and discipline errant aides there.

Just before the midterm elections of 1990, he forced the dismissal of GOP strategist Ed Rollins from the Republican Congressional Campaign Committee. What infuriated Bush was Rollins's contention in a political newsletter that Republican candidates must divorce themselves from the White House because of the alleged involvement of Neil Bush, one of the president's sons, in a savings and loan scandal that was getting big headlines at the time. Because of Neil, Rollins said, the Bush name was not helpful.

"President Bush went through the roof," recalls a senior aide, feeling that his innocent son had been maligned. While aboard *Air Force One*, he called Guy van der Jagt, chairman of the House campaign committee, who Rollins was working for, and started yelling at the top of his voice, a rarity for the usually composed president. Van der Jagt at first didn't want to fire Rollins, saying that penalty would be too harsh. But Bush declared, "If you don't fire him, I will never sign another fund-raising letter for you as long as I am president." Then he hung up. Van der Jagt relented, and Rollins was released.

In late 1991, Bush forced the resignation of then White House Chief of Staff John Sununu after Sununu's arrogance, bullying ways, and secretive, dictatorial style had alienated him from conservatives and other natural allies.

Earlier that year, I had broken a story in *U.S. News* about how Sununu was misusing government aircraft for personal business and vacation trips, at taxpayer expense. He refused to apologize, and his enemies used the flap as a bludgeon to attack him in the news media and spread the word to Bush that he was becoming an embarrassment. Just as important, Bush's popularity was sinking amid a painful recession, and he needed all the friends he could get, adding to Sununu's vulnerability.

By November, Bush was getting the word from his allies and friends that Sununu had to go; no one, it seemed, wanted to work with him in the upcoming 1992 reelection campaign. George W. Bush, the president's son and political troubleshooter (who would later win election as the 43rd president), told

Sununu privately that he had lost virtually all support for continuing as chief of staff. At first the abrasive former governor of New Hampshire refused to resign gracefully. But after a failed attempt to rally congressional support on his behalf, he gave up.

The end came on December 3, 1991, as *Air Force One* was cruising from Florida to Meridian, Mississippi. Sununu gave Bush his letter of resignation in a tense final scene in the president's airborne office. Bush sat behind his big mahogany desk and the outgoing chief of staff took the high-backed leather chair opposite him, with press secretary Fitzwater on the couch across the room. Everyone was terse and composed but after Sununu and Fitzwater returned to the senior-staff cabin, the former governor began to weep silently, with tears running down his cheeks. He said it was the press's fault. "They'll be celebrating, I suppose," he said, then added sadly: "I didn't think they could get me."

THE PERSIAN GULF crisis showed Bush at his best.

When Iraq invaded Kuwait in August 1990, his senior advisers initially were not too concerned. The day after the attack, at a hastily convened meeting of the National Security Council, there was a consensus that the invasion was a fait accompli and there was little or nothing the United States could do about it. The war zone, after all, was halfway around the world, and any U.S. intervention would draw widespread condemnation in the Arab world.

Bush wasn't happy with the meeting. But he was scheduled to give a speech in Aspen, Colorado, that afternoon, and he broke off discussions to chopper to Andrews Air Force Base. It turned out that the airstrip at the Rocky Mountain resort was too short to accommodate the 747, so Bush flew there in a small executive-style aircraft called a Jetstar. This meant that, during the worst crisis of his presidency, he was traveling with only one senior foreign-policy adviser aboard—Brent Scowcroft.

They sat knee-to-knee in the small cabin, and Scowcroft decided to speak his mind. The national security adviser, a diminutive man with soft brown eyes and a gentle voice, talked with surprising passion. He had been "very disturbed" by the tone of resignation expressed at the NSC meeting that morning. "We can't accept this as a fait accompli," he said. He suggested having another meeting as soon as they got back, to revisit the issue.

Bush felt the same way. The president said vital U.S. interests were at stake—oil supplies and the stability of the entire Middle East—and he would not allow Saddam Hussein's invasion of Kuwait to stand.

After conferring with British prime minister Margaret Thatcher in Aspen, and finding her in complete agreement, Bush drew a line in the sand a few days later and declared that the invasion was unacceptable.

From then on, Bush played his role as commander in chief masterfully. He built an international coalition against Iraq, including Arab states such as Saudi Arabia, and he sent 500,000 U.S. troops to the region over the next four months. He gave Saddam Hussein every chance to avoid war by pulling out of Kuwait. He let the generals figure out the best military strategy and let them do their job. And he persuaded Congress and the American people that war was the honorable and necessary course.

After a massive air campaign in January and a brief ground assault, the Iraqi forces were rolled back, Kuwait was liberated, and the war was over. It was all set in motion by that conversation between Bush and Scowcroft on the president's plane en route to Aspen. It was the high point of the Bush presidency.

YET BUSH APPEARED TO BE NEGLECTING the domestic side of his job. As the recession deepened, he seemed powerless to stop it and insensitive to both the pain that middle-class families were suffering and the profound sense of economic uncertainty that was spreading across the country. Bush's popularity was dropping, and even Republican conservatives were upset because the president had broken a campaign promise by agreeing to raise taxes in order to reduce the mushrooming federal deficit. The signs of political trouble were everywhere.

Returning from a disappointing trip to Japan in January 1992, an unsettled Bush decided to discuss the upcoming reelection campaign with Robert Teeter, his chief campaign strategist, and Sam Skinner, his new White House chief of staff. He hadn't been paying much attention to his political team, assuming that his strategists were doing their jobs and would figure out how to win.

As he took a seat in the senior-staff compartment, Bush was in a sour mood—with good reason. Teeter's plan to bring corporate executives along on the trip had backfired; the businessmen had bad-mouthed the president's economic policies at nearly every stop. Worse, Bush had gotten some extraordinarily bad publicity when he contracted stomach flu and vomited in the lap of the Japanese prime minister at a dinner. The embarrassing photos had been carried in the news media around the world.

Bush said he hoped an upcoming trip to New Hampshire, site of the first presidential primary in just a few weeks, would start to turn things around. Yet polls showed that he might lose this first test.

"Where do we go from here?" Bush asked.

Teeter, a pollster by profession, and Skinner, a former businessman, disagreed about what to do. As Bush fumed silently, they squirmed in their first-class seats and blamed each other for the president's sagging political fortunes. They couldn't agree on who was responsible for what, and neither seemed willing or able to take charge. As things got tense and their voices rose, Bush bit his lip and frowned—then walked out in a huff and closed the door behind him as he entered his private cabin.

When word of the disarray got around to other Bush strategists about how neither Teeter nor Skinner wanted to take responsibility for the campaign's problems—and Skinner in particular didn't know what role he was supposed to play—there was shock and dismay. A senior Bush adviser said, "All I could think of was, it's over. How can we possibly run an election with these two guys not liking each other and not being able to work together and neither one wanting to be responsible? It was the damnedest thing in my mind. I'd heard of people fighting for power, but here were these two guys fighting *not* to be in charge."

AS CRITICISM OF his distance from everyday Americans intensified, Bush's façade of good cheer began to crack. On a trip to Cartagena, Colombia, he was still fuming at a fresh round of attacks in that morning's newspapers as *Air Force One* left Washington. "I think we've had too many press conferences," Bush peevishly told the traveling reporters. "I'm not going to be burned for holding out or doing something deceptive." He refused to answer even the most benign questions, such as whether he had slept well the night before. "I can't go into the details of that," he said sharply, "because some will think it's too much sleep and some will think it's too little."

Actually, Bush was under even more pressure than his critics knew. He had been told that terrorists in Colombia had placed a $30 million bounty on his head, and his Secret Service team was very worried about security. Chief flight steward John Haigh was so concerned that he wrote out his last will and testament that morning before departing, had a friend witness it, and left it in a desk drawer. When *Air Force One* landed, Haigh stood on the tarmac with Bush's garment bag, as was his custom, and looked around nervously. "I felt like a turkey in a turkey shoot," he said. "I thought they might make me the example." However, the trip went off without incident.

TOWARD THE END of his 1992 campaign, Bush increasingly occupied something of a dream world, reinforced by his isolation on *Air Force One*. On a trip to Atlanta, he needed instruction from one of his few African-American aides on the proper terminology for referring to black people. She told him the preferred usage was African American, and he dutifully used that term in his speech later that day.

The isolation was infectious. During a flight to Maine for a family event after the president had deftly helped thwart an attempted coup in the Soviet Union, there was gloating on the plane. "Do you think the American people are going to turn to a *Democrat* now?" said George W. Bush, the president's eldest son.

Of course, that's exactly what they did in November.

THE SUNDAY NIGHT before the balloting, Bush was flying from Louisiana to Houston for his final rally in an atmosphere of denial. The polls showed him losing the race to Bill Clinton, but the die-hard Bush staffers on *Air Force One* couldn't admit it to themselves. Bush sat in the conference room with a handful of loyal advisers, including George W. Bush, press officer Mary Matalin, and old friend Ron Kaufman. "The polls were not encouraging," Kaufman recalls, "but we had believed that in the end the country would not vote for what Mary Matalin called that draft-dodging, philandering son of a bitch."

The Oak Ridge Boys, a popular Country and Western band, were aboard the plane, and they began singing a medley of gospel songs, ending with "Amazing Grace." Suddenly, it hit everyone, except the president, that the race, and the Bush administration, were about to end. "We were all crying," Kaufman says. "No one said it, but we had the feeling, it's over. It was a very poignant, bitter-sweet moment."

Recalls George W. Bush: "I think a lot of us felt in our guts that he was going to get beat. . . . There were just a lot of tears in people's eyes. . . . People just knew that this good man was fixing to go down to defeat."

January 20, 1993, was Bush's last day in the White House, and his final flight on the presidential plane was a sad one, as it is for all defeated presidents. He recalls being "emotionally drained" and "a little bruised" that day, and describes the routine details of his final flight with vivid precision: how Ranger and Millie, his two dogs, bounded up the stairs, scrambled left into the first couple's bedroom, and jumped into the president's bed, where they liked to sleep. How the crew was gracious to the end. How he tried to say thanks to friends on board but choked up. How he considered taking a final shower on the plane but was too depressed for such a symbolic gesture.

"Barbara and I sat at our bedroom desk, across from each other, each of us lost in our own thoughts," Bush says. "We looked at each other, but we didn't speak much. Ours had been a wonderful chance to serve, a wonderful opportunity. I hope history will show I did some things right, but on that flight I kept thinking of where I had let good people down—of how I had lost the presidency three months before."

CHAPTER ELEVEN

BILL CLINTON: THE BABY BOOMER

WILLIAM JEFFERSON CLINTON TOOK office in January 1993 promising to be a combination of Franklin Roosevelt and John Kennedy. Eight years later, after he was impeached by the House of Representatives for lying about his affair with former intern Monica Lewinsky, he seemed more a combination of Hugh Hefner, founder of the *Playboy* empire, and Otter, the charming but irresponsible fraternity boy in the movie *Animal House*. His presidency was a roller-coaster ride of ups and downs. He was by turns brilliant and reckless, endearingly suave and occasionally vulgar, endlessly inquisitive and profoundly self-centered.

Clinton started out with big ideas and overreached, particularly with his hugely complex, government-centered health-care reform plan of 1993. He placed his wife, Hillary Rodham Clinton, in charge of formulating and winning approval for the package, and it died miserably on Capitol Hill. Partly as a reaction to the White House's display of political ineptitude and arrogance, the voters in 1994 gave Republicans control of Congress for the first time in a generation.

This forced Clinton from the left to the political center, where the country wanted him to be, and the GOP made him look even more moderate by shifting to the hard right. He went on to easily win a second term in 1996 by adopting centrist policies, such as balancing the budget, fighting crime, and promoting free trade. The economy boomed. Thanks in part to his conservative predecessors who helped to vanquish the Soviet Union, the United States emerged as the lone superpower. His job-approval ratings among voters soared. Yet Clinton's undisciplined character became his tragic flaw.

For years there had been accusations that he was an adulterer but he always denied it. Yet he committed a remarkable act of stupidity by having an affair with Lewinsky, a talkative and immature admirer in the West Wing, at a time when his enemies were looking for as much dirt about him as they could find. Through this self-indulgence, he handed them a potentially lethal issue. Independent Counsel Kenneth Starr issued a scathing report to Congress in late 1998, detailing Clinton's adulterous and deceptive conduct, and the House of Representatives impeached the president following a bitterly divisive debate. But the Senate acquitted him, deciding that impeachment by the House was enough punishment, and he remained in office. All this provided drama and controversy worthy of a TV sitcom, and Clinton continued to be an object of fascination even among his adversaries.

CLINTON'S BEHAVIOR ON *Air Force One* reflected all his positives and negatives, and there were abundant examples in each category because he was the most-traveled president in history. Over eight years, he flew a total of 1,409,090 miles. This was more than twice the mileage of the next most-traveled president, Ronald Reagan, who flew 675,640 miles during his eight years, according to records of the White House Military Office. Clinton made a total of 133 visits to foreign countries, averaging nearly 17 trips annually. During his two terms, in fact, Clinton made more foreign visits than Presidents Eisenhower, Kennedy, Johnson, and Nixon combined over the course of more than two decades. Clinton spent a total of 229 days in foreign countries, and his most extensive travel year was 1998, when he was trying to burnish his image to divert attention from the impeachment proceedings.

The only president to come close to Clinton's rate of foreign travel was

George Herbert Walker Bush, who loved foreign policy more than any other facet of the presidency. Bush made 60 visits to foreign countries in four years, but his rate of travel—15 trips per year—still fell short of his successor's 17.

Habitually late, Clinton would alternate frenetic activity with periods of wasted time. He preferred to leave on a lengthy trip in the evening and travel all night, during which he would chat with aides, read, play cards, watch movies, and cadge a few hours of sleep. He would arrive the next morning and go right to his official schedule. This pattern guaranteed that he and the staff would arrive at nearly every destination bleary-eyed.

"The problem was that it didn't matter really how much or how little sleep he got at night," says a longtime aide. "He was always tired in the morning and wide awake at night. His body just took half a day to wake up." He would swallow a sleeping pill or two so he could nap for five-hour blocs, a technique he coordinated with his staff and White House doctors. Even that couldn't break the pattern.

As a result, Clinton considered *Air Force One* the perfect venue for all-night bull sessions—monologues, really, rather than LBJ-style harangues. He would exhaust members of his staff, who felt obliged to listen to his tales about the leaders he had just met, the places he had seen, the issues that were on his mind, and anything else that struck his fancy. One topic, especially with his closest confidants, was women, who always seemed eager to get near him, trying to shake his hand, hug him, wave at him, and otherwise capture his attention. And as he traveled, he would sometimes regale aides and friends with a review of the female sights he had seen in receiving lines, in crowds, or in welcoming committees, according to some of his traveling companions.

He occasionally let his volcanic temper erupt on the plane, although the tantrums passed quickly. En route to Chicago in mid-1993, Clinton noticed in his briefing book that his aides had nixed a visit with Mayor Richard M. Daley, who had wanted to see him. "Who the hell could make such a dumb fucking mistake?" the president yelled. His rage built on itself, and some of his aides thought he might even get violent. "Why are we not organized to do this?" shouted Clinton, his face beet red. He complained that he was constantly over-scheduled and was getting bogged down in trivia, while the really important people were given short shrift. But his anger dissipated in a few minutes after the meeting with Daley was hastily arranged by phone from the plane.

In this case, Clinton was correct on the substance. Someone *had* made a stupid mistake by failing to set up the meeting with Chicago's most powerful politician, and the Clinton White House *was* chaotic. But these larger issues were ignored as soon as the president calmed down. It became business as usual.

"There is a certain sort of camaraderie that happens on the plane that leads you to unburden yourself, and I often did that," Clinton told me in a September 2002 interview. ". . . And there's a certain way that people feel freer to say whatever it is they're thinking when you're on that plane. . . . It was like a safe community. . . . I just had a lot of really, really good conversations that spanned the gamut from what I thought about the players in a given peace process or a conflict to various things about our kids."

His mood ranged from grand highs to extreme lows. A pet peeve on foreign trips was that his staff would trap him in hours of official meetings when they knew he wanted to participate in events with everyday people or visit cultural sites. He loved museums and historic places, from the Louvre in Paris to the pyramids outside Mexico City, and public markets. "We just spent seven hours in a hotel room," he once shouted while in Europe. "I could have been in Kansas City!"

"Partly, it was because of his curiosity," says Sandy Berger, his national security adviser, "partly it was his instinct that appreciating the culture of the place to which you are going is a sign of respect, and he always wanted to do that."

CLINTON AND HIS TEAM came into office with many lessons to learn. They initially disdained the military, partly because many of them had been antiwar activists in their younger days and few of them had any direct experience with life in the armed forces. "I believe that when they first came in office that the staff looked at the career military as people who couldn't get jobs on the outside," says Howie Franklin, a career Air Force noncommissioned officer who rose to chief steward on *Air Force One*. ". . . But I saw them change their minds and realize that the professional military person was indeed a professional. The Navy's running the White House. The Air Force is running *Air Force One*. The Marine Corps is running *Marine One*. We were the only guys in town who did what we said we were going to do."

ONE OF THE MOST embarrassing episodes of his first few months was the "Haircut Incident." In his motorcade back to the airport after a busy day in Los Angeles, Clinton decided he wanted a haircut from Christophe, the LA-based stylist to Hollywood stars who had also become the president's favorite "barber." Aides hastily arranged for the stylist to do the trim aboard the plane, which sat idling on the tarmac while Christophe worked his magic. This postponed *Air Force One*'s departure. Clinton later said he asked his aides if this would disrupt air traffic, and they said no.

"I think the pilot assured him that it would not be a problem when indeed it obviously was," said Mack McLarty, then White House chief of staff. "So I think he was probably innocent in terms of intending to inconvenience others, and very, very naïve. But you do rely on what people tell you." McLarty added that Clinton had made only about a dozen *Air Force One* trips at that point, so he and his staff were still rookies.

When word reached the media, hell broke loose. It turned out that one of Christophe's haircuts cost an estimated $200, contradicting Clinton's self-styled image as a populist. And even though his aides insisted that air traffic was not delayed, other sources said some commercial planes were indeed held up for at least a few minutes. In any case, given the extraordinary security surrounding *Air Force One*, there was always a good chance that everyday citizens would be inconvenienced, and Clinton should have known better.

"The perception was more powerful than the reality, and the underlying truth—that Clinton had been self-indulgent and insensitive to the image of having a Hollywood hairstylist cut his hair on a busy airport runway, and that his staff had been too stupid to stop it from happening—was bad enough," said senior Clinton adviser George Stephanopoulos. "The controversy also created new leads for the press, such as, Did the President pay for his pricey haircuts?

Finances were Hillary's department, and her staff said I was supposed to tell reporters that the Clintons had a 'personal services' contract with Christophe. *Oh, that'll help*. Naturally, they wanted to see the contract, which nobody would give me—because it probably didn't exist."

When the new administration fired seven key members of the White House Travel Office for alleged accounting irregularities a short time later, on May 19, things got worse. These people had been responsible for taking care of the media on the road, and they were popular with the press corps. Now it appeared that Clinton cronies, including his distant cousin Catherine Cornelius and his entertainment-industry pal Harry Thomason, were maneuvering to take over the operation. Suddenly it looked like Clinton not only was a hypocrite but had declared war on the press.

The furor eventually died down, but at considerable cost to the president's image. From then on, Clinton and his staff tried to think very seriously about everything they did on the plane, to avoid more embarrassments.

TIME AND AGAIN, CLINTON used *Air Force One* to decompress after pressure-packed events. At the end of long trips, he would venture into the staff compartments, wearing jeans and a T-shirt, an unlit cigar clamped between his teeth, with his eyeglasses perched at the end of his nose, and ask who was available to play a game of hearts, to chat, or to watch a movie. Gene Sperling, his chief White House economic adviser, compared it to college kids after exams—a sort of "after-finals release."

This sense of decompression prevailed after his first meeting as president with the blustery Russian leader Boris Yeltsin in Vancouver, Canada. At first the two men didn't get along, largely because Yeltsin felt that Clinton was too young and inexperienced. "He just wasn't sure that this young president was his equal, and it showed in their general demeanor and exchange," recalls Mack McLarty. With one day left in their summit, McLarty got together with Russian officials and said surely something could be done to build rapport; there were too many important issues to resolve. The Russians apparently agreed, because the next morning Yeltsin greeted Clinton with a big grin and handshake. "I am ready to get down to business, Beel," he said. It was the first time he had called his American counterpart by his first name, and the ice was broken.

Just after *Air Force One* took off and headed home, Clinton summoned McLarty into his cabin. "Mack," the president said, "I think I'm really beginning to establish relationships with these other world leaders." McLarty was less impressed. "You're gaining ground, but you have some more ground to gain," the chief of staff ventured. They chatted for 20 minutes, during which Clinton expressed intense pleasure that he had made the grade, at least in his own mind. Then Clinton shut the discussion down. "That's it," he said. "I'm exhausted and I've got to go to sleep." McLarty left.

That wasn't the end of the episode. McLarty took his chair next to Secretary of State Warren Christopher in the senior-staff compartment. They ate dinner and each drank a glass of wine, whereupon Christopher fell asleep. By this time it was almost midnight. Then the phone calls began arriving from U.S. officials, who were very upset. It turned out that some of the young president's off-the-cuff comments to Yeltsin had been translated by local journalists from transcripts made by Russian note-takers; they found that Clinton had made disparaging comments about the Japanese. "You know, sometimes when the Japanese say yes, they really mean no, and vice versa," Clinton had said.

The story was being spread by the news media, and McLarty woke Christopher up to contain the damage. The secretary of state spent 45 minutes making calls to senior Japanese officials to smooth things over. The officials were quite understanding, and McLarty knocked on the president's door, entered the cabin, and told him about the ruckus and how it had been "finessed." Clinton's reaction: "I didn't mean it offensively."

Clearly, the new president's earlier self-satisfaction had been misplaced. He had a lot to learn about diplomacy.

THE CLINTON TRAITS of brilliance, curiosity, and a willingness to make excuses for himself were on constant display during his airborne adventures. On a long flight in late 1994, after his Democratic party had lost control of Congress, Clinton admitted he was hurt but tried to put it all into perspective. Some of those who listened to him believed he was trying not only to persuade them that things weren't as bad as they seemed, but to convince himself that he wasn't the first president to screw up.

He launched into a monologue, several hours long, in which he discussed every president from Lincoln to George Herbert Walker Bush, analyzing what they and their Cabinet officers had done right and wrong. "People were just sort of stupefied by it, both by his knowledge, but also just by his desire to talk," says David Gergen, a senior adviser to Clinton at the time. "He was nursing the wounds of that defeat in '94. It was quite an extraordinary performance. . . . You see those sometimes on these planes. You get a revelation. On the road, on the plane, you get a chance to see a president in a very different way. For many people on the staff there was an intimacy that you didn't get in the White House."

Clinton would take "decision memos" aboard the plane—memoranda asking him to check off "approved" or "disapproved" on legislation, regulations, appointments, and other matters. He enjoyed ticking off the appropriate boxes and piling up the forms as evidence of his productivity. At other times, he would work on speeches, rewriting passages in his left-handed "curl." One could never tell when he would abruptly dismiss aides from his private cabin so he could fall asleep, usually within a few seconds, only to wake from his catnap an hour later and call in advisers for more policy discussions.

Some of his White House aides had a name for the late-night president: "Clinton unplugged." He looked at *Air Force One* as a haven where he could operate on his own schedule and in his own manner. Clinton's wandering eye was a constant fact of life. Nina Burleigh, who covered the White House for *Time* magazine, related an incident in 1997 when he admired her legs on *Air Force One*. Writing in *Mirabella* magazine about Clinton's sexual allure, Burleigh said it happened when she was playing hearts in the front cabin with the president and his longtime confidant Bruce Lindsey. "The president's foot lightly, and presumably accidentally, brushed mine once under the table," she said. "His hand touched my wrist while he was dealing the cards. When I got up and shook his hand at the end of the game, his eyes wandered over to my bike-wrecked, naked legs. And slowly it dawned on me as I walked away: He found me attractive."

She added: "No doubt the president's lawyers and spin doctors would say I wishfully imagined that long, appreciative look. But we all know when we're being ogled." In a remarkable admission for a journalist, she said she enjoyed the attention and added, "I'd be happy to give him [oral sex] just to thank him for keeping abortion legal." Apparently, nothing ever came of the incident.

But when Clinton let his guard down at such moments, particularly during his lengthy card games, he revealed himself as he rarely did anywhere else. One of his card-playing buddies said the president wanted to shed his official responsibilities at those times, and be one of the boys, talking about sports, movies, women, and other politicians. And he encouraged good-natured banter. Analyzing an upcoming college basketball game on one flight, an aide heard Clinton pick the University of Arkansas to win and blurted out, "You must be crazy." Clinton didn't miss a beat, and argued his case with renewed vigor. "One of his most important traits as president was to let aides disagree with him to his face on policy issues," says the aide. "And in this case, what he wanted at that moment was not three subservient staffers around him but three friends. He wanted to have a few people to relax with. The president is a human being."

WHEN HILLARY WAS aboard, Clinton would spend much of his time with her, talking policy or reading quietly, and he was generally subdued. His time with Chelsea, his teenaged daughter, provided special moments for both of them.

"When Chelsea was there, you almost didn't want to enter his cabin," recalls Gene Sperling, the chief White House economics adviser who briefed the president often on the plane. He recalled many cases of the two sitting next to each other, reading, or Chelsea sitting on a table with her arm around her dad as they chatted amiably. "They both seemed so happy and serene and proud," Sperling added.

But when neither Hillary nor Chelsea was aboard, the atmosphere changed. Clinton's *Air Force One* became a fun house, especially late at night. Clad in a T-shirt and jeans, the middle-aged president would sometimes hang out with his twentysomething aides, including, over the years, Josh King, Kris Engskov, Steve Gooden, Jeremy Gaines, and Andrew Friendly.

Frequent fliers described the conference room as a sort of recreation center and town hall. The president liked to sit at one end of a long rectangular table where he would hold forth, play cards, or watch a movie—sometimes all three at once, in addition to working out a crossword puzzle. Meanwhile, some of his staffers would be watching the movie or reading at the other end of the table. Often, exhausted aides would be sleeping on one or both of the two long couches at the sides of the room.

One of the young staffers told me: "People like myself would let him regress a little bit. He could get far away from the policy people who would come in and out of his office in the White House. This was his basic chill-out time with young guys, sort of a university crowd. He could get rid of the cares of the world because we could always be relied on to talk about movies, TV shows, and sports. I got my closest exposure to him in that setting as opposed to the White House. I would sit with the president in jeans and a sweatshirt, and certainly very few of the public and very few of the White House staff ever saw that. You heard droplets of conversation, things that he might have said to Chelsea in the living quarters; 'I feel good' . . . 'I gotta lose a couple of pounds.' . . . 'That was a great golf game but I'm still slicing it.'"

The staff mostly listened, and that was the point.

Clinton loved to keep track of popular culture, especially through movies, even ones that had no redeeming social value. Realizing this, before many long trips, aide Josh King would select 15 or more films from his own collection or bring along classics that he rented at a video store, to supplement the list available on board. The president loved the extra options.

He preferred that aides acquire first-run films without having them censored "for airline use," as his predecessors had done. He wanted to enjoy the bawdy scenes.

Aides would regularly approach the president's cabin and hear him laughing uproariously at a film the critics had ripped apart. He enjoyed what aides called cheap-thrills movies, like *Die Hard* and various Arnold Schwarzenegger flicks. It was mindless entertainment that let him forget his official duties for a while.

Sometimes policy making and show business intersected. En route to

Cologne for a series of meetings with other world leaders, Clinton called Sperling into his office. He asked if the United States was doing enough to help Third World nations reduce their financial debts. It turned out that Bono, the Irish rock star, had sent Clinton a number of letters urging him to endorse debt relief, and Clinton wanted more information. After Sperling's briefing, Clinton was satisfied that his administration was doing as much as it could.

And there were times, however few, when the president schmoozed with the reporters in the rear cabin. As often as not, this tended to backfire when he got too candid or theoretical. On September 22, 1995, as he leaned against a bulkhead in the press compartment, he regaled the journalists with a lengthy monologue about the condition of society, and he said Americans appeared to be in a "funk." This produced a round of stories comparing his remarks to Jimmy Carter's infamous speech declaring that the nation was in a malaise. Like Carter, he seemed to be blaming the voters for his own failures.

SOME CLINTON loyalists weren't always happy with his let-it-all-hang-out approach, including Harold Ickes. As deputy chief of staff, Ickes was a tough-minded New York liberal, but he also had a traditional side. He was, after all, the son of former Interior Secretary and FDR confidant Harold Ickes, who was a stern authority figure.

"It was like being at home with the president," Ickes recalls. ". . . I had the feeling once you got in the environment of *Air Force One* there was a different set of rules. There was much more informality. You did not have to worry about the pesky Fourth Estate lurking around the background. You didn't have to worry about them snapping a picture of your mouth gaping or something like that. But it was Clinton's attitude that lent itself to this. I thought that the White House staff was too informal around Bill Clinton. It bothered me. I always made a habit that when he came into a room I would stand up. Most of the staff never bothered to stand up when the president of the United States walked in, and that used to piss me off—seeing George [Stephanopoulos, a senior adviser] sitting there with his fucking feet on the table and [he] would sit that way when Bill

Clinton would come in and sit down. But part of that is Clinton, because he is so informal . . . almost, I think, unpresidential in some sense."

Leon Panetta, who was one of Clinton's chiefs of staff, agreed. He said the atmosphere on the plane was too much like a "private club," especially at the end of long trips when aides would "really let their hair down." Some would drink too much, some would play music too loud, some would get too raucous; and the staff would sometimes leave the cabins a mess.

"I would be offended because some of the staff people would treat it as just another plane," Panetta said. "I would have to pull some of the staff people aside and say, 'Look, dammit, this is the presidency of the United States and you've got to behave that way." His advice was simple: Everything that happens in the White House or on the plane has the potential to appear on the front page of *The Washington Post* or *The New York Times*, and everyone had to behave accordingly.

Panetta had another concern, a familiar one over the years of *Air Force One* travel. "When I first became chief of staff, what I found was that staff were climbing on *Air Force One* that frankly didn't have much business being on board. Everybody was able, one way or another, to kind of wheedle through it. So one of the first things we decided was that we had to get very disciplined about who would or who would not go."

CLINTON GENERALLY MANAGED to compartmentalize his life and focus his energies where he had to, but he found it difficult to pace himself. When his mother died during his first term, Clinton attended the funeral in Arkansas, then left for a long-scheduled trip to Moscow even though he was understandably distraught. He also had to cope with the presence aboard *Air Force One* of *Nightline* host Ted Koppel and a film crew, as they prepared a story on the making of a superpower summit.

Clinton talked to Koppel, discussed the Moscow trip in detail with his staff, read a variety of memos designed to prepare him for the visit, and then, as the plane soared over northern Europe, went to his private cabin for some sleep.

He had been resting for two and a half hours when chief steward Howie

Franklin slipped into his room. No one else on the staff had the nerve to be the designated "wake-up" caller. Franklin knew the room's layout by heart, so he walked softly through the darkness to the president's motionless form. "I go in and lean on him," Franklin recalls, "and he kind of moaned a little bit—I'm standing over the top of him and he's nuzzled down underneath these covers. It's about three o'clock in the morning body time. And I said, 'Sir, I sure hate to do this.' "

Clinton snapped, "Well, don't do it."

Franklin knew the president well enough to resort to good-old-boy language. "Sir," he said firmly, "it's time to get your butt up and go to work."

The president rolled slowly out of bed, and Hillary suddenly came awake in the other bed. "Hillary's peeking out of the covers with a semi 'Oh dear' look on her face," Franklin recalls. The steward announced firmly that the couple had 90 minutes to get ready before they had to face the Russians and the news media in Moscow.

It didn't end there. Clinton, as with most presidents, had a valet to pack his clothes but the valet was on a backup plane on this particular trip. Franklin was designated to rummage through the president's wardrobe to find a specific tie and shoes that Clinton wanted to wear. After the president and the First Lady took showers, he settled on his clothes at the very last minute.

In 1996, Clinton scheduled a two-day trip to Colorado Springs and Billings, Montana, that started at 7 A.M. when Clinton and his senior aides met at the White House Diplomatic Room for a brief discussion of the itinerary. He showed up on time but was extremely grumpy. As everyone knew, he hated early-morning events, and it turned out that he had been up late again the night before, reading and watching TV, so little was accomplished at the briefing.

After the 10-minute *Marine One* flight to Andrews, Clinton bounded up the stairs of *Air Force One*, entered his private cabin, and kept to himself for the outbound trip. Upon arrival, he spoke at the Air Force Academy, shook 2,600 hands, and met with federal workers. Flying from Colorado Springs to Billings, he took a nap and fell into a deep sleep. This time it was Ickes's turn to rouse him, and, wanting to give his boss as much rest as he could, entered the cabin as the plane was making its descent. "Mr. President, we're starting to land," Ickes whispered.

Clinton groggily asked for a quick summary of what was coming up, and Ickes told him he had to give a speech—and the event was only six minutes from the airport. The president had been hoping to make some final revisions in his text during the limousine ride, and now he realized there wouldn't be enough time. "Jesus Christ," Clinton fumed, "why didn't you get me up earlier?"

Ickes sputtered that he knew the president was tired, and an angry Clinton sent him away. After hurriedly getting dressed, Clinton kept his arrival hosts waiting for 15 minutes as he reviewed his speech before disembarking. Following the address in a sweltering gym, he met with Native American leaders, had dinner with former governors and policy experts on Western issues, and held a few other private meetings.

After spending the night in Billings, Clinton attended a breakfast meeting the next morning, visited two ranches, held an outdoor roundtable discussion of regional concerns, played golf, was briefed again on local issues by his staff, held another roundtable, and concluded with a lengthy bout of hand shaking as a crowd lingered around him.

By the time the White House group climbed aboard *Air Force One* late that day, everyone was exhausted except Clinton. As one staffer after another nodded off, he appeared in the doorway to the conference room in jeans and a T-shirt and asked the dreaded question: "Who wants to play hearts?"

His longtime confidant Bruce Lindsey and Roy Romer, then governor of Colorado, dutifully agreed. When Ickes returned from a nap three hours later, as the plane descended into the Washington area, Clinton was analyzing his partners' hands and giving them tips on how to improve their games. Clinton insisted on playing one more hand before disembarking, played still another hand on *Marine One*, and got to the White House at 2 A.M., wide awake.

CLINTON WAS AN INVETERATE shopper and gift buyer. On his many trips to foreign cities, he would insist on going to a market or a commercial zone, where he would enter one shop after another looking for prizes he could take home. (He would pay in cash or an aide would submit a credit card and get reimbursed later.)

At some point during nearly every foreign trip, his aides would gather up all the carefully wrapped presents and tchotchkes the president had acquired and unpack them aboard *Air Force One*. Clinton would proudly review each of his purchases for family members, friends, and staffers, and his aides felt obliged to compliment him on his taste and generosity.

Sometimes an adviser would show off his own purchases, and the president would get envious. One aide remembers him gazing longingly at an Uncle Sam carving.

"Is that mine?" the president said, half joking.

"No sir, that's my acquisition," an aide replied.

"Damn, I like that," Clinton said, and he went looking for something similar at the next stop.

OVER EIGHT YEARS of covering him, I got some revealing glimpses of Clinton aboard the plane.

En route to the funeral of assassinated Israeli leader Yitzhak Rabin, I was a member of the *Air Force One* press pool. At one point, I found myself in a small compartment in front of the press section writing a report and, when I finished, headed back to the press area. Suddenly I saw the president, wearing jeans and a sweatshirt, walking down the hall. He took me aside and, with tears in his eyes, told me of his broken heart at the death of the Israeli prime minister, whom he considered a mentor and a historic peacemaker. "Thanks for being here," he said. "He was a great man."

White House Chief of Staff Panetta, who was on the trip, said: "Not only did he develop a close professional relationship with Rabin, but more importantly, he recognized that Rabin was a powerful force that brought about the agreements that we were able to achieve in the Middle East. . . . It was President Clinton's nature to really feel the sense of loss from things like that. He was deeply moved by not only the consequences of that death but what it meant for the future, and that's what concerned him more than anything."

Chief steward Tim Kerwin also had a private moment with the grieving president during that trip. At about 2 A.M., Kerwin entered the front galley from a dimly lit corridor where staff members were sleeping, and, a few seconds later, was joined by the president. Clinton sat down and began quoting Bible verses, explaining that it would be next to impossible to understand "where these people are coming from" if one wasn't familiar with Old Testament accounts of how the Israelites were expelled by the Pharaoh, and how the Palestinians have their own traditional stake in the land claimed by Israel today.

This was the same trip during which House Speaker Newt Gingrich, Clinton's Republican nemesis, got himself into hot water by complaining that the Clintonites made him leave the plane through the rear exit instead of the front door. Feeling snubbed, Gingrich said he was so upset that he might even prolong a government shutdown that was brewing in a dispute over the funding of Clinton's policies. Gingrich was pilloried in the media, portrayed as a spoiled brat and a crybaby.

ON A RETURN TRIP from Australia, I found myself the only journalist still awake in the press compartment in the wee hours. I walked to the galley for a soda, and stood in the aisle sipping it and stretching my legs when I heard that distinctive, raspy voice.

"Hey, man, how you doin'?" said the president, standing a foot away. He had eluded or exhausted his handlers and was getting himself a soft drink, obviously wide awake and eager to chat.

I had a decision to make: Let him talk one-on-one, or wake up my fellow reporters, which would destroy the spontaneity of the situation and maybe even chase the president back up front. So I opted to let everyone sleep and go with the flow. Clinton proceeded to chitchat for 15 minutes. There was nothing earthshaking (I later briefed the other journalists about what he had said), but his musings provided fascinating insight into his natural curiosity. He talked about holding koalas, of cradling baby kangaroos, of the rain forests, and the deserts of Australia. He gave a detailed explanation of the ecology of the Great Barrier Reef, then effused about how he had gone snorkeling the previous afternoon. "I swam over a giant clam," he said. "It was huge!"

· · ·

"WE HAD QUITE a lot of eventful decisions that had to be made on *Air Force One*," Clinton told me in a recent interview.

In May 1995, he was flying to Ukraine, a former Soviet republic, and was told of a serious security threat. Russian intelligence had passed along to the CIA word that rebels in the region were well armed, possibly with handheld missiles, and might make an attempt on the president's life. The threat had been confirmed by the CIA. The question was whether Clinton should cancel his scheduled visit to Babi Yar, site of a mass grave where the Nazis had buried 100,000 of their murder victims, many of them Jewish, during World War II.

Clinton talked about it at great length, and decided to take the chance. The outdoor event went off without a hitch, but several senior staffers who had participated in the final discussion aboard *Air Force One* were jumpy. Every time something crunched under foot, McLarty, wearing big galoshes to prevent him from slipping on the pathway, would look up suddenly, expecting to see an incoming missile.

EVEN MORE HARROWING was Clinton's trip to Islamabad, Pakistan, in March 2000. For weeks prior to departure, the Secret Service warned the White House that the situation would be extremely dangerous. The early plan was for Clinton to leave India for a quick trip to the Pakistani capital to meet with General Pervez Musharraf, the country's ruler. As U.S. intelligence picked up more and more signs of a possible attack against the president, the Secret Service finally recommended in the strongest terms that the visit be scrapped. "They were really freaked out," recalls Sandy Berger, Clinton's national security adviser. ". . . They were adamant about not going to Islamabad."

But Berger and other foreign-policy specialists felt that meeting with Musharraf would be valuable. For one thing, every American president was expected to visit Pakistan for every time he visited India, its traditional rival. Second, there were important issues to discuss, from nuclear nonproliferation to India-Pakistan relations to Pakistan's role in fighting terrorism. Finally, no one wanted the public to think the president was afraid to travel.

Secret Service officials persisted, arguing that there were many terrorists in and around Pakistan, including operatives of al Qaeda and Osama bin Laden (who would later orchestrate the attacks of September 11, 2001). They would like nothing better than to knock a president from the sky. The landing and takeoff at the Islamabad airport would be especially perilous because terrorists could hide in the surrounding hills and fire at *Air Force One* with handheld, ground-to-air missiles. The Secret Service also expressed grave doubts about trusting the Pakistani military with secret information about the president's itinerary and the plans to protect him. "The threat was not abstract," Berger recalls. "It was real intelligence. It was the only time that I really thought during the eight years (of Clinton's presidency) that something might happen." At one point, a senior agent said he would resign if the president went to Pakistan. (He would later relent.)

At a final Oval Office meeting with Berger, Secret Service leaders, and other U.S. officials, all the arguments were presented again. The Secret Service's chief representative said, "We cannot guarantee that we can protect you in this environment. Ultimately, it's your decision."

Clinton looked at his foreign-policy advisers and paused. Then, in a rare case of a president overruling the Secret Service, he announced that the reasons for going outweighed the risks, and he would make the trip. He said he was glad his wife, Hillary, would not be on the journey but realized his daughter, Chelsea, would be accompanying him. "We'll go," the president said. "But I don't want Chelsea to be on this leg."

Then he turned to his national security adviser. "Okay, Berger," he joked. "You think this is such a good idea, you're coming with me." Berger smiled weakly.

Departing from India, the Americans used a ruse to confuse would-be attackers. The original plan was to have two cargo planes on the tarmac in Bombay before departure to Pakistan. The president was to board one of them, then walk out a different door, and board a smaller C20 corporate-style jet holding 20 passengers. But this plan was scrapped when White House Press Secretary Joe Lockhart pointed out that since the press contingent was to travel on one of those cargo planes, it might look as if the media were being used as a decoy.

What actually happened was that Clinton walked to the door of one military cargo jet and shook hands with well-wishers but never got on. He hustled around the front of the plane to board an unmarked, white Air Force C20, out of sight of reporters and spectators. As an added precaution, several other decoy planes made the flight. The hour-long trip was nerve-wracking; the Americans used gallows humor to relieve the tension, asking each other if their life insurance was paid up. But since the exact time and place of the president's arrival were not known to the Pakistanis, the Secret Service thought they had surprise on their side. Still, the pilot zoomed from 10,000 feet to the tarmac in 12 seconds, to avoid being an easy target.

The press contingent aboard its cargo plane had more of a problem than the journalists ever knew. U.S. military spotters thought they saw a flash on the ground—possibly evidence of a ground-to-air missile that had just been launched. This was immediately relayed to the pilot, who released "countermeasures"—airborne decoys designed to divert incoming missiles. To this day, no one can be sure what was actually seen, possibly the sun glinting off a metal surface in a field below the cargo plane. But no one was taking any chances that day.

The president's departure from Islamabad a few hours later was the next challenge. By that point, it was clear where Clinton was, and his takeoff route could be easily predicted. Once the American party was aboard, they were told to immediately take their seats and, as they strapped themselves in, the jet began gaining speed along the runway. "It felt like we were going straight up in the air," says Berger. "We went, *foof!* and you could actually feel the pressure and the force on your body."

After a few seconds, the small cabin filled with relieved chatter. As the plane left Pakistan air space, Berger called Larry Cockrell, chief of the president's Secret Service detail who was still on the ground, and said, "We're out of Pakistan, Larry. You can get out of the bathroom." Cockrell laughed, not so much at Berger's joke but because the ordeal was over.

Clinton later told me: "That's the only time I really thought we were, based on the intelligence I'd seen, at some significant risk. But I had no question that I should be doing it. The only thing I hated was putting those pilots and other aides [at risk]—you know, people that served us, that worked in the mess, and my young staff members, I didn't like the idea. I just wished that somehow that I could have magically gone by myself."

Such a thing is never possible for the commander in chief.

A PARTICULARLY REVEALING moment was Clinton's decision to send armed federal agents to seize a 6-year-old Cuban refugee named Elian Gonzalez from his relatives in Miami. The boy had left Cuba with his mother in a desperate seaborne escape attempt that ended in the mother's death. But Elian was taken in by relatives in Miami, and a dramatic legal struggle ensued when his father in Cuba, who had been estranged from his mother, sued to win his return.

The struggle put the Clinton administration in a quandary. Clinton didn't want to alienate the politically powerful Cuban-American community in South Florida, which wanted Elian to remain with his American relatives. Opposition from Cuban Americans could cost Vice President Al Gore key support in Florida in the 2000 election. But at the same time, the law and common sense seemed to favor returning the boy to his father. Complicating matters was the fact that Attorney General Janet Reno, who would have to enforce whatever decision was made, was from Miami and hoped to run for governor of Florida.

Elian had been living with his Miami relatives for weeks when the issue reached the boiling point. The Clinton administration decided that, by law, he had to join his father back in Cuba, but his Miami relatives refused to surrender him. This produced fierce demonstrations and increasing pressure in Miami for a resolution that would keep the boy in the United States. "We were trying to find a time to get Reno and the president together," recalls former White House press secretary Joe Lockhart.

On April 5, 2000, en route to Washington after the dedication of a memorial for bombing victims in Oklahoma City, Chief of Staff John Podesta decided it was time to make the final decision.

Halfway home on *Air Force One*, Clinton asked Reno to come to his airborne office. Clinton was wearing his blue "commander in chief" windbreaker and he was playing a jazz CD. Reno walked somberly into the cabin and took a seat in the leather-upholstered chair across from the president's wraparound desk, to his left. Lockhart sat to Clinton's right. Deputy Chief of Staff Steve Ricchetti sat on the floor, a casual gesture he hoped would relax everyone.

But the tension was thick. Reno knew that she was expected to bring up the Elian case, and she did, in an unexpectedly emotional way. The laconic and usually stoic attorney general said she was torn about the case and after 10 minutes she started to weep. Twisting her gangly, 6-foot-1 frame in the chair uncomfortably, she talked about how wonderful Miami was, how many friends she still had there, and how much she wanted to move back after her time was up in Washington. Yet she said her friends were deeply split about what to do with the sweet-looking little boy from Cuba. "Things are so divided," Reno said amid sobs.

Having a Cabinet member break down was awkward enough. But Clinton never had a close relationship with Reno; far from it. He considered her too independent from the White House and altogether too unpredictable. Making things even more discomfiting was Clinton's hearing problem. Even though she had pushed her chair to the edge of the president's desk, her voice dropped to a whisper and more than once he had to ask her to repeat herself.

Clinton let her go on for another 10 minutes, then said quietly, "This must be hard for you." (He later told aides he wondered how he would have felt if he had been president during the school integration crisis in Little Rock, Arkansas, his hometown, a generation earlier. That would have torn him up, too, he said.) But now it was time to decide.

"We need to bring this to a conclusion," Clinton said, noting that the controversy over Elian had dragged on for too many weeks. "But," he added, "I have some concerns that this be done properly." He was worried that someone would get hurt in any raid to snatch the child from his relatives. But that seemed to be the better of the two choices available. The other was to keep negotiating even though all sides were hardening their positions. It quickly became clear that Clinton had lost patience with that approach because it was making him look vacillating and weak.

Reno agreed that a raid could be dangerous; intelligence sources said some people in the house where Elian was being held were armed. Clinton insisted, again, that it was time to act, and he told her to proceed with the raid. In fact, it was conducted efficiently and with no injuries, but it spawned even more criticism from Cuban Americans who said Clinton and Reno had betrayed the little boy. It also would hurt Vice President Al Gore's 2000 presidential campaign in Florida, quite possibly costing him the state and the White House. But the special atmosphere of *Air Force One* had helped bring everyone to the decision point.

"I can't imagine they would have had that conversation about Miami in the Oval Office," Lockhart told me later. "It wouldn't have seemed appropriate. There's an atmosphere somewhere between casualness and intimacy on that plane."

ANOTHER IMPORTANT DECISION on *Air Force One* was Clinton's order to bomb Iraq during the impeachment crisis in December 1998. En route home from a trip to Israel, Clinton considered an attack on Iraq because Saddam Hussein was again balking at allowing United Nations weapons inspections. "We knew there would be screaming about the decision," Lockhart recalls, because it could so easily be seen as an attempt to divert attention from the impeachment crisis and possibly sway votes in the House by showing that Clinton was an effective commander in chief.

About two hours after the start of the 12-hour flight, Clinton made the decision to strike. National Security Adviser Berger and Secretary of State Madeleine Albright sat with him in his office as he talked by secure phone to other members of his senior staff, including Gore and Defense Secretary Bill Cohen. Everyone recommended an attack.

White House adviser Doug Sosnik and Lockhart were sitting on the couches in the corridor outside the president's office when Berger emerged and told them that military action was approved. "Okay," he added, "how are we going to explain this?"

Lockhart replied, "It'll be tough, but if we don't strike Iraq because of the political situation, it'll be worse."

Sosnik agreed. As Lockhart recalled later, "Everybody came to the conclusion they were going to criticize us no matter what we did, so we ought to do what was right."

Hundreds of cruise missiles struck Baghdad on December 16, and the House, after delaying its final debate by one day, impeached Clinton December 19.

ON THE LIGHTER SIDE, Clinton's vanity would clearly emerge on the plane. He thought he looked cool in casual clothes, so he would wear jeans and a sweatshirt or T-shirt as often as he could. Trouble was, they made him look overweight and undignified, but the staff didn't have the heart to tell him.

As an aging baby boomer, he hated to admit that his hearing had faded over the years; he attributed it to listening to too much loud rock 'n' roll music in his youth. At first, his aides were perplexed that he preferred to make phone calls when he landed rather than on the plane, which seemed more convenient. Then they realized he simply couldn't hear phone conversations very well. The plane may have state-of-the-art acoustics, but it was still difficult for a hearing-impaired person like Clinton to pick up every word.

"The communications on the plane were terrible," says Sandy Berger. "It drove him crazy and it drove me crazy. There were secure 'coms' on the plane and there was always a backlog of calls involving foreign leaders, returning calls or making calls. . . . The phone system on *Air Force One* was so bad and the disconnect rate was so high that he would be truly embarrassed when he was on the phone with a foreign leader and it would be like when you get your cellphone and you hit a patch and suddenly you can't hear. Here was the president of the United States, leader of the greatest nation, and he can't make a phone connection!"

The problem, which remains today, is not with making regular phone calls from the plane, which can been done easily and with good quality. The problem comes with secure communications, which involve patching calls through encryption systems and scrambling devices. That takes time, and the quality of the connections is often primitive. In the end, White House aides agreed that the president was right to discourage important phone calls on the plane because this secure communications system, coupled with his hearing problem, could have easily caused serious misunderstandings.

Clinton also loved to play jazz and rock 'n' roll CDs in his private cabin. Among his favorite artists were B. B. King, Wynton Marsalis, and various gospel choirs. Trouble was, he didn't use earphones and just turned the music up to such a high volume that his aides would have trouble hearing him when they entered the compartment. He would do the same thing in the staff cabin when he played the card game of hearts. He liked to have the music blaring as he played hand after hand and held forth on one topic after another, always the center of attention. More than one staff member begged off from the card game with a headache.

"We never had a president who listened to a lot of music before Clinton," says former chief steward Howie Franklin. "But here's a musician [a longtime saxophone player] who comes along. And he wants to listen to music on a regular basis and we found out that if he listens to music in his stateroom [on the internal *Air Force One* sound system] you would have to listen to the same music that he's listening to in the back. . . . We're talking about rock 'n' roll, like the Four Tops, and sixties and seventies rock 'n' roll. . . . And he'd like to crank it up. So we went out and bought him a CD player that he could carry with him. And then he would listen to it in the stateroom and we had two of them so he could bring it off the airplane because that's how much he liked listening to music."

The stereotype was true that Clinton loved junk food, especially hamburgers and fries from McDonald's. But over time his eating habits changed, especially after he damaged his knee on March 14, 1997, in a fall at the Florida home of golfer Greg Norman. His doctor and physical therapist told him that such an injury often caused patients to stop exercising and gain weight. Since Clinton was already miffed at all the "fat jokes" told at his expense, he took their advice to work out on an exercise bike and cut down on calories. His meals on *Air Force One* improved: He often ate veggie burgers, salads, and roast chicken, all specially prepared in the senior-staff galley at midships. The rest of the passengers routinely ate more standard (and less nutritious) fare.

. . .

IN MANY WAYS, the end of the 1996 reelection campaign was the high point of Clinton's eight years on *Air Force One*.

For one thing, everyone at the White House seemed euphoric as it became increasingly clear that Clinton would be the first Democratic president since Franklin Roosevelt elected to a second term. The crowds were big and enthusiastic, and Clinton was enjoying himself immensely.

Mark Penn, Clinton's pollster and one of his senior political advisers, was on the plane for virtually every trip in the two months leading up to the election. "The days never ended," Penn told me. ". . . We'd try to hit as many cities as possible. The question was, how do you continue to do all your work when the plane would stop, everybody would get off, you'd load into a motorcade, go see 20,000 people, and get back on? The work part of the day was always the first part of the day, because you had to make sure you were clear on where the messages were, what the speech was going to be, what else was going to happen. . . .

"We were essentially the flying campaign. All of the media message decisions were really being made on the plane. . . . If you think of a typical day, maybe the president had done some exercise but essentially you'd have a speech prep in the morning on the plane and go through what the events were, what the messages were, what the policy issues were. Something else could be happening that day but you'd assume if you were traveling for an hour and a half, he might spend a half hour alone, a half hour on other business, and a half hour of campaign-related stuff . . . what [Republican challenger Bob] Dole's up to, what the overnight polls are showing, and what we need to do today."

Sometimes, the president and his brain trust would sit in the conference room or in his private office and watch suggested TV ads. He would accept or reject them on the spot, and sometimes make alterations. And within a 48-hour time span, sometimes less, the group would decide his itinerary for the next few days. "We could decide that we were going to show up in any community in America," Penn said. Local TV stations would track the plane for 20 minutes prior to its arrival, carrying the landing live. Clinton and his staff would frequently watch the coverage in his cabin.

On the last leg of the campaign—from a final rally in South Dakota to Little Rock, Arkansas—at about 2 A.M. Election Day, a party atmosphere prevailed. Clinton, surrounded by two dozen jubilant aides in the conference room, had changed into casual clothes, sat down at the head of the table, and started his customary card game. Suddenly, he turned to Penn and said jovially: "Okay, Mark, so what's going to be the final prediction?"

Penn, who had just reviewed his final polls, said Clinton would win with 49 percent to Dole's 41, and the remainder for liberal insurgent Ralph Nader and minor candidates. This turned out to be true, but it wasn't what Clinton wanted to hear. He had been eager to break the 50 percent mark so he would not go down in history as a "minority president." Disappointment flashed in the president's eyes, the room quieted down, and Clinton returned to his card game.

HIS SECOND TERM held the potential for some historic achievements, such as reform of Social Security and Medicare. But Clinton's personal appetites got the best of him.

Previous presidents had had their share of sexual liaisons, but the media kept them quiet. The media during Clinton's era had become more salacious and graphic, and his adversaries were bent on his political destruction—so his affair with former White House intern Monica Lewinsky almost led to his removal from office. Beyond that, his misbehavior and subsequent lies resulted in a squandered year of his presidency and a fiasco for the nation to endure. He was able to compartmentalize the scandal, and continued to work hard on policy issues, even if little was accomplished.

Air Force One provided a window on the sordid mess, particularly after Clinton was forced to admit his sins publicly on August 17, 1998. The next day, the president went off to what had been billed as a family vacation at Martha's Vineyard. As Bill, Hillary, and Chelsea Clinton made their way from the Diplomatic Entrance across the White House lawn to *Marine One* on the way to *Air Force One*, it was clear how strained their relationship was. Clinton managed a weak smile for the TV cameras as he walked, holding the leash of Buddy, his new chocolate-colored Labrador. Hillary stared firmly into the distance as she walked awkwardly at his side. Between them, tightly grasping each of their hands, was their 18-year-old daughter, Chelsea, as a sort of human link holding together their troubled marriage. As they stepped into the helicopter, Hillary walked brusquely past her husband as he tried to assist her by holding her right elbow.

Once aboard, the president held on to Buddy and scarcely looked at his wife. "It was clear that there was a lot of reckoning ahead in that family," said one of their flying companions. The silence was so uncomfortable and the moment so poignant that press secretary Mike McCurry at one point said awkwardly, "So, I've never been to Martha's Vineyard, what should we do?" Chelsea, as embarrassed as everyone else, started to talk about the beaches and the restaurants, but it did little to relieve the tension.

When they reached Andrews Air Force Base, they found not the big 747, or the backup 707, but a much smaller C9, a twin-engine executive-style government jet that was small enough to land on the airstrip of the New England resort. Just before they arrived, Kris Engskov, the president's personal aide, rushed into the front section and turned that day's newspapers over so the banner headlines on the front pages, screaming "Lewinsky," wouldn't generate another moment of embarrassment to the first family.

They had no private compartment. Clinton sat in the first row of the forward section with a national-security aide. Hillary and Chelsea sat in the row behind them, chatting quietly. The rear section, open to the front, held staff and Secret Service agents, and a handful of journalists. The first family was clearly visible to everyone in the plane if they stood up or moved about.

The unhappy couple made the hour-long ride largely in silence, as Chelsea made small talk with those around her. For a while, Mrs. Clinton slept as the president read *The General*, a military novel by Patrick A. Davis. He also worked on *The New York Times* crossword puzzle and at one point turned to McCurry with a laugh as he pointed to 46 down, "meal for the humble" in four letters. The answer was "crow," and Clinton said, "Here's one that's appropriate for today." McCurry managed a weak laugh. Tim Kerwin, the normally talkative chief steward, stayed mum, fearing he might say something wrong.

This was the same weekend that Clinton was secretly planning to strike against suspected al Qaeda terrorists in Sudan and Afghanistan, and he briefly returned to Washington to supervise the air raids the next day. White House officials later told me that Hillary Clinton, knowing of the imminent military operation, decided not to quiz her husband on the Lewinsky affair or his testimony before a grand jury because she realized the pressure he was under. "She basically said we're not going to deal with this until you do what you have to do," recounted a senior White House aide at the time. "She had some appreciation that he was under an enormous amount of stress."

The August 20 attacks were criticized as an attempt to divert attention from Clinton's personal woes, just as his missile attacks on Baghdad the following December would be criticized for the same reason. And they did bear an eerie similarity to *Wag the Dog*, a movie that summer about a president who creates a phony war to distract attention from a sex scandal. But the attacks failed to kill terrorist leader Osama bin Laden, just as the president's personal campaign failed to heal his troubled marriage that weekend.

IN HIS FINAL DAYS as president, Clinton had a hard time letting go. He got little sleep as he sorted through papers and memorabilia, signed executive orders, created eight new national monuments, nominated nine federal judges, approved hundreds of new federal regulations, and, most controversial, granted 140 pardons and worked out a deal with a special prosecutor to drop the criminal case against him for lying under oath about having sex with Monica Lewinsky.

His last trip on *Air Force One* was a sentimental journey to Little Rock, Arkansas, where he had gotten his start in politics. He walked the length of the plane, inspected the cabins, the galley, and the conference rooms, and even paid a visit to the press compartment. "You got anybody you want to pardon?" he quipped. "Everybody in America either wants somebody pardoned or a national monument."

After the inauguration of his successor, he spent two hours at Andrews Air Force Base saying good-bye to all comers. "When you leave the White House," he declared, "you wonder if you'll ever draw a crowd again." Then he boarded the 747 and began his new life. En route to his new residence in New York, he took a brief nap and began still another round of farewells with the crew. "It was really emotional because it was so short," Clinton told me. "You know, you couldn't watch a movie or play a game or pretend it wasn't happening. It was going to be over in a minute."

At that point, the aircraft was no longer called *Air Force One* because the designation is only used for planes carrying the president. It was now Special Air Mission 28000. After taking William Jefferson Clinton to New York, the plane returned to Washington, ready to serve the 43rd president, George W. Bush.

CHAPTER TWELVE

GEORGE W. BUSH: COMMANDER IN CHIEF

THE MOST DRAMATIC AND important events in the history of *Air Force One* happened on September 11, 2001.

President George W. Bush got up at 6:30 A.M., feeling great. It was a balmy morning at the Colony Beach and Tennis Resort, a Gulf Coast complex on Longboat Key near Sarasota, Florida, where he had spent the night. He was in a particularly good mood since he had enjoyed a rollicking evening the night before with his brother, Jeb, the governor of Florida. They had handicapped Jeb's reelection race in 2002 and decided no one could beat him.

Bush decided to take a run, put on shorts and a T-shirt, and jogged around the golf course in a brisk 17 minutes. As he finished, a sweating and smiling president told the small pool of reporters waiting to ask him a few questions that he was feeling especially energetic.

He would need all the vigor he could muster for the challenge that would confront him two hours later.

Bush returned to his hotel suite, had orange juice and toast, showered, and put on a dark blue suit, pale blue shirt, and iridescent orange tie. At 8:30 A.M., he stepped into his limousine, and his motorcade sped off to his first appearance of the day, a visit to a second-grade class at Emma E. Booker Elementary School in

Sarasota, to promote his ideas about education reform. During that 15-minute ride, as the president looked over the text of his remarks, his aides in other limousines got a flurry of pages and cellphone calls from the White House.

Something terrible had happened in New York.

WHEN THE MOTORCADE reached the school, Karl Rove, Bush's chief political strategist, walked quickly up to the president in a narrow corridor. A plane had crashed into the North Tower of the World Trade Center in New York City, Rove whispered. Basing his report on erroneous television reports passed along by his aides in Washington, Rove said it appeared to be a small twin-engine plane. Bush shook his head sadly and said the pilot must have had a heart attack.

He walked into a classroom and took a seat on a stool in front of a dozen second graders who took turns reading aloud. A few minutes after the program began, Chief of Staff Andrew Card, his hands folded primly across his stomach, walked gingerly up to the president, in full view of television cameras covering the event, and whispered into his right ear as Bush turned his head so the microphones couldn't pick up what was being said. "A second plane hit the second tower," Card whispered. "America is under attack."

Bush's face grew taut and pale, his lips pressed together in a grim line. His first thought, he said later, was, "They had declared war on us, and I made up my mind at that moment that we were going to war."

Meanwhile, his traveling aides were in a small room at the school, watching the shocking TV images of two huge Boeing 767's—American Airlines Flight 11 and United Airlines Flight 175—crashing into the World Trade towers. A short time later, at 9:39 A.M., a third hijacked airliner, a 757 designated as American Airlines Flight 77, hit the Pentagon. It was growing tragically clear that this was the worst terrorist attack in U.S. history, and there would be thousands of casualties.

Bush made a brief statement at Booker Elementary, telling the country he was aware of the events and would say more later, and boarded his limousine. His motorcade sped to Sarasota's Bradenton International Airport.

· · ·

AFTER BUSH WALKED briskly up the long mobile staircase and entered his cabin on *Air Force One*, a tense Secret Service agent said, "Mr. President, we need you to get seated as soon as possible." But first Bush talked by secure telephone to Vice President Dick Cheney and National Security Adviser Condoleezza Rice in Washington, and conferred briefly with Card and Rove on the plane. He was eager to get a better picture of the crisis, but there was no clarity. In fact, rumors abounded that other government sites had been hit, including the White House and Camp David.

Bush and his staff took comfort in simply being aboard the plane. It seemed a secure refuge, protected by the Secret Service and the Air Force and operated by one of the best flight crews in the world, and no one thought a hijacking was even possible. "There was this surreal, serene, quiet, peaceful feeling," recalled White House Communications Director Dan Bartlett, who accompanied Bush on that fateful day. "Everybody exhaled once we got on the plane. . . . When we were on the ground, at the school, and hauling ass to the airport, there was tension, but as soon as everybody got on the plane, there was a comforting feeling. Everybody felt safer."

Adds chief White House photographer Eric Draper: "When we got airborne I was thinking, how could anyone hit a moving target?"

As the day wore on, he wasn't so confident. Fighter escorts got closer and closer to *Air Force One* as a protective measure in case someone tried to shoot it down. No precaution seemed excessive, because the situation was so confused. "We didn't know if *we* were going to be attacked," Andrew Card told me later. "We didn't know if the White House was going to be attacked. What happened in New York was horrific enough, but then when you heard about the Pentagon, and then you heard about Flight 93 [which had been hijacked by terrorists and crashed in the Pennsylvania countryside after passengers put up a fight], it was just, 'Okay, what's next? When will it stop?' I'd call back and get reports on what was happening in Washington. It was, like, there was a fire in the Old Executive Office Building. Well, somebody burned a trash can, but I mean, when I first heard it, I envisioned flames coming out the windows and everything else. And then I heard, the State Department has been attacked. There was all of this stuff coming to us, and you just didn't know. And you'd call back to the office and no one's there to answer the phones." It turned out that the White House had been evacuated.

Card, who quickly emerged as the conduit of information to the commander in chief, didn't tell the president every rumor, only what seemed important for him to know. Above all, Card wanted to keep Bush safe. "You can't go back to Washington until we know," Card told the president as *Air Force One* made its steep climb out of Sarasota. "You've got to let the dust settle."

Bush replied, "I've got to go back. Andy, I'm going back to Washington."

MOMENTS AFTER TAKEOFF, Bush removed his suit jacket, sat down at the big brown wraparound desk in his flying office, and called Cheney again. By this time, the vice president had been moved from his West Wing office, shuffled to the White House basement, and rushed through a tunnel and into a bunker under the White House designed to hold the president, the vice president, and other senior government officials under emergency conditions.

Cheney said Air Force jets had scrambled into the air around Washington in case they were needed, but the pilots were awaiting instructions. Should they shoot down any other civilian airliners that seemed to be hijacked and threatening to crash into a populated area or a historic monument? Hundreds of airplanes had been grounded around the country, but some were still flying. It was possible that the military pilots could make a horrible mistake and destroy a harmless plane. And even if another airliner had been hijacked, shooting it down could kill hundreds of innocent people.

It was the biggest decision of Bush's presidency up to that point.

The president and vice president agreed very quickly that approval had to be given for the pilots to destroy threatening aircraft. "You have my authorization," Bush told Cheney, and he repeated the same words for emphasis a few moments later. But the president said he wanted a bit more clarity on exactly how this dangerous process would work.

After hanging up with Cheney, he called Defense Secretary Donald Rumsfeld, holding the phone to his left ear and waving his right hand for emphasis.

Swiveling his chair to face a window behind his wraparound desk, Bush gazed at the clouds racing by beneath him as he asked Rumsfeld exactly what procedures the Air Force pilots would use in trying to force a plane to land before firing at it.

Rumsfeld, as always, was concise (just as he had been all those years ago on *Air Force One* when, as Gerald Ford's chief of staff, he broke the news to Betty Ford that someone had tried to assassinate her husband): The pilots would try to contact any suspicious aircraft by radio to order a landing at the closest airport. If that failed, the military pilot would use visual signals, such as hand gestures from cockpit to cockpit or flying his jet in front of the other plane to force a change of course. If the suspicious aircraft continued flying in the direction of what appeared to be a target destination with "hostile intent," the military pilot would be authorized to destroy it. For the third time, Bush reconfirmed his authorization for a shootdown under those procedures.

But the matter still weighed heavily on him. When he was told a few minutes later that the fourth airliner, United Flight 93, had crashed in the southwestern Pennsylvania countryside, he asked, "Did we shoot it down or did it crash?" No one could be sure. Two hours later, the Pentagon confirmed that Flight 93 had not been fired upon, and Bush sighed in relief.

AT 10:32 A.M., less than an hour after leaving Sarasota, Bush got a call from Cheney with another chilling development. *Air Force One*, he said, appeared to be the next target. This seemed perfectly credible at the time, given all that had happened. Not only had there been four hijackings and four plane crashes that morning but, as Card said, there had been many rumors of other disasters. Now there were even more rumors—that a plane had crashed at Camp David, the presidential retreat in rural Maryland; that still another jet had gone down near the Ohio-Kentucky border, that a car bomb had exploded outside the State Department. It seemed like the terrorists might be everywhere.

Someone had called the White House, Cheney told Bush, and apparently used the military codeword "Angel" for *Air Force One* in warning that the plane was "next." Cheney and others immediately concluded that terrorists had inside information that could jeopardize the president's life aboard his plane. Card, after talking to military officials, told Bush it would take up to an hour and a half to get fighter jets alongside *Air Force One*.

Bush fumed at the terrorists, telling aides, "They're not going to get away with this. . . . We're going to find out who did this. . . . They will pay." He repeated the same phrases frequently throughout the day.

At 10:41 A.M., Cheney called Bush again. "There's still a threat to Washington," he said. Condoleezza Rice agreed in a separate phone call, and Card made it unanimous. The president reluctantly accepted his advisers' suggestion to fly to Barksdale Air Force Base in Louisiana, a secure location where he could talk further with his aides, assess the situation, and have the plane refueled. Card told the pilot.

Air Force One then banked sharply to the left, changing from a northward course toward Washington and heading southwestward toward Barksdale.

Most of those aboard weren't sure what was happening. "I overheard someone saying, 'Angel is the next target and that means us,'" recalls Eric Draper, who was sitting in his assigned seat, No. 37, in a staff cabin. By this time, every person seemed to have a telephone to his or her ear, trying to get information or to let loved ones know they were all right. All the TV monitors were tuned to the news, but the reception kept cutting off. The onboard television system at the time could only pick up local stations as the plane flew over large cities and towns, which frustrated the worried fliers. (That system has since been improved.)

At one point, Colonel Mark Tillman, the pilot, mistakenly thought an airliner was heading for *Air Force One* and diverted his course. He worried that terrorists might be listening in on his radio communications, so he refused to tell air traffic controllers his precise position, assuming rightly that they would track it on radar. He was so concerned about what might happen next that he asked for, and received, an armed guard outside the cockpit door.

Occasionally, Bush would emerge from his office and see how the staff was holding up, sometimes giving a frazzled aide a hug, at other times seeking a bit more information to coordinate the federal response. "What stood out to me was how cool, calm, and collected he was under the circumstances," Draper says.

In the end, the threat to *Air Force One* turned out to be exaggerated. An anonymous caller had indeed threatened the plane, U.S. officials later said, but the caller had never referred to the aircraft as "Angel." Somehow a White House operator or someone in the chain of command had inserted the codeword in passing along the threat, and by the time it reached senior officials, including Cheney, it was garbled. Everyone thought the caller had used the internal call sign of "Angel." But on September 11, no one was taking any chances.

The president and his flying team soon got another shock. They had seen TV footage of the hijacked planes crashing into the twin towers, which was bad enough. But no one was prepared for the collapse of the buildings, in huge, gray plumes of smoke and dust. Everyone on board seemed to have the same thought: How many people had died?

AS BUSH'S PLANE approached Barksdale, White House Press Secretary Ari Fleischer, who was on board, drafted another statement for Bush to read on his arrival at the base. The nation was waiting to hear the president, and it would be an important moment. (Bush had briefly considered making a statement by phone from the plane directly to the radio and TV networks, but rejected the idea because it might look like he was afraid to land.)

Fleischer called Karen Hughes, Bush's longtime counselor, in Washington, for some ideas. At one point, he started to read her a phrase he was considering: "This morning we were the victims of—" But Hughes cut him off. "Wait a minute," she snapped. "We aren't the victims of anything. We may have been the targets, we may have been attacked, but we are not victims." The phrase was deleted, which reflected Bush's thinking perfectly.

At another point in the confusion, Hughes tried to reach Bush directly through the White House operator but the call didn't go through. "We can't reach *Air Force One*," the operator reported to a distressed Hughes. What if the plane has been blown up? she thought. Actually, Hughes had gone through the White House civilian communications system, not the military network that was the proper procedural way to reach the plane in a crisis. Hughes quickly got an update from an aide: Nothing was wrong with *Air Force One*.

In fact, as the plane began its descent into Barksdale, Bush and his staff stood at the windows lining the right side of the plane and watched as fighter jets fanned off into the distance. It was a comforting sight.

At Barksdale, Bush called his wife, Laura, at a secure location in Washington and was told that she and their twin daughters were fine. He also talked again with Cheney. At 12:36 P.M., Bush walked quickly into a conference room near the base commander's office and, as hastily assembled TV cameras rolled, read the five-minute statement prepared by Hughes and Fleischer. He seemed grim and hesitant, but he ended on a forceful note. "The resolve of our great nation is being tested," the commander in chief declared. "But make no mistake: We will show the world that we will pass this test."

THROUGHOUT THE DAY, there was little time to ruminate or reflect, but this was the perfect environment for Bush. It required quick, instinctive judgments, and Bush prided himself on his decisiveness. As always, *Air Force One* reinforced the solitary nature of the presidency in a time of crisis.

Bush took off his suit coat but didn't roll up his sleeves or loosen his tie. He allowed a few trusted aides, including Card, Rove, and Bartlett, to flow in and out of his office, and he had near-instant access to hundreds of policy makers in Washington. But as the day wore on, Bush felt the full weight of the crisis was on his own shoulders. As he looked out the small porthole windows in his cabin at the endless expanse of cities, suburbs, and farmland 40,000 feet below (a mile higher than usual, at an altitude where most missiles supposedly could not reach the plane), Bush felt especially alone. In nervous agitation, he drank bottled water and munched unsalted popcorn, sometimes filling his mouth with handfuls of it as kernels scattered on the floor.

Air Force One proved to be an effective mobile command center as, for the first time, a president actually directed the government and sought to guide the nation in a crisis from his flying White House. "Almost every nook and cranny on the plane was being used for some kind of meeting, which is unusual," said Card. At one point, the chief of staff even used Bush's bedroom to meet with Secret Service agents and Bush's military aide about where the plane should fly next, and to assess the latest intelligence reports.

. . .

JUST AFTER 1:30 P.M., *Air Force One* took off from Barksdale heading for Offutt Air Force Base in Nebraska. The president and his advisers decided it still wasn't safe for him to return to Washington, and he could preside over a meeting of his National Security Council via a secure videoconference from Offutt.

But Bush was getting impatient. "I want to go back home ASAP," he told Card aboard the plane. "I don't want whoever did this holding me outside of Washington." Bush emphasized that he would return to the White House after his stop at Offutt unless some new and extraordinary threat was discovered that would change his mind.

Bush itched to take action. He called his advisers in Washington for more updates and grew even more angry as he and his staff watched TV coverage of the attacks, which by this time included the horrific images of the collapsing buildings, repeated again and again.

At one point, speaking again to Rumsfeld by phone, he said he had been preoccupied with the attacks in New York and was stunned to see all the damage to the Pentagon and to learn more details of what had happened there. "Wow," he told the defense secretary, "it was an American airliner that hit the Pentagon. It's a day of national tragedy, and we'll clean up the mess, and then the ball will be in your court and Dick Myers's court to respond." Air Force General Richard B. Myers was scheduled to become the new chairman of the Joint Chiefs of Staff in three weeks.

At 2:30 P.M., Bush reached his father on the phone. "Where are you?" the president asked. The former commander in chief said he and his wife, Barbara, had been on the way to Minneapolis but were at that moment in Milwaukee.

"What are you doing in Milwaukee?" President Bush asked.

"You grounded my plane," his father replied.

President Bush went on to say his crisis team was "functioning well" and he knew just what the nation needed to do. "We're going to be fine," he summed up.

Both father and son found the call comforting.

Just before *Air Force One* landed at Offutt at 2:50 P.M., Bush told his lead Secret Service agent on the plane, "We need to get back to Washington. We don't need some tinhorn terrorist to scare us off. The American people want to know where their president is."

His cowboy swagger had returned.

EN ROUTE BACK to Washington, Card cleared Bush's suite so the president could put the finishing touches on his address to the nation that night. But when the plane began its descent into Andrews Air Force Base, Bush opened the door to his office and aides filtered in. For several long minutes, the president and his staff again lined the sides in the presidential cabin and the senior-staff compartment, looking out the windows.

The wingtips of the fighter jets this time were amazingly close to the wingtips of *Air Force One*, one escort on each side—so close, in fact, that one of the pilots' late-afternoon stubble could be clearly seen on his face as he slightly tipped his wings as a salute to his commander in chief. Bush saluted silently. "It's great," Bush said, in recognition of the awesome military power at his disposal.

In an interview for this book a year later, Bush said, "I never felt like my life was in danger. . . . I'm the kind of guy, my attitude is, if your number is up, it's up, you know? And you just be prepared for it. I don't walk around saying there's a guy with a gun around every corner. I just don't think that way. But I've never worried about my safety. The pilots on *Air Force One* are the best."

THE EVENTS OF September 11 proved several things—among them that *Air Force One* could function well as a flying command post, that the aircraft's emergency procedures were workable, and that Bush himself was an effective commander in chief. There had been doubts about this last point since Bush was declared the winner of the disputed campaign of 2000. For weeks after Election Day, Bush and his Democratic opponent, Vice President Al Gore, had waged a furious legal and political battle to determine who had carried the state of Florida. In a controversial 5–4 decision, the Supreme Court ruled in Bush's favor, giving him the slimmest of majorities in the Electoral College, and the White House.

Yet until September 11, Bush had been unable to completely erase the hard feelings and establish his legitimacy. Gore had, after all, won the popular vote nationwide by 500,000 ballots, and many Democrats argued that he was the real winner, the "people's president."

As he struggled to govern, Bush implemented several theories about presidential leadership that broke with the immediate past. One was that, after the turbulent Clinton years, Americans didn't want the president to be constantly hogging the headlines and calling attention to himself. As a result, the Bush White House would go for long stretches without the president making the front pages or leading the evening news. This was just fine with Bush.

"He has a very basic belief that if he does his part—gets the information, makes the choices—the results are somehow with God," says chief White House speech writer Michael Gerson. "He believes there's something broader going on. He does his best and the outcome is out of his control." This gives him a sense of peace and enables him to make decisions crisply and without anguish.

In his personal habits and predilections, Bush seems to be the picture of humdrum, everyday normalcy, as does his inner circle. "We're a pretty dull crew," says White House Press Secretary Ari Fleischer. Bush, trying to move beyond the party-boy reputation he gained as a hard-drinking youth, reinforces this image of sobriety in just about everything he does. A teetotaler for many years, he goes to bed by 10 P.M. every day and gets up at 6 or 6:30. He doesn't throw fancy parties and rarely holds state dinners, and he disdains the George-town social circuit. In pointed contrast to his predecessor, he shuns the Hollywood types that Bill Clinton couldn't get enough of.

Bush sees *Air Force One* as his private place, as all presidents tend to do. "It's their sanctuary," says White House Communications Director Bartlett. "You can almost see both the president and the staff let their guard down once they get on the plane."

In his private moments, Bush appears to be more of an average Joe than most presidents like to admit. He is not a voracious reader of books, managing to plow through one biography or historical volume every two or three weeks. In early 2002, for example, he read Edmund Morris's *Theodore Rex*, a biography of

Theodore Roosevelt, and Bernard Goldberg's *Bias*, an insider's account of an alleged liberal slant in network television news.

He has little interest in following the news day-to-day on TV. When he wanders into an *Air Force One* staff cabin and notices the news on a monitor, he will often frown and snap, "Turn that off." Like most presidents, he doesn't think he gets a fair shake from the media and tries to ignore the coverage as much as possible. He scans a few newspapers every morning but prefers to have his press staff summarize, orally or in writing, whatever he needs to know beyond his daily security and intelligence briefings. His favorite TV fare is major-league baseball, and before trips his staff occasionally videotapes one or two games, especially those involving his former team, the Texas Rangers, so he can watch the replay on *Air Force One*. He is an enthusiastic reader of the box scores, especially for the Rangers. (He was once part owner of the team.)

Bush hates sitting still. Before landing, he has a habit of pacing impatiently in his airborne office or waiting just outside the door as the plane completes its taxiing (even though this violates air-safety rules that require passengers to remain seated and strapped in until the aircraft comes to a stop). If the mobile staircase takes longer than he anticipates to roll up to the doorway, he will start complaining. "Let's go," he will say. "What's going on?"

Several months into his administration, Bush added a special feature to *Air Force One*: a treadmill. Bush uses the machine often in his airborne conference room or in his bedroom, especially on long flights, when he will work up a sweat that soaks through his T-shirt. "He likes a serious workout," Fleischer says.

Bush admits that he gets restless easily, and finds that using the treadmill calms him down. "Being a 'Type A' personality," he told me, "I can get kind of caged in."

Another innovation is Bush's interest in the board game Risk, in which players amass armies and try to conquer the world. En route home from Europe in July 2001, Bush supervised a particularly competitive game. The president encouraged each participant to take the biggest risks possible and to attack each other mercilessly. At one point, he goaded his military aide, supposedly an expert on military maneuvers and strategy, to take some chances. When he did so and found his armies annihilated, Bush teased the aide for being the first to lose. Supervising another game, the commander in chief yelled, "You're a wimp. Go get 'em."

Bush also likes to play bridge, but most of the time he can only persuade Condoleezza Rice and First Lady Laura Bush to participate, and that isn't enough. Few others on the White House staff know how to play, so they almost always lack a foursome. Some goals are beyond even the president of the United States.

"*Air Force One* is a comfortable environment for the president," said White House Chief of Staff Card in an interview. "It's less formal than the West Wing of the White House. And for example you can walk into the president's office on *Air Force One* and he will be dressed in casual attire. It's very, very rare to walk into the Oval Office and find the president dressed in casual attire. I mean, it's not the Oval Office, but it is the president's working office. It's also his living room on the plane, and just like you can relax and have a conversation in your living room with friends, he invites people to his living room on *Air Force One* as friends. The living room also has some formality to it, and that's when he might convene a meeting of some of his senior advisers or some of the folks on the plane to talk policy and it's a little more structured. But I tend to find the more structured meetings tend to be in the conference room rather than in the office up in the front."

"Having traveled with the president all across the country in the campaign in a much smaller, much less user-friendly airplane, I remember thinking 'Wow!'" says Karen Hughes, Bush's longtime adviser, recalling her first time on board. "It's an airplane, but you can actually work and get a lot of things done. There are workstations and computers and office space and a conference room and a conference table. And that's an enormous advantage in helping you work, as opposed to sitting balancing a laptop in your seat, which is the way I spent most of the year and a half before."

Hughes says another big advantage to traveling on *Air Force One* is that the staff gets to know each other very well amid the informal atmosphere of long flights. This is where the staff first got a taste of Rice's sense of humor. Leaving El Salvador on one trip, the president was running early, as usual—in this case, an hour ahead of schedule. "We run so early," Rice quipped, "that our first term is going to be over in three years and six months."

It was on the long flights that White House colleagues learned that Rice is, in Hughes's words, "a good catnapper—Condi can fall asleep anywhere," but she usually prefers to stay in her first-class seat, as does Card. Secretary of State Colin Powell prefers to stretch out, so he usually lies on the floor.

As for Bush, he has little trouble dozing wherever he is, and he arranges his sleep schedule according to the advice of his doctors and his staff. After boarding an early-morning flight to Elmendorf Air Force Base in Alaska on February 16, 2002, en route to Asia, Bush's military aide advised the president and his traveling party to sleep for about two hours, then stay awake for the rest of the long flight. That way, they could go to bed again when they arrived in Tokyo on Sunday night and sleep through. Bush followed the directions and felt fine when he started his official visit on Monday morning. He generally follows this pattern on long trips—start early and doze briefly on the plane, stay awake until landing, and then get a good night's sleep at his destination.

WHEN HE RECEIVES a briefing on the plane, he follows the same pattern that he does at the White House. "I think people would be surprised by the questions he asks at a briefing," says Nick Calio, Bush's first congressional liaison, "because they come oftentimes at a torrent. He can also cut you off fairly quickly if you're going on too long or if he's already got where you're going and he wants you to move on. He's also funnier than hell," making jokes and self-deprecating remarks.

He will usually make a variety of phone calls to advisers back home, to members of Congress, or to foreign leaders. On very lengthy flights, he might watch a movie, and during the months after September 11, he seemed drawn to films with military themes, such as *Behind Enemy Lines* and *Hart's War*. At other times, he thumbs through the *Air Force One* movie guide and gives spot reviews of movies he has seen or read about, making pronouncements such as "terrible" and "chick flick." One non–action-adventure film he did like was *Analyze This*, a comedy starring Billy Crystal that parodies organized-crime movies.

AS HE SHOWED on September 11, Bush apparently has no qualms about moving decisively, even if it means reversing himself. This flexibility came across en route to Berlin on May 22, 2002, during a trip to solidify European support for his war on terrorism. During the flight, Bush approved the reorganization of the federal government that was to become a hallmark of his second year in office.

Meeting in the president's airborne suite, Card briefed the president and presented him with an inch-and-a-half-thick binder containing eight policy options for the reshuffling, designed to enhance the anti-terror campaign at home. Bush accepted nearly all the recommendations, including one for a Department of Homeland Security, a Cabinet-level department that he had initially opposed. In the end, his concern about bigger government was outweighed by the bureaucratic impediments that he felt were hampering his campaign, and he opted for the new department.

Typically, in making the choices, he followed the advice of Card and other key aides, and felt no need for exhaustive briefings and explanations of each proposal.

MOST AMERICANS PROBABLY realize that Bush has a spiritual side. He makes frequent references to his "born-again" Christianity and once said the philosopher he admired most was Jesus Christ. But the depth of his Christian commitment may take many by surprise. Knowing that he hates to miss church on important occasions, Condoleezza Rice, Card, and Karen Hughes suggested to Bush that they conduct an informal religious service on the flight from San Salvador to Washington on Palm Sunday, 2002. Bush enthusiastically agreed.

What followed aboard *Air Force One* was possibly unprecedented in the travel history of the presidents. Rice and other senior aides spread the word on the plane shortly after takeoff that there would be a service for anyone who wanted to attend. White House Staff Secretary Harriet Miers and a young press aide named Reed Dickens helped draw up a program, which was reproduced and distributed to the three dozen officials who huddled in the conference room. As President Bush, Mrs. Bush, and six aides sat around a rectangular table, senior staffers made remarks.

Card, whose wife is a Protestant minister and who reads verses from the Bible each day, as does Bush, started the proceedings. "I opened it up with greetings and a prayer and call to worship," Card told me. The group—which included Secretary of State Powell, members of the flight crew, and lower-level aides—then sang hymns and religious songs led by Rice, an accomplished musician and singer. There were readings and prayers by different officials from the Old and New Testaments, and Hughes gave what one attendee called a "wonderful little sermonette."

Speaking from notes she had hastily prepared just before the service, Hughes talked about how Christ had been warmly welcomed by the people of Jerusalem on Palm Sunday, yet only a week later he was rejected by those same people. Her point was indirect but clear: Bush was riding high in the polls, but public opinion can be very fickle.

Two other recurring themes in the spoken remarks were thanksgiving both that the trip had gone well and that they were united in the service of their country, and recognition of the family and friends who were not able to join them. At the end of the spoken presentations, everyone sang the Christian hymn "Amazing Grace," and members of the group, including the president and the First Lady, exchanged hugs and kisses in a gesture of solidarity and fellowship.

Some staffers said later they felt a bit uncomfortable about the unusual service, which they considered Christian in tone, although no one who practiced a different faith was excluded. They were concerned that Bush critics might portray the service as an inappropriate blending of church and state.

"I feel guilty talking about it—I don't know why," Card said during our interview, "because the president made sure that all the staff on the plane was invited to attend, the Air Force staff as well as his staff. I reminded people of the celebration of Jesus coming into Jerusalem [on Palm Sunday] and that wherever people are gathered in his name there is a church, and so you didn't have to be in a church to have a church on the plane."

Others were even more effusive. "It showed the humanity of the president," recalled Noelia Rodriguez, First Lady Laura Bush's press secretary, who attended the ceremony. "None of us could be in church that day, and this was the president's way of honoring our spirituality. You could feel this connection with everybody, and we were so close to heaven that it was very special and moving." Dickens said everyone seemed to experience "a heavenly feeling."

For his part, Bush remembers the experience warmly. "There were a lot of religious people on the plane," he told me. ". . . It was just a packed house. . . . And to be able to worship with people with whom you work in a unique spot is a special moment." He added: "You know, I did feel the presence of God amongst my friends on *Air Force One*. . . . and it was a lovely ceremony. It was a very touching moment."

Yet Bush mostly keeps his innermost feelings to himself—a family trait he shares with his father. Unlike Bill Clinton, who would emote late at night on long flights, Bush resists unburdening himself as much as he can. "He is not the emotive type," says Fleischer. "He's emotional. He'll tear up or cry, but no, he doesn't exactly start spilling his guts to the staff or anybody else just because he is on *Air Force One*."

BUSH'S RELIGIOUS FEELINGS notwithstanding, he can't escape the R-rated side of popular culture. Sometimes the films available on *Air Force One* have a distinctly raunchy side that might surprise his culturally conservative allies.

This caused a flap during a flight from Michigan to Washington in May 2002. A pool report written by Joseph Curl of *The Washington Times* noted that a film shown in the press cabin and a Secret Service compartment, called *Not Another Teen Movie*, revealed "a fully naked female displaying her full nudity (in a frontal manner)."

After *The Washington Post* picked up the item in a gossip column, the film was pulled from the plane's inventory; but reporters and, apparently, Secret Service agents (mostly male in both categories) raised a fuss, and a few weeks later, bare breasts returned in another movie.

A White House official told me the films chosen for the plane are generally available in theaters across the country, even if some are R-rated. "We're not prudes," he said.

CONTRARY TO HIS carefully cultivated populist image, Bush loves the perks of office, as most presidents do, and this trait is especially clear on *Air Force One*. After taking off his suit jacket upon boarding, he customarily puts on a lightweight blue windbreaker-style jacket with AIR FORCE ONE over the right breast and "President George W. Bush" embroidered on the left. His father loved to wear the same distinctive jacket on the plane, as did Bill Clinton. It has become an airborne presidential uniform—prized by the owners because only one man in the world gets to wear it. On lengthy flights, he changes into a sweat suit or slacks and a golf shirt.

"He's always an affable person and that continues aboard the plane," says Fleischer. Bush starts off most trips in his cabin and sometimes invites friends, members of Congress, or special guests there for a while. On day trips, he prefers leaving Washington early in the morning so he can get home early enough for dinner with his wife, Laura; he generally spends his evenings quietly in the East Wing residence.

On what some of his aides call a flying day, Bush generally gets his daily military or intelligence briefing as his first order of business on the plane, conducted in the conference room, as he would do in the Oval Office. Aides say Bush looks forward to these sessions because he has more time to ask questions on the plane, when the schedule is more relaxed than in the White House.

Afterward, he usually comes back to chat with advisers in the senior-staff cabin and visits with members of Congress when they are aboard, then he returns to his private cabin or his bedroom to read or take a nap. But sometimes he gets so involved in chatting up his guests that he will refuse to sit down and fasten his seat belt, so he will sometimes be standing and swaying in the aisle as the plane takes off or lands. He generally waits until the last minute to change back into his business suit, but he is almost never late under any circumstances.

Early on, Bush ordered aides to keep his traveling entourage to a minimum in a clear contrast with Clinton, who often would fly with a huge crowd of officials, guests, and hangers-on. "We don't fill the aircraft all that much," says Mark Rosenker, former director of the White House Military Office. ". . . This president likes a small 'footprint' when he travels. That's his style and that's how he's able to function best."

For those who do accompany him, Bush enjoys giving impromptu tours of his quarters, as do most presidents, pointing out his shower, his desk, the medical clinic, and his exercise equipment. Knowing the limits of his self-control, Bush banished the Heath bars, Reese's peanut butter cups, and other candies—treats that the Clintonites enjoyed—from his cabin and the senior-staff area. He realized he couldn't resist the temptation after catching himself munching the sweets when he passed by. Still, he snitches a snack or two when he finds them farther back in the plane among the junior aides.

Says Nick Calio: "We see a very different person than the public sees on a day-to-day basis. . . . It's a more informal setting and he can relax more. And he's not so guided. In the West Wing, he can't get up and walk out of a room without somebody following him, and on the plane he has the luxury of having more freedom. . . . It's clearly quite different than anything at the White House. If he really doesn't want to do something, he doesn't have to. There's usually not much scheduled on the plane. So if he wants to go back and spend the whole trip with members of Congress or if he wants to call them up to the front for a while, he can."

Adds Bartlett: "He understands the symbolism of the plane and its usefulness as far as being part of the presidency, the effectiveness it can have, whether it be lobbying or whatever."

A trip to Billings, Montana, in early 2001 was pivotal. Bush looked out a window and saw cars lined up for miles around the airport so local folks could catch a glimpse of his plane. Since then, he has made a habit of adding a riff in his arrival remarks about how he has just flown in on *Air Force One*. He knows the connection is powerful.

So do the politicians who clamor to ride with him—and be seen on TV as they disembark. "I would have crawled on broken glass," said Matt Salmon, the GOP candidate for Arizona governor who traveled with Bush on *Air Force One* during the 2002 mid-term campaign.

Bush's staff also has installed a presidential seal and more sophisticated lighting in the conference room so the president can record a statement and drive home that it is from *Air Force One,* at a time of crisis or political necessity. On touchdown, the videocassette containing the statement can be sent immediately to the TV networks.

AS A MATTER of routine, Bush rarely ventures into the press compartment. He told Press Secretary Fleischer that he would gladly talk with the media folks there if he could do it off the record, or at least off camera. That way, he would not have to mind every word and gesture, and neither would the reporters. They could get to know each other in a more informal setting. But journalists for the wire services and some TV correspondents object to such arrangements. They always want the president on the record and on camera, which can stifle conversation. So Bush's contact with the airborne press corps is minimal.

This is a shame, because from Roosevelt to Bush, no accounting of the presidency is complete without an examination of what happens on *Air Force One* and the plane's hold on our presidents.

"It was like you had your own little community there," recalled Bill Clinton. "The experience took on a life of its own because we worked there, we played there, we slept there. . . . It became like a floating family."

"When you're abroad and in strange lands," Ronald Reagan said, ". . . you're very busy and then you arrive back at the airport—and your first glimpse of this plane and that flag up there—yes! It's a little bit like hearing the national anthem and you swell a little with pride."

Added George Herbert Walker Bush: "When you taxi up in our country or in some other country, there is a great emotion. . . . I love when I [went] up and [shook] hands, you know, at the rope lines with some kids . . . and you can really tell that they were moved. . . . It is the mobile symbol of the presidency and thus the country."

Jimmy Carter summed it all up: "Everywhere we've been in the world on *Air Force One*, and we've been many places, I can see within the eyes and the demeanor of those who welcomed us that they sensed that *Air Force One* at that moment *was* the United States of America."

CODE NAMES USED BY THE SECRET SERVICE

Air Force One: Angel

The White House: Crown

The President's Limousine: Stagecoach

U.S. Capitol: Punchbowl

Harry Truman: General; Supervise

Bess Truman: Sunnyside

Dwight Eisenhower: Providence

Mamie Eisenhower: Springtime

John F. Kennedy: Lancer

Jacqueline Kennedy: Lace

John F. Kennedy, Jr.: Lark

Caroline Kennedy: Lyric

Lyndon Johnson: Volunteer

Lady Bird Johnson: Victoria

Lynda Bird Johnson: Velvet

Luci Baines Johnson: Venus

Richard Nixon: Searchlight

Pat Nixon: Starlight

Gerald Ford: Passkey

Betty Ford: Pinafore

Susan Ford: Panda

Michael Ford: Professor

Jack Ford: Packman

Jimmy Carter: Deacon

Rosalynn Carter: Dancer

Amy Carter: Dynamo

Ronald Reagan: Rawhide

Nancy Reagan: Rainbow

George Herbert Walker Bush: Timberwolf   George W. Bush: Trailblazer
Barbara Bush: Tranquility   Laura Bush: Tempo

Bill Clinton: Eagle
Hillary Rodham Clinton: Evergreen
Chelsea Clinton: Energy

ENDNOTES

CHAPTER ONE *THE ROLE OF* AIR FORCE ONE

2   "It's a majestic symbol": Author's interview with President George W. Bush, Oct. 1, 2002.

2   "It has," says pollster Bill McInturff: Author's interview with Bill McInturff, Aug. 7, 2002.

3   "I can get more done": Reagan was quoted in *Air Force One: The Planes and the Presidents, Flight II*, written, produced, and directed by Elliott Sluhan, Public Broadcasting Service, May 20, 1991.

3   "I think in general": Author's interview with President Bill Clinton, Sept. 2, 2002.

3   "Behind all these other changes in the middle years": Dwight D. Eisenhower, *The White House Years: Mandate for Change 1953–1956*, Garden City, N.Y · Doubleday & Company, Inc., 1963, p. 491.

4   "The White House is now a glass house": Author's interview with Doug Brinkley, Aug. 16, 2002.

5   "In a sense": Author's interview with Karl Rove, Jan. 31, 2002.

5   "This is a place": Author's interview with David Gergen, June 26, 2002.

7   "To the extent": Author's interview with Mark Penn, Apr. 15, 2002.

8   And it has served as a political reward: Agence France Presse, "Big Clinton campaign donors hitched rides on *Air Force One*," Apr. 15, 1997. See also Brian McGrory and Michael Kranish, "Donors flew on *Air Force One*, records show," *The Boston Globe*, Apr. 15, 1997, p. A17.

8   "I think you get a relatively complete": Author's interview with Andrew Card, Apr. 15, 2002.

8   "Every *Air Force One* reflects": Author's interview with Leon Panetta, Apr. 8, 2002.

8   "I rarely had that much unimpeded": Author's interview with President Bill Clinton, Jan. 28, 2002.

8   "There's something about the power": Author's interview with Doug Sosnik, Dec. 26, 2001.

9   "He had been through a trial by fire": Author's interview with Robert Dallek, Feb. 8, 2002.

9   Once, his aides said, he got "euphoric": Robert Dallek, *Flawed Giant: Lyndon Johnson and His Times 1961–1973*, New York: Oxford University Press, 1998, pp. 82–83.

10   "We had actually quite a lot": Author's interview with President Bill Clinton, Jan. 28, 2002.

11   "He *is* a smart guy": Author's interview with Sandy Berger, March 7, 2002.

11   They sat for 18 hours: This account of the trip to the Sadat funeral is based on separate interviews that the author conducted with Presidents Jimmy Carter and Gerald Ford on Jan. 25, 2002.

12   "Of course he had": Author's interview with President Jimmy Carter, Jan. 25, 2002.

13   Ford has a similar recollection: Author's interview with President Gerald Ford, Jan. 25, 2002.

14   "I saw it as the symbol": Author's interview with President George Herbert Walker Bush, Feb. 5, 2002.

14   "With President Clinton": Author's interview with Joe Lockhart, Dec. 18, 2001.

CHAPTER TWO *THE* AIR FORCE ONE *EXPERIENCE*

15   "Coming back from an economic summit": Hedrick Smith, *The Power Game: How Washington Works*, New York: Ballantine Books, 1988, pp. 75–76.

15   "It's almost a mythical place": Author's interview with Doug Brinkley, Aug. 16, 2002.

16   "The entire government": Author's interview with Stan Greenberg, Apr. 23, 2002.

16   "For friends and supporters": Author's interview with Bill Galston, Apr. 24, 2002.

17   78 percent of adults: Survey conducted by Frank Luntz of Luntz Research Companies for this book, May 2002.

17   The mystique grows: Ibid., Luntz poll, May 2002.

17   In a separate survey: Survey conducted by Bill McInturff of Public Opinion Strategies for this book, August 2002.

18   "300 to 400 government officials": Hedrick Smith, *The Power Game: How Washington Works*, New York: Ballantine Books, 1988, pp. 75, 11–12.

20   Security and safety measures: This section on security is drawn largely from my own nearly 20 years of covering the presidency and flying on *Air Force One*. I have interviewed many government officials, crew members, and security authorities about the security arrangements, but most preferred to remain anonymous. Ralph Albertazzie, who was Nixon's pilot, provided extensive information in an interview July 17, 2002. Also see Ronald Kessler, *Inside the White House: The Hidden Lives of the Modern Presidents and the Secrets of the World's Most Powerful Institution*, New York: Pocket Books, 1995, p. 23. In addition, see J. F. terHorst and Ralph Albertazzie, *The Flying White House: The Story of Air Force One*, New York: Coward, McCann & Geoghegan, 1979, pp. 98–99, 194–98.

23   Just after midnight on May 27, 1997: Paul Hoverstein, "Unfriendly skies know no president," *USA Today*, June 4, 1997, p. 6A.

27   "We make sure that anything": Author's interview with Howie Franklin, May 24, 2002.

28   "It makes a big difference": Author's interview with Tim Kerwin, Aug. 6, 2002.

29   "Every president that I worked for": Author's interview with Howie Franklin, May 24, 2002.

30    $348 per hour: Unbylined article, "Columbine Cost Cited: Hagerty Itemizes Expenses of President's Planes," *The New York Times*, July 24, 1957, p. 28.

30    $1,995 per hour: J. F. terHorst and Ralph Albertazzie, *The Flying White House: The Story of Air Force One*, New York: Coward, McCann & Geoghegan, 1979, p. 83.

30   Since 1991, the Air Force has estimated: Charles Babcock, "Campaigning via *Air Force One*: Public Foots Much of the Bill," *The Washington Post*, Dec. 31, 1991, p. A15. Also, Ronald Kessler, *Inside the White House: The Hidden Lives of the Modern Presidents and the Secrets of the World's Most Powerful Institution*, New York: Pocket Books, 1995, p. 23. My own reporting comes up with similar numbers.

31   "This is probably the most unique airplane": Author's interview with Mark Rosenker, June 18, 2002.

31–32   "*Air Force One* is adventure": Author's interview with Howie Franklin, May 24, 2002.

32   Its four General Electric: Robert F. Dorr, *Air Force One*, St. Paul, Minn.: MBI Publishing Company, 2002, p. 130.

33   Air Force Colonel Mark Tillman: Author's interview with Mark Tillman, June 18, 2002.

33   And the plane is not immune: By *The News-Gazette*, "Clinton stays longer in area than planned," *The News-Gazette*, Jan. 28, 1998.

36   at a cost of more than $660 million: Robert F. Dorr, *Air Force One*, St. Paul, Minn.: MBI Publishing Company, 2002, p. 109.

37   "The president doesn't need a bigger plane": Author's interview with Brent Scowcroft, Apr. 19, 2002.

37   "There's no plan": Author's interview with Mark Rosenker, June 18, 2002.

38   "It's slowly going to be modified": Author's interview with Mark Tillman, June 18, 2002.

CHAPTER THREE *THE FIRST "FLYING PRESIDENTS"*

39   until Theodore Roosevelt sailed: J. F. terHorst and Ralph Albertazzie, *The Flying White House: The Story of Air Force One*, New York: Coward, McCann & Geoghegan, Inc., 1979, p. 64.

40   On January 11, 1943: terHorst and Albertazzie, pp. 127–30. This book contains a description of FDR's first trip by plane, to which I refer in this chapter.

40   "He was about to see a new continent": James MacGregor Burns, *Roosevelt: The Soldier of Freedom*, New York: Smithmark Publishers, 1996, p. 316.

41   The trip, described later by pilot Howard Cone: Burns, pp. 128–33.

41   After takeoff at dawn: Ibid.

41   The seaplanes first flew: Burns, pp. 129–33.

42   Otis F. Bryan, the pilot on the final: Burns, pp. 130–31.

43   "All has gone well": Burns, p. 324. See also Doris Kearns Goodwin, *No Ordinary Time*, New York: Simon & Schuster, 1994, p. 409.

43   In her memoirs, Eleanor: Eleanor Roosevelt, *This I Remember*, New York: Harper & Brothers, 1949, p. 279.

43   The redesign included a wheelchair lift: Robert F. Dorr, *Air Force One*, St. Paul, Minn.: MBI Publishing Company, 2002, pp. 32–34.

45   He rode his first airplane in the 1920s: Timothy R. Gaffney, "Truman Remembered at 50th Anniversary," *Dayton Daily News*, Sept. 19, 1997.

45   His mother also had a bit of trouble: Harry Truman, *Memoirs by Harry S. Truman, Volume One: Year of Decisions*, Garden City, N.Y.: Doubleday & Company, Inc., 1955, p. 219.

45   In a letter to his mother and sister: *Memoirs by Harry S. Truman, Volume One: Year of Decisions*, pp. 295–96.

45   In his memoirs: Truman, *Memoirs, Volume One*, pp. 332–33.

46   "I decided to make the journey": Truman, p. 333.

47   Still, Truman made good use: Truman, p. 339.

47   No other president: David McCullough, *Truman*, New York: Simon & Schuster, 1992, p. 406.

47   For the remainder: terHorst and Albertazzie, p. 144.

48   In 1946, Truman's advisers: terHorst and Albertazzie, pp. 159–60.

48   With its four propeller engines: terHorst and Albertazzie, pp. 160–62.

49   Naming the aircraft: terHorst and Albertazzi, p. 161.

50   "I had breakfast:" *Memoirs by Harry S. Truman, Volume Two: Years of Trial and Hope, 1946–1952*, Garden City, N.Y.: Doubleday & Company, Inc., 1956, pp. 363–64.

50   He was the first chief executive to watch television aboard: Truman, *Memoirs, Volume Two*, p. 497.

51   He once told his pilot: terHorst and Albertazzie, pp. 153–54.

51   On one occasion, he ordered Myers to buzz the White House: terHorst and Albertazzie, pp. 154–56. Also Special to *The New York Times*, "Col. Henry T. Myers, 61, Dies; Pilot for Roosevelt and Truman," *The New York Times*, Dec. 10, 1968, p. 47.

52   At about 10 P.M. on Saturday [account of the start of the Korean War]: *Memoirs by Harry S. Truman, Volume Two: Years of Trial and Hope, 1946–1952*, Garden City, N.Y.: Doubleday & Company, Inc., 1956, pp. 331–33.

53   In all, Truman made 61 flights: Unbylined article, "Events of Interest in Aviation World," *The New York Times*, Feb. 7, 1953, p. 31.

53   Ike chose as his regular aircraft: Robert A. Searles, "Eisenhower's Aviation Legacy," *Business & Commercial Aviation*, published by McGraw-Hill Companies, Inc,. Vol. 83, No. 3, Sept. 1998, p. 116.

54   The plane, decorated in a drab color scheme: Dale Lezon, "Ike's Plane Lands in Santa Fe," *The Albuquerque Journal*, April 4, 1997, p. 1.

55   Sometimes he slurped his soup: terHorst and Albertazzie, p. 182.

55   Bill Draper would even tell: terHorst and Albertazzie, p. 179.

56   Eisenhower was the subject of criticism: Special to *The New York Times*, "Butler Deplores President's Trips," *The New York Times*, June 4, 1956.

57   "Both in size and speed": Dwight D. Eisenhower, *The White House Years: Waging Peace 1956–1961*, Garden City, N.Y.: Doubleday & Company, Inc., 1965, pp. 415–16.

58   "He was hooked": Stephen E. Ambrose, *Eisenhower: Soldier and President*, New York: Simon & Schuster, 1990, p. 490.

58   only one out of 10 Americans had ever been aboard an aircraft: Robert F. Dorr, *Air Force One*, St. Paul, Minn.: MBI Publishing Company, 2002, p. 49.

58   "Travel, just for its own sake": Ambrose, p. 488.

59   "Not for a moment": Eisenhower, *The White House Years, Waging Peace 1956–1961*, p. 489.

59   Ike admitted that: Eisenhower, *The White House Years, Waging Peace 1956–1961*, pp. 512–13.

CHAPTER FOUR *JOHN F. KENNEDY: THE PRINCE AND THE POWER*

62   "This aircraft told everyone": Author's interview with Jeffery Underwood, Aug. 15, 2002.

64   It was Jackie, with the advice of industrial designer Raymond Loewy: Robert F. Dorr, *Air Force One*, St. Paul, Minn.: MBI Publishing Company, 2002, p. 59.

64   People who thought the presidency was the toughest: Richard Reeves, *President Kennedy: Profile of Power*, New York: Simon & Schuster, 1993, Chapter 47.

64   "He had a big bed back there": J. F. terHorst and Ralph Albertazzie, *The Flying White House: The Story of Air Force One*, New York: Coward, McCann & Geoghegan, Inc., 1979, p. 202.

64   Kennedy allowed the black Labrador: Ronald Kessler, *Inside the White House: The Hidden Lives of the Modern Presidents and the Secrets of the World's Most Powerful Institution*, New York: Pocket Books, 1995, p. 36.

65   True to his nature: Various sources, including Kessler, and Hugh A. Mulligan, Associated Press dispatch, Dec. 27, 1987.

65   "They had learned to keep themselves": William Manchester, *Portrait of a President: John F. Kennedy in Profile*, Boston: Little, Brown and Company, 1962, pp. 20, 21.

66   "hatless, coatless, on-the-ball vigor": Manchester, p. 14.

66   "John F. Kennedy was a happy President": Theodore C. Sorensen, *Kennedy*, New York: Harper & Row, Publishers, 1965, p. 366.

66   One Saturday in October 1963: Arthur M. Schlesinger, Jr., *A Thousand Days: John F. Kennedy in the White House*, Boston: Houghton Mifflin Company, 1965, pp. 1015–16.

67   "It was with difficulty": Theodore C. Sorensen, *Kennedy*, New York: Harper & Row, Publishers, 1965, pp. 367–68.

68   "We'll never have another day": Sorensen, p. 601. Also confirmed in author's interview with Sorensen, Oct. 17, 2002.

68 he wore a medical corset: William Manchester, *Portrait of a President: John F. Kennedy in Profile*, Boston: Little, Brown and Company, 1962, p. 40.

68 "His doctors had told him": Michael R. Beschloss, *The Crisis Years: Kennedy and Khrushchev 1960–1963*, New York: Edward Burlingame Books, 1991, pp. 186–87.

69 "One might feel admiration": Kenneth R. Crispell and Carlos R. Gomez, *Hidden Illness in the White House*, Durham and London: Duke University Press, 1988, p. 201.

69 "On one level": Robert Dallek, "The Medical Ordeals of JFK," *The Atlantic Monthly*, Dec. 2002, p. 49.

69 In Paris, he soaked: Beschloss, p. 189.

69 Beschloss cites evidence: Beschloss, pp. 189–90. Robert Dallek, "The Medical Ordeals of JFK," *The Atlantic Monthly*, Dec. 2002, p. 60.

70 "Kennedy had never encountered": Arthur M. Schlesinger, Jr., *A Thousand Days: John F. Kennedy in the White House*, Boston: Houghton Mifflin Company, 1965, pp. 374–75.

70 "It was like riding": Beschloss, p. 225.

70 "We're stuck in a ridiculous situation": Beschloss, p. 225.

70 "All wars start from stupidity": Kenneth P. O'Donnell and David F. Powers with Joe McCarthy, *"Johnny, We Hardly Knew Ye": Memories of John Fitzgerald Kennedy*, Boston-Toronto: Little, Brown and Company, 1970, 1972, pp. 338–40.

71 After meeting in London: Beschloss, p. 229.

72 In the evening," Beschloss says, "he entertained": Beschloss, p. 235.

73 "God, I wish you could think of": Beschloss, pp. 665–66.

73 "You two guys": Beschloss, p. 669.

74 When the Kennedy party got on the plane: Kenneth P. O'Donnell and David F. Powers with Joe McCarthy, *"Johnny, We Hardly Knew Ye": Memoirs of John Fitzgerald Kennedy*, Boston: Little, Brown and Company, 1970, 1972, pp. 33–44.

74 Joe Chappell, the flight engineer: Author's interview with Joe Chappell, July 13, 2002.

75 When *Air Force One* landed, Attorney General Robert Kennedy: O'Donnell, Powers, and McCarthy, p. 44.

CHAPTER FIVE *LYNDON B. JOHNSON: KING OF THE COWBOYS*

77 "Now let's get airborne": Charles Roberts, *LBJ's Inner Circle*, New York: Delacorte Press, 1965, p. 36.

77 "He wanted to have a picture taken": Author's interview with Jack Valenti, Jan. 15, 2002.

77 While Mrs. Kennedy and the slain president's: Roberts, *LBJ's Inner Circle*, p. 36.

77   He conferred with Larry O'Brien: Roberts, p. 122.

78   This latter phone call: Robert Dallek, *Flawed Giant: Lyndon Johnson and His Times 1961–1973*, New York: Oxford University Press, 1998, p. 50.

78   "Robert Kennedy was less cooperative": Dallek, p. 50.

79   523,000 miles: LBJ Library, Austin, Tex.

79   "Johnson's all-embracing style": J. F. terHorst and Ralph Albertazzie, *The Flying White House: The Story of Air Force One*, New York: Coward, McCann & Geoghegan, Inc., 1979, p. 242.

80   Once he ordered a root beer: Ronald Kessler, *Inside the White House: The Hidden Lives of the Modern Presidents and the Secrets of the World's Most Powerful Institution*, New York: Pocket Books, 1995, pp. 24–25.

80   "He had episodes of getting drunk": Kessler, p. 31.

80   "Jack Kennedy always wanted soup": Kessler, p. 32.

80   "We were serving roast beef": Kessler, p. 30.

81   "I'll have them niggers voting Democratic": quoted in Kessler, p. 33.

81   "President Johnson's attitude was": Author's interview with John Haigh, Aug. 19, 2002.

81   "He was like a dog": Author's interview with Joe Chappell, July 13, 2002.

81   "He had this crude manner": Author's interview with Robert Dallek, July 22, 2002.

81   Former steward Gerald Pisha: Pat Murkland, "Desert mayor has memories of high times with five presidents," *The Press-Enterprise* (Riverside, Calif.), May 15, 1996, p. C01.

81   "He was totally naked": Quoted in Kessler, p. 36.

82   "I need some more goddamn ball room": Quoted in Kessler, p. 36.

82   "fooling around": Kessler, p. 37.

82   "Johnson was not a man to sublimate": George Reedy, *Lyndon B. Johnson: A Memoir*, New York: Andrews and McMeel, Inc., 1982, p. 32.

82   "I can't do the job alone": Frank Cormier, *LBJ, The Way He Was*, Garden City, N.Y.: Doubleday & Company, 1977, pp. 4–5.

83   He once bit down on: terHorst and Albertazzie, p. 243.

83   Cormier recalled the day: Quoted in Hugh A. Mulligan, Associated Press dispatch from Washington, D.C., Dec. 27, 1987.

83   "Look around the world": terHorst and Albertazzie, p. 247.

84   "He insisted that they were 'spies' ": George Reedy, *Lyndon B. Johnson: A Memoir*, New York: Andrews and McMeel, Inc., 1982, pp. 64–65.

85   But the relationship soured: Reedy, p. 65.

85   "At four o'clock": Author's interview with Ron Nessen, Apr. 1, 2002.

85   Walter Mondale: Author's interview with Walter Mondale, Mar. 13, 2002.

86   "We want to be always safe": Author's interview with James Cross, Feb. 1, 2002.

87   Borrowing ideas from Eric Goldman: Robert Dallek, *Flawed Giant: Lyndon Johnson and His Times 1961–1973*, New York: Oxford University Press, 1998, p. 81.

88   Charles Roberts of *Newsweek*: Roberts, *LBJ's Inner Circle*, pp. 96–97, 98.

88   "Johnson's euphoria rested": Dallek, p. 83.

89   "While in Asia": Joseph A. Califano, Jr., *The Triumph and Tragedy of Lyndon Johnson: The White House Years*, New York: Simon & Schuster, 1991, pp. 150–51.

89   After ordering his aides: Califano, pp. 152–53.

89   "I am willing": Califano, pp. 151–52.

90   By the end of 1966: Califano, pp. 152–53.

90   In the fall of 1967: Dallek, pp. 494–96.

90–91 The president secretly called Jack Valenti: Author's interview with Jack Valenti, Jan. 15, 2002. This account of the December trip comes largely from Valenti.

92   On March 31: Dallek, p. 529.

CHAPTER SIX *RICHARD NIXON: THE SOLITARY BROODER*

95   On February 23, 1969, a month after: Henry Kissinger, *White House Years*, Boston: Little, Brown and Company, 1979, pp. 243–47.

96   "That's a Kennedy song": Richard Reeves, *President Nixon: Alone in the White House*, New York: Simon & Schuster, 2001, p. 52.

97   "Are there any non-Jews here?": Reeves, p. 434. This account of the China trip comes partly from Reeves.

97   "Nixon oscillated between anxiety": Kissinger, p. 1054.

98   a burly staffer blocked the aisle: Kissinger, pp. 1054–55.

98   he fell into a funk: Kissinger, p. 1093.

99   "Triumph seemed to fill Nixon with a premonition": Kissinger, p. 1471.

99   "On the way back," Nixon wrote: Reeves, p. 499.

99   Yet, the next morning, Nixon insisted: Reeves, p. 49.

99   "The opposition line will be": Reeves, pp. 541–42.

100   "Freeze them": Reeves, p. 543.

100   "He wants total discipline": H. R. Haldeman, *The Haldeman Diaries: Inside the Nixon White House*, New York: G. P. Putnam's Sons, 1994, p. 532.

100   "He wants to be sure the IRS": Haldeman, p. 533.

100   "That's it!": Quoted in Reeves, p. 35.

100   His flight crew was overburdened: J. F. terHorst and Ralph Albertazzie, *The Flying

White House: The Story of Air Force One, New York: Coward, McCann & Geoghegan, Inc., 1979, pp. 78–79.

101   He was a Spartan eater: For an interesting account of Nixon's habits and the atmosphere on the plane, see Ronald Kessler, *Inside the White House: The Hidden Lives of the Modern Presidents and the Secrets of the World's Most Powerful Institution*, New York: Pocket Books, 1995, pp. 44–45, 57, 59, 62.

101   "His staff was a buffer": Author's interview with Jim Bull, July 30, 2002.

102   "He stayed pretty much in his cabin": terHorst and Albertazzie, p. 259.

102   "an incredible stack of little white note sheets": Haldeman, p. 209.

102   "He was the most unmechanical": Author's interview with Brent Scowcroft, Apr. 19, 2002.

103   "H [shorthand for Haldeman]: Tricia job": Quoted in Reeves, p. 124.

103   "On October 10, 1972": Reeves, pp. 24–25.

104   "Then he told me to make a note": Haldeman, p. 423.

105   Former White House counsel John Dean recalls flying: Author's interview with John Dean, Mar. 27, 2002. Also, John W. Dean III, *Blind Ambition: The White House Years*, New York: Pocket Books, 1976, pp. 147–48.

105   In fact, Dean argues: John W. Dean III, *Blind Ambition*, pp. 57–59.

106   When the new *Air Force One*: Dean, *Blind Ambition*, p. 170. Also, author's interview with John Dean, Mar. 27, 2002.

106   It was an updated Boeing 707, but reconfigured: terHorst and Albertazzie, p. 34.

107   On February 8, 1973: Reeves, pp. 570–71.

108   "Within minutes—or was it seconds?—word came": David Gergen, *Eyewitness to Power: The Essence of Leadership: Nixon to Clinton*, New York: Simon & Schuster, 2000, p. 73.

109   There were 34 passengers aboard: terHorst and Albertazzie, pp. 43–44. Much of this account of Nixon's final flight aboard *Air Force One* comes from terHorst and Albertazzie's book.

109–10   Just remember, he told Simmons: terHorst and Albertazzie, p. 49.

110   "Is everybody enjoying the flight?": Author's interview with Ralph Albertazzie, July 17, 2002.

CHAPTER SEVEN *GERALD FORD: EVERYMAN*

111   "He was a homespun": Author's interview with Howie Franklin, May 24, 2002.

111   "President Ford probably treated": Author's interview with Charles Palmer, July 14, 2002.

112 "Gerald R. Ford was an ordinary man": James Cannon, *Time and Chance: Gerald Ford's Appointment with History*, New York: HarperCollins Publishers, 1994, p. 411.

112 "Nixon, by nature, was a recluse": Gerald R. Ford, *A Time to Heal: The Autobiography of Gerald R. Ford*, New York: Harper & Row, Publishers, 1979, p. 126.

113 "Everyone knew it as *Air Force One*": Ford, p. 127.

113 "Ford wanted to be": Author's interview with Ron Nessen, Apr. 1, 2002.

114 "Ford was President for 895 days": Cannon, p. 393.

114 "The years of suspicion": Ford, pp. 124–25.

115 "What happened was this": Ford, p. 289.

116 "I mean": Author's interview with Ron Nessen, Apr. 1, 2002.

117 "[T]he press turned on him with ridicule": David Gergen, *Eyewitness to Power: The Essence of Leadership: Nixon to Clinton*, New York: Simon & Schuster, 2000, pp. 126–27.

117 "No man should have to clean up": Ron Nessen, *It Sure Looks Different from the Inside*, Chicago: Playboy Press, 1978, p. xiv.

117 There also were the dark moments: These accounts of the assassination attempts largely come from Ford's autobiography and my interview with Nessen, Apr. 1, 2002.

120 "He was meeting with the Russian premier": Ronald Kessler, *Inside the White House: The Hidden Lives of the Modern Presidents and the Secrets of the World's Most Powerful Institution*, New York: Pocket Books, 1995, pp. 77–78. This story was confirmed for me in interviews with Charles Palmer, July 14, 2002, and with Bill Gulley, former chief of the White House Military Office, on Aug. 23, 2002.

120 It was when a military aide: J. F. terHorst and Ralph Albertazzie, *The Flying White House: The Story of Air Force One*, New York: Coward, McCann & Geoghegan, Inc., 1979, p. 74.

120 "There is no Soviet domination": Ford, p. 422.

121 "I can be very stubborn": Ford, p. 424.

121 "He made it sound": Author's interview with Brent Scowcroft, Apr. 19, 2002.

121 "It reinforced the bumbler image": Author's interview with Ron Nessen, Apr. 1, 2002.

CHAPTER EIGHT *JIMMY CARTER: THE PARSIMONIOUS PREACHER*

123 "a lonely peanut farmer": Author's interview with President Jimmy Carter, Jan. 25, 2002.

123   "Our commitment to human rights": Jimmy Carter, *Keeping Faith: Memoirs of a President*, Fayetteville, Ark.: University of Arkansas Press, 1995, pp. 22–23.

124   "We had some very dangerous times": Speech of Jimmy Carter at a forum for international students at Emory University, Atlanta, Ga., Jan. 23, 2002.

124   "That's an interesting fulcrum": Author's interview with Jody Powell, Apr. 30, 2002.

125   "Obviously, Watergate": Author's interview with President Jimmy Carter, Jan. 25, 2002.

126   "Carter was kind of an introvert": Author's interview with John Haigh, July 21, 2002.

126   "I never doubted": Zbigniew Brzezinski, *Power and Principle: Memoirs of the National Security Adviser, 1977–1981*, New York: Farrar Straus Giroux, 1983, p. 23.

126   He deeply admired Egyptian leader Sadat: Brzezinski, pp. 24–26.

127   "His memory was phenomenal": Brzezinski, pp. 22–23.

127   "I tried to cut down": Jimmy Carter quoted in *Air Force One: The Planes and the Presidents, Flight II*, Public Broadcasting Service, written, produced, and directed by Elliott Sluhan, May 20, 1991.

128   "They weren't": Author's interview with Charles Palmer, July 14, 2002.

128   He wanted to reduce the number of stewards: Ronald Kessler, *Inside the White House: The Hidden Lives of the Modern Presidents and the Secrets of the World's Most Powerful Institution*, New York: Pocket Books, 1995, p. 100. This was confirmed in my interviews with several stewards.

129   "Guess who had to vacuum it up?": Quoted in Pat Murkland, "Desert mayor has memories of high times with five presidents," *The Press-Enterprise* (Riverside, Calif.), May 15, 1996, p. C01.

129   "Her greatest thrill": Author's interview with Jim Bull, July 30, 2002.

129–30 "It took a year and a half": Quotes in Kessler, p. 95.

130   "The Carters sometimes got mad": Kessler, p. 96.

131   "The decision," Vance wrote: Cyrus Vance, *Hard Choices: Critical Years in America's Foreign Policy*, New York: Simon and Schuster, 1983, pp. 409–10.

131   "I will never forget the flight": Jimmy Carter, *Keeping Faith: Memoirs of a President*, Fayetteville, Ark.: University of Arkansas Press, 1995, p. 575.

132   "We don't need to tell the president *that*": Author's interview with Jody Powell, Apr. 30, 2002. Also see Hamilton Jordan, *Crisis: The Last Year of the Carter Presidency*, New York: Berkley Books, 1983, pp. 345–49.

133   "It is impossible for me to put into words": Carter, p. 16.

133   "It was very emotional": Author's interview with Phil Wise, Apr. 22, 2002.

134   "Usually after a foreign trip": Hamilton Jordan, *Crisis: The Last Year of the Carter Presidency*, New York: Berkley Books, 1983, pp. 393–95.

CHAPTER NINE *RONALD REAGAN: AMERICA'S LEADING MAN*

137   They spent: Author's interview with Tim Kerwin, Aug. 6, 2002.

137   "That's an offer one doesn't turn down": Peter Hannaford, ed., *Recollections of Reagan: A Portrait of Ronald Reagan*, New York: William Morrow and Company, 1997, pp. 70–71.

137   "He was extremely disciplined": Author's interview with David Gergen, June 26, 2002.

139   "*Air Force One* became a symbol": Author's interview with Fred Ryan, Apr. 10, 2002.

139   "People would come up": Author's interview with David Gergen, June 26, 2002.

139   "In many ways, Reagan was a loner": Author's interview with Ken Duberstein, Aug. 12, 2002.

140   "He was already a public person": Author's interview with John Haigh, July 21, 2002.

140   "He always had a smile on his face": Author's interview with Jim Bull, July 30, 2002.

141   "but he would always come in": Author's interview with Howie Franklin, May 24, 2002.

141   "I long for the days": Larry Speakes, *Speaking Out: The Reagan Presidency from Inside the White House*, New York: Charles Scribner's Sons, 1988, p. 116.

142   "He didn't like to travel": Author's interview with Marlin Fitzwater, Apr. 6, 2002.

144   "All she wanted": Author's interview with Jim Bull, July 30, 2002.

144   "The main difference was his personality": Author's interview with Marlin Fitzwater, Apr. 6, 2002.

146   "He's too short": Author's interview with Howie Franklin, May 24, 2002.

147   Fitzwater recalled proposing: Author's interview with Marlin Fitzwater, Apr. 6, 2002.

147   "My control over the departure times": Joan Quigley, *"What Does Joan Say?" My Seven Years as White House Astrologer to Nancy and Ronald Reagan*, New York: Birch Lane Press, 1990, pp. 82–83.

149   "he would flash the cuff links": Author's interview with Fred Ryan, Apr. 10, 2002.

152   As Speakes tells the story: Speakes, pp. 142–49. His account was confirmed by others in the Reagan administration in interviews with the author at the time.

153   "Iran-Contra was a very discouraging period": Author's interview with George Shultz, Aug. 22, 2002.

153   "It seemed to be trouble": Author's interview with Jim Bull, July 30, 2002.

154   "It came from a depth of conviction": Author's interview with George Shultz, Aug. 22, 2002.

155   "By protocol, only the President and Mrs. Reagan": Hedrick Smith, *The Power Game: How Washington Works*, New York: Ballantine Books, 1988, p. 76.

156   "I want you to know": Author's interview with Fred Ryan, Apr. 10, 2002.

157   "Well, I'm on shaky ground here": George Skelton, *The Los Angeles Times*, Apr. 20, 1988, Metro Part 2, p. 7.

159   "The airplane was an antique": Author's interview with Bob Ruddick, July 4, 2002.

CHAPTER TEN *GEORGE H. W. BUSH: THE FOREIGN-POLICY PRESIDENT*

162   "George Bush was in awe of the presidency": Author's interview with David Valdez, July 18, 2002.

166   "We were all huddled down": Author's interview with Andrew Card, Feb. 11, 2002.

166   "We were trying to agonize": Author's interview with Andrew Card, Feb. 11, 2002.

169   "Pretty soon everyone": Author's interview with Marlin Fitzwater, Apr. 6, 2002.

169   "The presidents clearly feel": Author's interview with Marlin Fitzwater, Apr. 6, 2002.

171   The end came on December 3, 1991: Marlin Fitzwater, *Call the Briefing!* New York: Times Books, 1995, pp. 188–92.

173   "I think we've had too many press conferences": Michael Duffy and Dan Goodgame, *Marching in Place: The Status Quo Presidency of George Bush*, New York: Simon & Schuster, 1992, p. 187.

174   "I felt like a turkey in a turkey shoot": Author's interview with John Haigh, July 21, 2002.

174   "The polls were not encouraging": Author's interview with Ron Kaufman, Aug. 1, 2002.

175   "I think a lot of us": Author's interview with President George W. Bush, Oct. 1, 2002.

175   "Barbara and I sat": George Bush, "Man Oh Man, Was It Comfortable," *Forbes*, Nov. 18, 1996, p. 122.

CHAPTER ELEVEN *BILL CLINTON: THE BABY BOOMER*

177   Clinton made a total of 133 visits: John Berthoud and Demian Brady, "Bill Clinton: America's Best-Traveled President, A Study of Presidential Travel: 1953–2001," National Taxpayers Union and NTU Foundation, Policy Paper 104, March 16, 2001.

178   En route to Chicago in mid-1993: Bob Woodward, *The Agenda: Inside the Clinton White House,* New York: Simon & Schuster, 1994, p. 278. My reporting confirms Woodward's account, particularly my interview with David Gergen on June 26, 2002.

179   "There is a certain sort": Author's interview with President Bill Clinton, Sept. 2, 2002.

179   "Partly, it was because of his curiosity": Author's interview with Sandy Berger, Mar. 7, 2002.

179   "I believe that when they first came in office": Author's interview with Howie Franklin, May 24, 2002.

180   "I think the pilot assured him": Author's interview with Mack McLarty, Mar. 19, 2002.

180   "The perception was more powerful than the reality": George Stephanopoulos, *All Too Human, A Political Education,* Boston: Little, Brown and Company, 1999, p. 144.

183   "People were just sort of stupefied": Author's interview with David Gergen, June 26, 2002.

183   "The president's foot lightly": Recounted in Howard Kurtz, "Media Notes: A Reporter With Lust in Her Hearts," *The Washington Post,* July 6, 1998, p. C01.

184   "When Chelsea was there": Author's interview with Gene Sperling, Aug. 7, 2002.

186   "It was like being at home with the president": Author's interview with Harold Ickes, May 16, 2002.

187   "I would be offended": Author's interview with Leon Panetta, Apr. 8, 2002.

188   "I go in and lean on him": Author's interview with Howie Franklin, May 24, 2002.

188   This time it was Ickes's turn: Author's interview with Harold Ickes, May 16, 2002.

190   "Not only did he develop a close professional relationship with Rabin": Author's interview with Leon Panetta, Apr. 8, 2002.

192   "We had quite a lot": Author's interview with President Bill Clinton, Jan. 28, 2002.

192   Every time something crunched: Author's interview with Mack McLarty, Mar. 19, 2002.

192   "They were really freaked out": Author's interview with Sandy Berger, Mar. 7, 2002.

193   "The threat was not abstract": Berger interview, Mar. 7, 2002.

194   "It felt like": Berger interview, Mar. 7, 2002.

194   "That's the only time": Author's interview with President Bill Clinton, Sept. 2, 2002.

195   "We were trying to find a time": Author's interview with Joe Lockhart, Dec. 18, 2001.

197   "I can't imagine": Lockhart interview, ibid.

197   "We knew there would be screaming": Lockhart interview, ibid.

198   "The communications on the plane were terrible": Author's interview with Sandy Berger, Mar. 7, 2002.

199   "We never had a president who listened": Author's interview with Howie Franklin, May 24, 2002.

200   "The days never ended": Author's interview with Mark Penn, Apr. 15, 2002.

202   "Here's one that's appropriate for today": Peter Baker, *The Breach: Inside the Impeachment and Trial of William Jefferson Clinton*, New York: Scribner, 2000, p. 47.

CHAPTER TWELVE *GEORGE W. BUSH: COMMANDER IN CHIEF*

205   President George W. Bush got up at 6:30 A.M.: This account is based in part on the author's separate interviews with Karl Rove on Sept. 14, 2001, and Jan. 31, 2002, and with Andrew Card, Feb. 11, 2002. Journalists Dan Balz and Bob Woodward published an excellent description of the events of September 11 on Page One of *The Washington Post,* Jan. 27, 2002. I also based my account on interviews with Dan Bartlett, Karen Hughes, and many others.

206   "They had declared war": Balz and Woodward.

207   "There was this surreal, serene": Author's interview with Dan Bartlett, Feb. 7, 2002.

207   "When we got airborne": Author's interview with Eric Draper, Aug. 26, 2002.

207   "We didn't know if *we* were going to be attacked": Author's interview with Andrew Card, Feb. 11, 2002.

211   Fleischer called Karen Hughes: Balz and Woodward.

213   "I want to go back home ASAP": Author's interview with Andrew Card, Feb. 11, 2002.

213   "Wow," he told the defense secretary: Balz and Woodward.

213   At 2:30 P.M., Bush reached his father: Balz and Woodward.

214   "We need to get back": Author's interview with Karl Rove, Sept. 14, 2001.

214   "I never felt like my life": Author's interview with President George W. Bush, Oct. 1, 2002.

215   "He has a very basic belief": Author's interview with Mike Gerson, Nov. 29, 2001.

215   "We're a pretty dull crew": Author's interview with Ari Fleischer, May 9, 2002.

215   "It's their sanctuary": Author's interview with Dan Bartlett, July 29, 2002.

216   "Being a 'Type A' personality": Author's interview with President George W. Bush, Oct. 1, 2002.

217   "*Air Force One* is a comfortable environment": Author's interview with Andrew Card, Apr. 15, 2002.

217   "Having traveled with the president": Author's interview with Karen Hughes, Apr. 29, 2002.

218   "I think people would be surprised": Author's interview with Nick Calio, Apr. 2, 2002.

220   "I opened it up": Card interview, Apr. 15, 2002.

220–21 "I feel guilty talking about it": Card interview, Apr. 15, 2002.

221   "It showed the humanity of the president": Author's interview with Noelia Rodriguez, Apr. 9, 2002.

221   "a heavenly feeling": Author's interview with Reed Dickens, Oct. 16, 2002.

221   "There were a lot of religious people": Author's interview with President George W. Bush, Oct. 1, 2002.

221   "He is not the emotive type": Author's interview with Ari Fleischer, Mar. 14, 2002.

221   After *The Washington Post* picked up the item: Lloyd Grove, The Reliable Source, *The Washington Post*, May 7, 2002, p. C3. Also, Grove, The Reliable Source, *The Washington Post*, May 10, 2002, p. C3.

222   "He's always an affable person": Author's interview with Ari Fleischer, Mar. 14, 2002.

223   "We don't fill the aircraft": Author's interview with Mark Rosenker, July 2001.

223   "We see a very different person": Author's interview with Nick Calio, Apr. 2, 2002.

223   "He understands the symbolism": Author's interview with Dan Bartlett, July 29, 2002.

224   "I would have crawled": Quoted in Elisabeth Bumiller, "Peace and Political Status at 39,000 Feet," *The New York Times*, Oct. 29, 2002, p. A24.

224   "It was like": Author's interview with Bill Clinton, Sept. 2, 2002.

224–25 Quotations from Reagan, Bush, and Carter are from *Air Force One, The Planes and the Presidents, Flight II*, written, produced, and directed by Elliott Sluhan, Public Broadcasting Service, May 20, 1991.

BIBLIOGRAPHY

Ambrose, Stephen E., *Eisenhower: Soldier and President*. New York: Simon & Schuster, 1990.

———, *Nixon, Volume Three: Ruin and Recovery 1973 1990*. New York: Simon & Schuster, 1991.

Baker, Peter, *The Breach: Inside the Impeachment and Trial of William Jefferson Clinton*. New York: Scribner, 2000.

Bernstein, Carl, and Woodward, Bob, *All the President's Men*. New York: Touchstone, 1974.

Beschloss, Michael R., *The Crisis Years: Kennedy and Khrushchev 1960–1963*. New York: Edward Burlingame Books, 1991.

Bourne, Peter G., *Jimmy Carter: A Comprehensive Biography from Plains to Postpresidency*. New York: Scribner, 1997.

Brzezinski, Zbigniew, *Power and Principle: Memoirs of the National Security Adviser, 1977–1981*. New York: Farrar Straus Giroux, 1983.

Burns, James MacGregor, *Roosevelt: The Soldier of Freedom*. New York: Smithmark Publishers, 1996.

Califano, Joseph A., *The Triumph and Tragedy of Lyndon Johnson: The White House Years*. New York: Simon & Schuster, 1991.

Cannon, James, *Time and Chance: Gerald Ford's Appointment with History*. New York: HarperCollins Publishers, 1994.

Carter, Jimmy, *Keeping Faith: Memoirs of a President*. Fayetteville, Ark.: University of Arkansas Press, 1995.

Cormier, Frank, *LBJ, The Way He Was*. Garden City, N.Y.: Doubleday & Company, 1977.

————, *Presidents Are People Too*. Washington, D.C.: Public Affairs Press, 1966.

Crispell, Kenneth R., and Gomez, Carlos R., *Hidden Illness in the White House*. Durham and London: Duke University Press, 1988.

Dallek, Robert, *Flawed Giant: Lyndon Johnson and His Times 1961–1973*. New York: Oxford University Press, 1998.

Dean, John W. III, *Blind Ambition: The White House Years*. New York: Pocket Books, 1976.

Dorr, Robert F., *Air Force One*. St. Paul, Minn.: MBI Publishing Company, 2002.

Drew, Elizabeth, *On the Edge: The Clinton Presidency*. New York: Simon & Schuster, 1994.

Duffy, Michael, and Goodgame, Dan, *Marching in Place: The Status Quo Presidency of George Bush*. New York: Simon & Schuster, 1992.

Eisenhower, Dwight D., *The White House Years: Mandate for Change 1953–1956*. Garden City, N.Y.: Doubleday & Company, 1963.

Eisenhower, Dwight D., *The White House Years: Waging Peace 1956–1961*. Garden City, N.Y.: Doubleday & Company, 1965.

Fitzwater, Marlin, *Call the Briefing!* New York: Times Books, 1995. Philadelphia, Pa.: Xlibris, 2001.

Ford, Gerald R., *A Time to Heal: The Autobiography of Gerald R. Ford*. New York: Harper & Row, 1970.

Gergen, David, *Eyewitness to Power: The Essence of Leadership: Nixon to Clinton*. New York: Simon & Schuster, 2000.

Gilbert, Robert E., *The Mortal Presidency: Illness and Anguish in the White House*. New York: BasicBooks, 1992.

Goodwin, Doris Kearns, *No Ordinary Time*. New York: Simon & Schuster, 1994.

Haldeman, H. R., *The Haldeman Diaries: Inside the Nixon White House*. New York: G. P. Putnam's Sons, 1994.

Hannaford, Peter, ed., *Recollections of Reagan: A Portrait of Ronald Reagan*. New York: William Morrow and Company, 1997.

Hartmann, Robert T., *Palace Politics: An Inside Account of the Ford Years*. New York: McGraw-Hill Book Company, 1980.

Hoyt, Mary Finch, *East Wing: Politics, the Press, and a First Lady: A Memoir*. Philadelphia, Pa.: Xlibris, 2001.

Jordan, Hamilton, *Crisis: The Last Year of the Carter Presidency*. New York: Berkley Books, 1983.

Kessler, Ronald, *Inside the White House: The Hidden Lives of the Modern Presidents and the Secrets of the World's Most Powerful Institution*. New York: Pocket Books, 1995.

Kissinger, Henry, *White House Years*. Boston: Little, Brown and Company, 1979.

Manchester, William, *Portrait of a President: John F. Kennedy in Profile*. Boston: Little, Brown and Company, 1962.

McCullough, David, *Truman*. New York: Simon & Schuster, 1992.

Nessen, Ron, *It Sure Looks Different from the Inside*. Chicago: Playboy Press, 1978.

Nixon, Richard, *In the Arena: A Memoir of Victory, Defeat and Renewal*. New York: Simon & Schuster, 1990.

O'Donnell, Kenneth P., and Powers, David F., with Joe McCarthy, *"Johnny, We Hardly Knew Ye": Memories of John Fitzgerald Kennedy*. Boston-Toronto: Little, Brown and Company, 1970, 1972.

Quigley, Joan, *"What Does Joan Say?" My Seven Years as White House Astrologer to Nancy and Ronald Reagan*. New York: Birch Lane Press, 1990.

Reedy, George, *Lyndon B. Johnson: A Memoir*. New York: Andrews and McMeel, 1982.

Reeves, Richard, *President Kennedy: Profile of Power*. New York: Simon & Schuster, 1993.

Reeves, Richard, *President Nixon: Alone in the White House*. New York: Simon & Schuster, 2001.

Roberts, Charles, *LBJ's Inner Circle*. New York: Delacorte Press, 1965.

Roosevelt, Eleanor, *This I Remember*. New York: Harper & Brothers, 1949.

Schlesinger, Arthur M., Jr., *A Thousand Days: John F. Kennedy in the White House*. Boston: Houghton Mifflin Company, 1965.

Smith, Hedrick, *The Power Game: How Washington Works*. New York: Random House, 1988.

Sorensen, Theodore C., *Kennedy*. New York: Harper & Row, 1965.

Speakes, Larry, *Speaking Out: The Reagan Presidency from Inside the White House*. New York: Charles Scribner's Sons, 1988.

Stephanopoulos, George, *All Too Human, A Political Education*. Boston: Little, Brown and Company, 1999.

terHorst, J. F., and Albertazzie, Ralph, *The Flying White House: The Story of Air Force One*. New York: Coward, McCann & Geoghegan, 1979.

Truman, Harry S., *Memoirs by Harry S. Truman, Volume One: Year of Decisions*. Garden City, N.Y.: Doubleday & Company, 1955.

Truman, Harry S., *Memoirs by Harry S. Truman, Volume Two: Years of Trial and Hope, 1946–1952*. Garden City, N.Y.: Doubleday & Company, 1956.

Vance, Cyrus, *Hard Choices: Critical Years in America's Foreign Policy*. New York: Simon & Schuster, 1983.

Waldman, Michael, *POTUS Speaks: Finding the Words That Defined the Clinton Presidency*. New York: Simon & Schuster, 2000.

Walsh, Kenneth T., *Feeding the Beast: The White House Versus the Press*. New York: Random House, 1996. Philadelphia, Pa.: Xlibris, 2002.

Walsh, Kenneth T., *Ronald Reagan: Biography*. New York: Park Lane Press, 1997.

Woodward, Bob, *The Agenda: Inside the Clinton White House*. New York: Simon & Schuster, 1994.

Woodward, Bob, *Bush at War*. New York: Simon & Schuster, 2002.

Yeltsin, Boris, *Midnight Diaries*. New York: PublicAffairs, 2000.

INDEX

ABOUT THE AUTHOR

Kenneth T. Walsh has covered the presidency for *U.S. News & World Report* since 1986 and is one of the most respected journalists in Washington. He has logged more than 200 trips aboard *Air Force One*, both domestic and foreign, and traveled to more than 60 countries. He is the winner of the two most prestigious awards for covering the White House, the Aldo Beckman Award and the Gerald R. Ford Prize. He has won the Ford Prize twice. Walsh is the former president of the White House Correspondents' Association and has served as an adjunct professor of communication at American University in Washington, D.C. He lives in Bethesda, Maryland, with his wife, Barclay. They have two children, Jean and Chris.